THE
HEALER
BY GENNESARET

THE
HEALER
BY GENNESARET

a Novel

NIKI ADAMS

To order additional copies of this book, contact:
Xlibris Corporation
1-888-795-4274
www.Xlibris.com
Orders@Xlibris.com
38494

For Joy
and for all
others
who love God
and
know His Son,
Jesus Christ,
to be
the Savior
of the world

The Healer

John Greenleaf Whittier

To a young physician, with Dorè's picture
of Christ healing the sick

So stood of old the holy Christ
    Amidst the suffering throng;
With whom His lightest touch sufficed
    To make the weakest strong.

That healing gift He lends to them
    Who use it in His name;
The power that filled His garment's hem
    Is evermore the same.

For lo! in human hearts unseen
    The Healer dwelleth still,
And they who make His temples clean
    The best subserve His will.

The holiest task by Heaven decreed,
    An errand all divine,
The burden of our common need
    To render less is thine.

The paths of pain are thine. Go forth
    With patience, trust, and hope;
The sufferings of a sin-sick earth
    Shall give thee ample scope.

Beside the unveiled mysteries
    Of life and death go stand,
With guarded lips and reverent eyes
    And pure of heart and hand.

So shalt thou be with power endued
    From Him who went about
The Syrian hillsides doing good,
    And casting demons out.

That Good Physician liveth yet
    Thy friend and guide to be;
The Healer by Gennesaret
    Shall walk the rounds with thee.

Author's Note

There are dozens of books to be read about the life, miracles, and teachings of Christ Jesus, and I have read many of them over the years.

If in this book there is a likeness to any other author's works, it is because the life of Christ Jesus is an anthem from which any writer may catch the music and compose, without intention, a similar song.

Writing this book, I used only The Holy Bible and Davis and Gehman's *The Westminster Dictionary of The Bible* (Westminster Press, 1944.) for reference.

This is a work of fiction based on the New Testament Gospels and written from the imagination of my heart.

JESUS HEALING THE SICK

Chapter 1

The fleet was becalmed. Usually there was a brisk breeze, but late that night, not even a whisper of moving air. All around us on Lake Tiberias—sometimes called the Sea of Gennesaret—fishing boats rode unusually low in quiet, still waters. Our skiff was loaded with silver-bellied fish, and our nets were heaped on the stern. There was no room for more fish.

It had been a bountiful catch, with the waters roiling when my brother Simon and I, Andrew Bar-jona, pulled our dragnets into the boat. Eagerly we had commenced throwing the trash creatures and seaweeds back into the sea. It was sweet toil to plunder this lake. Three times we'd cast our nets and drew them filled to almost bursting.

Only when our boat could hold no more did we dip our fish-scented hands and arms into the water to cleanse them. Then we crawled into the bow of the boat and had a meal of flatbread, cheese curds, and dried grapes. We drank warm watery wine from the old skin bottle tethered to a rowlock.

We had worked for hours, breaking sweat upon our bodies. But now the air, so still and hot, denied us the usual relief, and we quickly tired. Our sail hung limply from the center post, drooping and withered. Simon and I just sat, waiting for the wind.

From time to time, we looked up to see John and James, Zebedee's sons. We would wave to them, and they to us. We had many friends among those who went to sea.

A small oil pot with a slow-burning wick was placed in the bow of each boat so we could see every vessel. They were scattered like pebbles on the placid surface of the lake, a few within calling distance one of another, but we were on the fringe and could only hear voices, not words.

Dawn would soon break, the dawn of what would become the most important day of our lives. Nothing would ever again be the same.

The eastern sky was turning from a velvet moonlit blackness to deep violet then to grey blue. A full moon was sliding westward toward the place where earth and sky embraced. We watched as the silver orb grew large and luminous and then settled downward and vanished from our sight below the near horizon.

We rarely saw a moonset from the lake. Usually by then, we were at the shore unloading our catch, sorting fish by size into baskets—fish that would sell at early market before the sun cooked them into rottenness.

But now we could see across the lake to the hills, where herdsmen kept watch over sheep and goats. Their watch fires still glimmered here and there. Now and again we heard dogs barking. But more often we heard foxes and wolves, close by on the nearest shore. They howled and squabbled, and herons and cranes rose up flapping noisily in escape from these predators. All sounds were increased by the stillness of the night and early morning air.

Simon moved to the stern of the boat and stretched his body atop lumps of sodden nets. He tried to sleep, but there was no shade from the brightening dawn. I watched him twist and turn, vainly seeking a comfortable position.

He had toiled very hard, much harder than I, as usual. I pitied him his restlessness. By nature I was less active, just as strong but more conservatively paced.

When the first rays of sunlight broke the horizon, the already stifling air, without wind to move it, was a blast of heat. Simon rose and plunged into the lake. The boat bobbed for a few seconds then idled while he swam. A few minutes later, he drew himself aboard with his greatly muscled arms. Momentarily dripping, he threw his damp body again over the nets, and this time he yielded at once to sleep.

I put on a tattered tunic and simply turned my back to the sun. Hunched over with my arms across my knees, I sat waiting for the land and sea to breathe again.

I must have slept. When I wakened, I found myself pitched forward into the mound of fish. I had stayed asleep until even in slumber I heard Simon's voice, grumbling.

He was throwing shriveling fish back into the sea.

"An ill-chosen trade we have," he complained. "Our best-ever haul, and the wind decides to sleep. In an hour or two the catch will begin to stink, and we'll have to feed them all back to the deep."

"I'll wager an hour from now we'll be plowing a wake toward port," I replied. "This calm can't last."

As we knew we must, we tossed the nets back into the sea and drew them out heavy and dripping wet. We spread them over the fish in an attempt to preserve the harvest. Our efforts made sense. Desiccated fish grow dull. Their eyeballs glaze with film then shrivel. No housewife will buy such specimens.

Hour after hour we labored. As the wind stayed away, the sweet smell of fresh fish began to give in to the fust of sure decay.

In the heat of midafternoon we reversed our work; we removed the nets and the top layer of fish, hoping to still find a breath of freshness in the depth of the catch. But there would be no harvest to bring to port that day. Not one fish fit for sale. No fish for women to buy and bake for supper. No fish to salt away. Every fish in every boat was being cast out and buried back in the sea. The work of a whole night and a day went to waste.

No sooner had the boats been unloaded and they rode higher in the water than the wind stirred. Not enough to fill the sails, but enough to allow the fleet to turn homeward. It had been too hot to even try to row. But by frequently jumping into the lake or tying sodden garments around our heads, we could weather the blast and move our oars.

Heated bodies barely withstand such effort without succumbing to sunstroke. We later learned two men on separate ships had passed out briefly, overcome by the merciless heat. On some other ships, there were enough hands to trade off rowing, but Simon and I were only two, and we rowed slowly.

Upon making it to port, every man went directly—silently and sadly—to his dwelling place. We were last to beach our vessel.

Simon and I stopped by our father's house to drink water and rest. We sat in the garden, in the dense shadow of a leafy tree. A sweet scent, like that of jasmine, came from turpentine, flowing from knife cuts made by our father in the tree's bark. We forgot the smell of rotting fish as we chewed the teil tree gum harvested that day.

Jona tried to cheer us. "When the Savior comes, he will teach us how to call or calm the wind when we need blessing," he said.

Simon could only mock our father's hope even though he shared it. "*When the Savior comes,*" he replied ironically.

Often while on the lake, when wind pulled the boat and we trolled the dragnets, we played a game of the hope we shared of the time when the Savior *would* come.

"When the Savior comes, I shall forsake this boat and swim to meet him," I once said.

"When the Savior comes, I shall stay right here, for the fish will be so happy they will leap into our nets, glad to fill our purses, our bellies, and to feed our souls," Simon replied.

Sometimes, instead of making a game, we spoke sincerely of what we would do if the Savior came in our time.

"No doubt, he'll need an army if he is to break the oppression of Rome," we'd agree and then pledge to be among the first to join in the warfare.

Between us, we decided that the first one to hear that the Savior had come could leave and travel wherever needed to learn of his plan of deliverance, and to determine how best we, sons of Jona, could enlist and offer to help.

Strange as it may seem, quite by chance that very evening after our fruitless night and day on the lake, I heard that the Savior, if not already on the scene, was surely on the way.

It happened like this: Simon left our father's house that afternoon and went to his own place to be with Adina, his wife, and the rest of the household.

On the other hand, I, who lived with my widowed father, returned to the shore to refresh my body in the lake. After bathing, I took a clean loincloth and tunic, and I dressed and walked along the shore to the port marketplace of our village.

A few fishermen were on the quay, mending nets in the dim evening light. A stranger sat near them upon an upturned basket. As I drew near, I heard him say "from Jericho."

"Are you from Jericho?" I asked.

"No," he replied, "just passed through. I was speaking of the strange traffic going each day from Jericho to the river. Deciding to see for myself where everyone was headed, I walked down to Bethabara."

"Is that a village?" I asked, showing my ignorance of Judea.

"It is just a place, where one might, or might not, find the baptizer whom many were seeking. Some went to a place called Bethany-Beyond-Jordan. Be that as it may, I reached the Jordan. Then walking a short distance southward toward the great Salt Sea, I came upon a curious scene.

"In the river, where it meanders and is rarely deeper than a man's waist, stood a wild man. His hair was a tangled mass far down his back. His beard, equally unkempt, reached into the water and was tugged along by the current. 'Repent!' the wild man called. 'The kingdom of God is at hand!' Then he would dip beneath the water anyone who came forward to him for baptism."

Hearing these words, the very hairs of my back and arms stood up. My voice sounded faint and hoarse as I asked, "The Savior? Was he the Savior?"

The traveler shook his head. "When asked that, the wild man said, 'No! No! I am not he who is coming! I am the voice speaking before him.'"

"These were his very words?" I asked.

"Yes. His very words. 'The time is at hand,' he cried out. 'All who seek the Savior must prepare their hearts and be cleansed of their sins.'"

"Then what?" I asked impatiently.

"Then penitent ones would come forward. One by one, each was dipped beneath the water and baptized."

"Were you?" I asked, immediately regretting my rudeness.

The stranger stammered, "I . . . I did not enter the water . . ."

"Forgive me," I said. "I should not have asked." I stood up. "I must go now to find my brother."

I left. Laughter followed me. I could hear the fishermen telling the traveler, "Those brothers . . . they are good at work on the sea, but in the Savior's army, well . . ."

It was quite dark when I knocked urgently on the door of Simon's house. His wife opened the door.

"I must see Simon at once."

"He has been asleep a long time," she answered. "It will soon be time to go out again. I dare not wake him."

"But he will want to hear my news," I protested.

She meekly stood aside. I went directly to his bed.

"Simon! Simon!" I urged. "Wake up. I have good news."

There was no response. I knew how weary and spent my brother was, but still I shook him.

"A man, preaching the Savior's time to come is at hand, is baptizing in the Jordan near the Jericho road!"

Simon barely roused. "Midnight is almost here . . . come back then Andrew . . . tomorrow . . . sleep . . . sleep now," he begged groggily. "Tomorrow," he repeated and went back to snoring. His wife shook her head and showed me to the door.

I went home, unrolled my bed, and lay down to rest. I could not sleep. I closed my eyes but could not silence my heart's loud beating. I gave in to wild imagination. I roamed as in a waking dream, searching for the one the traveler through Jericho had called the Dipper. I could put no face upon him or on my Savior, but I tossed constantly trying to do so.

At midnight, Simon came to me. "What were you so excited about last evening?"

I told him about the traveler from Jericho, en route to Damascus, who saw a strange man prophesying that the Savior was soon to come.

Simon grasped my arm. "Then you must find him. You would be too distracted to work the nets. I will get young Eliezer to help me."

I was rolling and tying my bed even as he spoke. Quickly I washed my face and arms and thrust my feet into sandals, put on my loincloth, and then donned my best leather girdle over a light tunic. Simon fetched a small but full wineskin and a drawstring scrip into which he put a dozen dried fish, a handful of dates, and some flatbread. Then he pressed into my hands a few coins. I put them with a change of clothing into a shoulder purse.

"I wish it were I who was going," he said as he grasped my hand. He held me close saying, "Go in peace. Find the Savior."

"Tell Father," I begged. But just then the older man came in. We told him our news, and tears came into his eyes. "Oh! That I might look upon the hope of Israel," he wept.

He held both of us in his embrace, then bade me go in peace and return in haste when my purpose was satisfied.

I took my bedroll and reached for the sturdy staff I had carved during many hours while waiting for our dragnets to encounter a school of fish.

I walked no more than ten paces when Simon caught my arm. "Come with me," he said, "I'll ferry you to where the lake empties into the Jordan, then fish my way back home."

Thus our search for the Savior unexpectedly began.

The lad named Eliezer was at the quay. We took him on and caught the wind blowing southward; soon we were far from shore, riding waves and white caps, talking all the while about finding the One who is to come, the hope of Israel, the prophesied deliverer, the promised of the Lord. We never noticed the time passing.

At last, we anchored close to the place where the lake waters funnel into the south-running stream. I'd been given time to think aloud of all the hazards I might encounter traveling through the rift valley—thieves hiding in the thickets along the banks of the Jordan, brigands camped in the bordering hills. Scorpions and buzzards, jackals and foxes, serpents and stinging nettles all along my path.

"Don't, by any means, cut oleander for any purpose, not for firewood or defense or shade. It is toxic in smoke in sap in petal and leaf," Simon warned me.

Simon gave me much good counsel. Then he committed me to the care of the Lord of heaven and earth. I felt safe, and we parted.

I waded through hip-deep water to the nearest shore. When I looked back, the skiff was already catching new wind and tacking across the Sea of Galilee homeward, and Simon was showing Eliezer how to position the nets for casting them into the depths. I waved, but he could not see me in the dark of the trees on shore.

Many times during the next few days, I questioned my wisdom in following the river. I could have walked westward to Tiberias then south along the western lakeshore road until I came to the great trade route through the Valley of Jezreel, leading to Jerusalem.

Days were hot. Nights were cold. The wind blew dust and sand and often made it hard to see or even follow the faint paths of animals and men. I knew not who or what may have walked this rough path before me. But I kept my goal in thought every time I was challenged.

The valley was green along the watercourse but sere not far away from it. There, rocks and cliffs and sometimes barren land lay naked under the blaze of cloudless days.

When I needed rest, I chose the shade. When I needed cool, I slipped into the meandering river. But I never let my guard down or strayed too far from my staff.

At night from my well-chosen resting places among sun-heated boulders, I could hear the voices of lions, the barks of foxes, and the scream of a small creature caught in an owl's talons or a jackal's paw.

By day I was often startled, sometimes fearful; and occasionally, I lost my way in a maze of rocks. But my feet always regained the path, and I journeyed steadily southward, as did the Jordan River which flowed on, leading me.

I knew immediately when I left upper Galilee. Desert crowded in toward the river. Barrenness sometimes took the place of verdure in the widening space between the upthrust of the land and the southward fall of the stream. I knew I was in a wilderness between the hill country of Judea and the region of the great rift border of Moab lowering toward the area of the lifeless sea whose water is brine.

When the Jordan valley widened again into another plain, I knew I was nearing the place called Bethany-Beyond-Jordan, or farther along, perhaps Bethabara, where my journey might end.

Getting there was wearying, but the prospect of learning about the Messiah lent me heart and strength. I never gave in to the soreness of my feet and bones or the gnawing hunger in my belly.

Then that night I stopped in a place above the river, where rocks rose as though tumbled across a small plateau. The valley of the river seemed narrow below and then opened to an expanse of tawny undulating desert as far as I could see in the light of the full moon. I wrapped myself in my tunic and pulled my bedroll over me for a cover. The boulders exuded warmth, and soon I fell asleep. I was utterly spent and wished only to be at my journey's end.

I did not dream or waken the whole night through.

At daybreak I heard a voice crying, "Repent! A new kingdom is close by and soon to come."

I couldn't believe my good fortune. I had camped near the very place I intended to reach.

I heard a man proclaim loudly, "I am the one Esaias spoke of, one called to proclaim in this wilderness a warning to all. Prepare your hearts to learn the way of the Lord. Make straight a path for his feet and your own hearts pure for his words."

I hid my staff, my bedroll, and purse among the rocks, and ran down to join a throng on the riverbank.

Rounding a large boulder, I came upon a strange sight: A man wearing only a girdle of leather about his loins was gnawing on a piece of honeycomb. Then he stripped dark beans from locust tree pods into his fist, put some into his mouth, and chewed them.

He held some of his food out to me as I came close. I took it and ate. And he clasped my thigh and bade me welcome.

It was as though he recognized me, even knew me.

"Come," he said to me. "My name is John, and I am the Dipper."

"I am Andrew, a fisherman on the Lake of Galilee."

I cast off my tunic and entered the stream behind him.

"First I will secure your heart," he said, "for I sense that you also are a seeker."

With that he bent me back into the water, and the surprise and pain of the cold was a shock. I felt a kind of death take hold of me. Then John pulled me up and said, "You are forever changed . . . made into a vessel to honor the Lord. Do not return to your sins."

"Hear me," he said. "Become one of my helpers. I have raised you up. Now you can help the others I baptize get back to shore."

Many people were waiting, gathered where sand and scrub willows banked the stream.

He beckoned a Sadducee in flowing robes to come to him in the water. When the man hesitated and drew back, John pointed a finger directly to him, saying, "O generation of vipers, you and you and you."

He raged on, pointing also to the Pharisees and others from Jerusalem who had come out to investigate the strange doings.

"Who warned you to flee from the coming wrath? You poison men with dangerous dogmas. Treacherous and malign are you all, like vipers. Henceforth, devote yourselves to changing your ways. It is not enough that you call yourselves the children of Abraham. The God of Israel is able to raise up sons of these very stones on the ground where you stand and make them sons of Abraham."

To a man, the crowd became very quiet. "Repent, I say. Bear fruit to a new way of life . . . for an axe is to be laid at the root of every fruitless tree. Unless you bring forth fruits of repentance, you too shall be hewn down and burned.

"I am not worthy to carry the Redeemer's shoes. He will baptize you with the divine Spirit that your souls may be cleansed, truly purified, and made holy," John continued.

"He comes with fan in hand to separate chaff from wheat, purging the earth of that which has no substance. He shall baptize you with fire that your evil may be consumed and true light be given you. You must bring forth fruit fit to be gathered into his heavenly kingdom after he has consumed your false doctrines. But first you must be made to see your fruitless designs—your hypocrisy and ungodliness. If you do not heed him, unquenchable trouble and afflictions will come as fire for your cleansing."

Thus days were to pass, as I and one other person worked with John while waiting for the Messiah to appear. A never-ending stream of people came early each day to be baptized. By noon our work was done, and we could rest as John reviewed the call he had given to the poor and the warning he had delivered to the haughty in Israel.

Day after day the Pharisees and Sadducees came to watch the Baptist, who, time and again, thundered his message pointedly toward them.

"You come to hear a strange prophet in the wilderness. You hoped to see a king come to save you from oppression. Whom do you find? Not a king, but a bath attendant offering to wash away your sins. I do this as a sign that you pledge to mend your way of thinking. The way to escape and overcome evil is to think differently about fear and enchantment. Only God is to be feared. If you were willing to change your thinking, you would not need to come to me, a wild prophet. Your own wisdom would be clear. You would be ready to recognize the Savior when he comes.

"Will you recognize him and heed his words? obey his commands? follow his leading? I say not. For you have not purified your hearts, forsaken your faults, cast out your greed, or put forth your hands to serve others in justice and truth through the Word of God in your hearts. I am not the Savior. Indeed, I am not worthy to touch, much less loosen, the thongs which bind his sandals to his feet."

A gasp went up in the crowd. One mentioning shoes and feet in a company of people must apologize. Offense is taken from reference to that which is unclean. Such is a law of mankind.

Feet, that part of man which touches the earth, are unclean. Man walks where beasts tread and defecate, where men cast sputum, and where vile garbage is left to rot. To speak of sandals and feet, one should first make an apology. Then the mention becomes abasement of self in utter humility.

But John did not apologize! He disavowed any claim to the messiahship. Some of those present were men who always claim the upper seats at feasts, and others who make great display of piety in the temple when casting their tribute or pray loudly in the street to show how devout they are.

Most people awaiting their turn in the river were not from the high and mighty. They were working men and weary women, even little children and family elders, from many different walks of life. Some were farmers; others merchants, dyers and weavers, and garment makers; iron workers, vintners, and wine sellers; shepherds and fishers; masons and wheelwrights.

To me it seemed that the whole world was present to prepare for the coming of the one promised to redeem Israel.

I was fascinated by John's exhortations, for he thundered his words and gesticulated wildly. "Repent! Repent to remission of your sins! Think! Mere confession is not enough! Think again! From a new viewpoint. Think righteously. One moment of thinking as the Almighty thinks brings salvation. Be willing to change your mind. Freedom comes not from armies. Ceremonies will not purify you, for ceremonies are empty traditions, leaving you free to repeat every offense.

"Set your hearts at work to purify your thoughts. Then you will be fit for the kingdom at hand. You have Isaiah who cried, 'Wash you, make you clean.' You have Moses, who, when bidden to sanctify the people of God, had them wash their garments before they received the covenant. Even so I prepare you to know your Redeemer when he comes. It is he who will baptize you with the Holy Spirit and with fire. It is he who will utterly change you and make you fit for the coming kingdom of God."

The throng of people listened, waiting patiently. They came one by one into the river, and John baptized each of them. When they came up from the depth, we who were helping led them dripping back to the riverbank. Most then turned homeward, already aflame with new hope.

All told, I stayed with this wilderness preacher for fifty days, helping to lift from beneath the water of the Jordan River many repentant ones newly committed to better lives. Through this ceremony of baptism, they pledged themselves to newness of thought, refinement of heart, ready to serve the promised Savior of Israel when he appeared.

When asked what further they might do, the Baptist told the people, "Give of your own possession that which will warm the man who has no coat." To the tax collectors he said, "Do not take more than is due and accept no bribes." To soldiers, "Do violence to no man nor accuse any falsely. Be content with what you've earned."

He was asked repeatedly, "Are you the Savior?" John always answered, "One is coming who will baptize you with fire and the spirit of God. He is the Savior."

One day I left the river to return to the place where I stashed my clothing and food. There I ate some dates and dried grapes. I was about to go down again to the river when I heard a sharp cracking sound like thunder. There were no clouds in the sky, and I thought maybe a boulder had been split by the heat of the sun, but there was no falling rock.

I ran down to the beach and saw John standing alone in the flowing stream. The people were gone. The day's work was finished.

The Baptist was almost weeping. He dragged his feet to the shore and fell upon the trodden sand. "I did not recognize my own kin."

"Who?" I asked urgently, and immediately I heard for the first time the name of the Anointed One.

John answered, "Jesus of Nazareth, my kinsman, the only true companion I had as a youth. As lads we spent many hours together, both of us speculating about our futures, both of us cautious in the presence of others but openhearted to one another. I did not recognize him." John fell to weeping aloud.

"Tell me," I begged. "Why does this hurt you so?"

I sat quietly beside him until his tears of regret were spent. Then he began to talk.

"We were bound together even before our birth. They say I leaped with joy within the womb when his mother came to visit mine. I do not remember this, of course, but I believe it, for it was often told to me by my parents. He is only a few months younger than I. But I never met him until our eighth year. He lived in Egypt during his early childhood. But when his parents returned to Israel, they came to Jerusalem each year to observe Passover. They stayed at our home in Ein Kerem. Our pretty village had a spring in the nearby vineyards where we played as children.

"We grew together into young manhood enjoying these visits. Sometimes we would sit for hours in the shade of a fig tree and speculate about the time to come. We had both been told we were to be special servants of the Most High God. In my tenth year, some years before my father died—God keep his sweet soul—he told me how an angel had appeared to him as he served at the altar in the great temple, and told him that I would be born. Though she no longer had the strength and time of life to bear a child, my mother, now long departed from this world, gave birth to me in her extreme old age," John said.

"Jesus was born of a slip of a girl-child who seemed barely old enough to raise a son. She and my mother were kin, both blessed by God; and blessing poured through them to us, for we were the first fruit of their wombs. I was orphaned at a still-tender age and was then cared for in a desert region by people who separated themselves from the impure and impious and trained me to revere the One Supreme God. I matured and followed the course set for me by the angel before my birth. Now I am to prepare the heart of mankind for response to the Anointed One promised by God. And so I am doing."

I could scarcely breathe. This wild man before whom I sat filled my ears with words hard to believe. He was indeed one crying in the wilderness of human hearts, preparing the way of the Lord. And the promised Son of God was, in truth, his cousin.

I trembled with joy and wept too with a heart more grateful to heaven than a fisherman could ever show, even when his vessel overflows with a prime catch.

"Will he return here, this Savior of Israel?" I asked.

"I think he is nearby and soon will come." He began to lament again. "How did I not know him when he came to me?"

John continued, "He has been around here for several days. I'm sure you beheld his presence among those who came from the city, with the scribes and publicans, Pharisees and priests, and wealthy Sadducees scattered among the common people." John spoke quietly.

My heart leaped! I had been terrified that perhaps I was too late to see him.

John continued, "I saw Jesus standing there. Watching me. When those who came for baptism today departed, he came walking to me in this very river."

My heart sank. He had come today while I was gone, but yes, I had seen among the throng a man who seemed different.

John went on, "As he came toward me, I saw a dove descend from high heaven. It came to rest briefly upon his shoulder. He said to me simply, 'I have come to be baptized.' It was then that I recognized my kinfolk Jesus. And hugging him, I said, 'I must be baptized of *you*, with fire and the Spirit of God to consume my worldly ways. How is it you come to me?'"

"I swear I heard him chuckle when I spoke of my worldliness. But he said, 'No, I must be baptized of you, for then I shall have fulfilled that which is a symbol that one has been made righteous, purged of this world's charms, and freed from its enticement. You are to witness my pledge. Thus I shall fulfill all righteousness.'

"I knew him for certain, just by his voice. This was he who shared assignment with me from God, from our very birth. He who would now increase as I must now diminish. He was indeed my kin, this Jesus of Nazareth, only now he is older and quieter. I looked deep into his eyes. I saw no fear. Only the light of love—a deep, unfailing, unflinching love.

"I reached out my arms, and he walked into my embrace and held me to his heart. I lowered him into the water, dipping deeply until it flowed over both of us. Then we rose up smiling, as rivulets dripped from our hair to our foreheads, into our eyes, down our cheeks and beards, thence to fall again into the stream. We waded ashore, our hands still clasped. I saw heaven open again, and a snow white dove descended to him. We heard a voice from heaven proclaim, 'This is my beloved Son, in whom I am well pleased. Hear his words.'"

John the Baptist laid his hand upon my shoulder. "Did you hear the thunder, Andrew?"

From the way my body trembled, he knew I had heard it.

"Is this why you have come to me?" he inquired. "Are you seeking God's anointed?"

"It is," I answered. "I am. I would follow him at once even though I have not seen him. But first I must find my brother and bring him. His heart is, like mine, pledged to serve him, to walk beside him, to help him put Rome out of our land."

"He is truly the Savior you seek," John said. "But do not forget, he will baptize you with fire as well as the Holy Spirit."

"I would serve him even unto death!" I cried eagerly.

"Then he will choose you, for he seeks the truly brave and the wholly ready. I perceive you know your need of him."

"Yes, I do. Where is he now?" I asked.

"I do not know," John said sadly. "Immediately after heaven opened upon him and we heard God's voice, he rushed from me into the wilderness. He will come forth in his time and seek his own. Go now, bring your brother, and keep in your heart all I have told you."

So I returned home to Capernaum via the road that led through Jerusalem, into hill country and through valleys, back to my town on the shore of that sweet lake in the north of Galilee.

The first day back in Capernaum, I went fishing again. As we trolled the lake, Simon had me tell him about the Baptist again and again.

That evening Jona said to us, "I can see your hearts are yearning to join this Jesus. I give you leave to go to him with my blessing. Others will help me harvest the lake. Follow your hearts. I will be cared for among our kin in the village. Would that my legs could carry me along with you. But they cannot. Take me in your hearts instead."

We left our father the next morning. Several days later, we had walked the distance from Galilee to Jerusalem, on to Jericho, thence to Bethabara, where the plain widens toward desert regions and the river flows gently and willow trees pour shade upon warm sandbanks.

John was glad that I returned, and he and my brother soon became fast friends.

Simon, I, and another disciple of John worked in the cool shallows of the river. Many came to be baptized.

Then one day weeks later, after our work was finished, we saw a tall, slender man walking nearby but not coming to where we were resting. Suddenly John stood up, saying quietly, "This is he of whom I bear witness." And he held out his arms to bar our rushing to the man. "Behold, the Lamb of God," he said. "Tomorrow you may go to him."

Neither Simon nor I could sleep that night. Quietly, so as not to disturb John, we talked of the Savior and wondered what sort of army he would need to wrest Palestine from the power of Rome.

Very early the next morning while it was still dark, Simon hurried to Jericho to purchase victuals. When he returned I told him that we had again seen the Lamb of God. He fell to the earth and pounded the sand with his fists, and was consoled only when I said, "He is staying close by; tomorrow you will see him."

And I did. But again Simon was elsewhere. I was at once on my feet.

I barely heard John say to me, "This is my dearly loved kin, the Lamb of God. His name is Jesus. Go! Follow him. You are his. Serve him with your whole heart."

Immediately I left John and followed Jesus as he walked away from the river. Suddenly, he turned. "What are you seeking?" he asked.

I answered, "Master, where do you live?"

"Come and see," was his simple answer.

We walked away from the river a short distance into the sere wilderness area of desert valleys between barren heights. He led me to a place where an outcropping of overhanging rock sheltered a small space between two large boulders shaded by an acacia tree.

"This is where I am staying," he said, "at least for the while. "In truth, I live where my Father dwells."

"Who is your father?" I asked.

"You know Him. He fills heaven and earth. Therefore, I am at home wherever I go. If you abide with me, I will show Him to you and you to Him."

"Are you the one to come?" I asked boldly.

"I am," was his gentle answer.

"Permit me, then, Master, to fetch my brother. He will also follow you, if you wish."

"Yes, go!" he said.

I hurried to the river. Simon was back, talking with the Baptist.

"Simon! Come!" I called. "We are staying with him today. Make haste!"

Without a word, John reached forth and, embracing Simon, bestowed a kiss on his forehead. Then Simon turned and came running to where I was waiting.

When we reached the Master's place in the rocks, Jesus saw us and greeted my brother, saying, "You are Simon, also a son of Jona, but I shall call you Cephas, which means 'a stone.' You are now Simon Petros—Simon Peter."

I recalled words I once heard from the Baptist as he railed against the Pharisees. "God is able to raise children unto Abraham of these very stones." Now I thought, *My brother is the first to be raised a stone in a new order being built by this man.*

So I left Simon with Jesus and wandered away. It was his turn to become acquainted. It was enough for me to see him where we both most wanted to be, at the feet of the Promised One. I was content.

We slept that night in the shelter of the rocks. When it was morning, Jesus said, "It is very early. Let us go again to John."

John welcomed us with an almost childlike joy. The morning air was already unbearably hot. "It will mean either no penitents today or many," he said. "Let's sit in the shadow of the willows and talk." He looked into Jesus's eyes and said, "I have many things to ask you."

Once we were sprawled comfortably beneath the trees, Jesus said, "What would you learn of me, John?"

John replied, "Where did you go when you left here so many days ago?"

Jesus sat silently, deep in thought for a few moments. It seemed he was praying.

When he spoke, he lifted his eyes to us. And his words came like a torrent after sudden heavy rain.

"No sooner had I risen from the water, John, and gained my foothold on the riverbank when the Spirit of my Father in heaven commanded me to flee into the wilderness, to be tested there.

"I hastened into the desert of Moab. When I sat down to rest, the Spirit said, 'Go farther.' I obeyed. I scarcely noticed the sun withdrawing as I ran ceaselessly, but night seemed to suddenly fall.

"In the dark I ran on, often stumbling; and it seemed I might break my shins against outcropping rocks, and my legs were pierced by thorny bushes.

"I ran through a small oasis inhabited by leopards. One chased me until I felt I would drop, but when I turned to face my fear, the leopard turned also and leaped atop a flat rock. It watched me while I sat to catch my breath, then it slept, and I crept away.

"Along the way foxes and jackals barked. I sometimes smelled the sharp odor of weasels and often heard coneys scurrying from my path. Altogether, it was not a pleasant passage deep into the wilderness. The night air was cold, my belly was empty, and I felt forlorn and wretched. But in my mind's eye, there was a single point of light to brighten the pathless waste. My only thought was of Almighty God, who sent me hither. He would lead me forth.

"The night around me was very dark as I moved on through many fears, conquering each by claiming the presence of God with me. I held on to that faint beam of light within. I thought if there is light within, one need never fear darkness.

"Light must always be there; this was my first lesson. I found light to be not in the air around me but in my mind. Not in sun or moon or stars or fire or candle or torch, for God made light to be present when there was as yet no heaven in which to place the orb of day or a moon mirror to shine at night. There were no starry points of light to beautify the vault above, hinting of other places, other glories. Out of darkness He called forth light. I learned that I must do so also."

"Master, you speak like the psalmist." This came from my brother.

Jesus turned to him. "Simon, I have all the Psalms in memory. You will do well to study them also, and learn every word spoken from the mouth of the Lord. Write them upon the table of your heart. In just this manner I have learned much that I know. Truth comes from God, for God is Truth and gives understanding to all who seek Him."

John said, "The very earth is crying for you. Israel gasps for air under the heel of Rome. The only hope for freedom is in God's promise of a Redeemer, and here you are!"

Jesus answered, "The Son of God is sent to put his heel upon the head of serpents. For this task my mother gave me instruction. My abba, Joseph, also helped, for he showed me how to recognize serpents."

"The wilderness is thick with vipers." It was Simon who spoke.

"I will teach you to handle the serpents which appear in your thoughts and are evil. Then they cannot harm. This also I learned in my youth."

"Tell us more about your days in the wilderness," John begged.

"That first night, I learned to subdue fear," Jesus said. "Then for many days, I lived in a cleft in the rocks. When wind raged, I quieted myself, and it would cease. When I was thirsty, I drank water from heaven, but not as you are thinking, for such water cannot be poured into a cup. It must be thought. Everything must be thought, for therein we have both possession and dominion. Can you understand this?"

No one answered yes except the Baptist. "Many times I have heard you reason like this, but for them this is new," he said, nodding to us.

"Then let me teach in small ways the large lessons and virtues given me by the Spirit of God in the wilderness. For, indeed, it was the understanding of God which delivered me from every danger and the snare of fears in the isolation and darkness of that first and every night following.

"Before I tell you though, let me explain this. From earliest years, I was taught scripture—first at home, and then in the synagogue school, even as you also were taught. My rabbi instructed me in the law of Moses. A few years later, I set out with my carpenter's skills and traveled wherever the wind blew to learn of the many things for good or for evil that live in the heart of mankind.

"Then I came back to the Galilee of my youth to ply my trade and meditate on what I had learned from the scriptures and of the world through which I had walked. John, you lived in the desert here but nearer the Dead Sea, among men seeking holiness and God. I visited you once, and we spent many hours both in conversation and thoughtful silence. At length we learned to hear the voice of God. Do you remember?"

John's eyes softened, and he nodded. "It was hard, was it not, to harness our young lives to divine will under the strain of rabbinical laws and teaching. I could hardly wait until the time came when I could come forth to speak of your coming."

Jesus gently touched John's arm. "But we did conform to the law, until our Father in heaven unleashed in you and me a new doctrine wherein the children of men may learn to fulfill all righteousness. We were both taught this truth: 'I AM the Lord, and there is none else. There is no God beside me.'"

Simon then spoke so softly I could hardly hear his words, "Master, is that how one comes to love all things one looks upon? In your thought, do you see God everywhere?" Jesus smiled and lovingly reached forth and this time touched my brother's hand, nodding yes.

Chapter 2

"Now then," Jesus said, "we must soon depart. But let me teach you a little more. The earth and all it holds is the manifestation of God who is divine intelligence, the eternal substance which does not scatter in the wind, or dislodge in the lift of an eagle's wing, or turn to ash in fire, or mold in the grave. One who learns this finds it is true. That which endures is spiritual. It abides ever the same yesterday, today, and forever, and we know its substance is divine Mind.

"I had to first learn and then prove God to be the source of all I think and see and hear. I had to learn to see through thought, not through this body's eyes. And to think as God thinks, for God's thoughts constitute only that which is real and nothing else.

"Yes, I ran fearfully into the wilderness day and night it seemed. Wildly at first, through the roaring wasteland of heat, with hunger, and terror, and temptation in my soul. I ran desperately. Thornbush and spine plants tore at my flesh and shredded my garment. I ran on and on. Desert creatures hissed, barked, or roared, and sprang at me. I usually ran until morning stars began to fade.

"Then one day a strange light seemed to obliterate the bleakness of the land. I saw cities and villages and seas and encampments at many green oases on the right hand and on the left. But it was all unreal. I was alone in a vast desert desolation, beholding what had no real existence.

"When I could run no longer, I simply collapsed and sat beneath a sheltering rock overhang in the wilderness for many days and many sleepless nights. Thinking. Reasoning. Affirming that you and I, and all men, are created to be the image of God. *Where would such truth lead me?* I wondered.

"I learned that intelligence and wisdom, not dust or flesh, are the substance of the man God calls into being. I pondered this. Gradually I noticed no passage of time, no heat or cold, no weariness, no hunger nor thirst, no loneliness, no uncertainty. Thus in quietness and confidence, I learned from God the work that I must do.

"I knew He would perform in me that which is appointed for me. Gradually my thoughts came back to earth, for I had been moved by God's thoughts into a heaven of great harmony and beauty and glory. I had no mind and no life but God. I had need for nothing other than His Love, and no purpose but His will. I glimpsed the infinity and eternality prepared for all who love God.

"One moment I was in a transport of glory and wonder, and in the next I saw around me the lifeless desert, the brittle thornbush, the viper's hole. As though it was my own voice, I heard words tempting me to forsake all I had seen of heaven. 'I hunger. If I am the Son of God, I can make the stones at my feet into bread.'

"But I knew that God is the one, the only creator. I rebuked the suggestion, answering aloud, 'It is written, man shall not live by bread alone, but by every word that comes from the mouth of God.' I screamed this to the wind again and again.

"Then it seemed that I was in the city of David, atop the temple at the very summit, on a spire too small for even a bird to rest upon. Again a voice, which *seemed* so like my own, said, 'If I truly am the Son of God, then, if I cast myself down, His angels will hold me up, and my foot will not strike against the stones below.'

"But the voice that was truly mine replied, 'It is also written, "You shall not tempt the Lord who is your God."' I was now on a very high mountain, so high I thought all the kingdoms of the world could be seen at once. The world was glorious, so to be desired as one's own possession.

"The suggestion came that all that I beheld in that vision would be mine if I would forsake God's purpose in me and worship the things of earth. At once I discerned the great evil and malice of the carnal mind toward God, trying to possess my will and use me to satisfy flesh rather than the Spirit of God.

"Evil would pretend to reward my spiritual infidelity with an abundance of things I could possess. Things which ultimately would be either lost, stolen, consumed, or destroyed, for such is the fate of earthly treasure. I thought of one, who, in the legend of earth's earliest paradise listened to the tempting suggestion that to be like God, eating fruit of a special tree would impart knowledge of evil as well as of good, thereby making mankind to be as gods.

"I declared, 'Never! Depart from me evil suggestion! You are not my thoughts! Not my mind! It is written, "Man shall worship the Lord our God and shall serve Him only."'

"At once the evil notions ceased, and angels as holy thoughts came to me. I felt strengthened, comforted, refreshed, and blessed, whereas before I seemed weak, tempted, hungry, and besieged. Thus I survived the wilderness temptations. Now I must work for God, the One who saved me. Let us go forth . . ."

We bade farewell to John the Baptist and set out on the road to Jericho.

As we walked away from the river, we saw a man standing beside the road. Simon and I knew him. He was a charioteer who worked with horses and was from Bethsaida, the village close to ours on the shore of the lake where we fished. He had heard from Jona, our father, that we had gone to find the Savior.

Jesus stopped where Philip of Bethsaida stood waiting and said directly to him, "Follow me . . ."

Not follow us, but follow me. All are to follow *him*, listen to *his* words, do *his* bidding, and prove our worth to *him*. Philip fell in step.

As we walked, Jesus spoke of the glory of the world around us—of shade, of sun, of shelter given by rocks, of the hardiness of persistent growth shown in blossoms on small plants growing in rock crevices, of the majesty of trees, each with distinct form and fruit. All these he praised.

We walked on.

Jesus watched the sky and saw a falcon diving from on high. He noticed clouds racing westward to evaporate in heat rising from the eastward desert of Moab.

"The earth is more than my Father's footstool," he explained. "He lives in all life and rests within the rocks."

We passed from Judea into Galilee and spent the night in the Jezreel Valley. We sat late into the night, talking around our small fire.

I remember we talked about the hope of Israel. How we were waiting with bated breath and eager yearning for the reign of God throughout the land given to us by God from the time of Moses.

We wanted freedom to live and worship the God of Abraham, Isaac, and Jacob—the God of our fathers, the God who had chosen Israel for an inheritance from heaven.

Jesus cautioned us, "It is not an earthly kingdom you must seek. Look for signs of a *coming* kingdom. I say to you, it is to be a spiritual dominion and must be established in every receptive heart and mind and become one's own consciousness.

"You think Israel's need is deliverance from oppression. I tell you this: The real need is to be delivered, not from the yoke of Rome, but from errant and mistaken ways of thought. Such ways are destructive and hold you in bondage to flesh and lead not to life, but to death.

"Of a truth I tell you, Israel is not just a people. It is a state of spiritual consciousness. The true children of Abraham are those who worship the God who is Almighty, supreme over all that is. Such as they must be willing to conform to the will of God. Israel as a people is chosen of God to show righteousness, through word and deed, to the whole world and all people on the earth."

None of us responded. We were lost in thought, pondering the words just spoken.

At length Jesus rose and went off to pray. With that, we each unrolled our beds, pulled our cloaks around us, and went to sleep.

Upon waking early the next morning, I saw that Philip had rolled up his pallet and left it leaning against the tree beneath which we slept.

Though we knew it not then, Philip had taken off at midnight to go beyond the village of Nazareth to Cana where a good friend of his lived. This friend also watched for the Savior. When Philip told him that Jesus of Nazareth was the one to come forth, Nathanael bar Tolmai (we later learned) asked, "Can any good thing come out of Nazareth?"

Philip simply said, "Come, and you will see." They hurried back as far as Nazareth and sat beneath an acacia tree at the edge of town near the highway to wait for Jesus to arrive in Nazareth, his hometown.

They saw us as we approached and ran to greet us.

Jesus said, "Behold, an Israelite who holds no cunning, no duplicity, no deceit in his heart." He spoke of the man who stood beside Philip.

Nathanael bar Tolmai of Cana asked, "From what place do you know me?"

Jesus answered, "Before Philip found you, I saw you sitting under a fig tree."

Nathanael was surprised. "Master," he said, "if you *saw* me, you are indeed sent of God to rule in Israel!"

Jesus responded with words that touched us all. "Because I said I saw you far off under a fig tree, you believe? I did see you talking to Philip at your abode. Do not marvel. You will be shown greater things than this. You will witness heaven opening before your eyes and will see angels of God ascending and descending upon me, though I also am born of flesh."

Nathanael said, "How shall it be! That I shall behold angels?"

Jesus replied, "You will see with your mind, not with your eyes."

It was late the morning of the third day after we left the Jordan River when we reached the village of Nazareth.

Jesus led the way to a house located on the edge of the village overlooking the valley below. Here he had lived as a child. He did not tell us much more than that. We looked around for a while. Then we walked on, talking among ourselves about our lives and homes.

Jesus was amused that Simon and I were acquainted with Philip, whose home in Bethsaida was not far from ours in Capernaum.

The people of the two close villages are well known to each other. Philip told Jesus he knew most of the fishermen in the area but wondered how it was that Simon and I so eagerly left our nets when we heard that the Savior might have come. Philip was also curious to know how our households would flourish without our nightly catch, for we were known to be skilled fishermen.

Thus we were jabbering as we walked. But then our tongues fell silent as if given a signal. Jesus suddenly left the path. He pushed through scrub brush to a rock formation, which rose up sharply a short way off.

We sought shade in the outcropping and were told to rest a bit. "Then," said Jesus, "I will begin to teach you from whence I come and what it means to be my followers."

Soon I and the others fell asleep. But later we came to when Jesus roused us to wakefulness and beckoned us to gather at his feet while he leaned against the sheltering boulder which cast coolness in the deep shadow.

"I have much to teach," Jesus began, "but we will journey together only as long as you can bear my message. I am sent to men who are willing to hear my words. Having heard, they must understand. Understanding will lead to practice, and practice will become a fruitful harvest.

"You have ears with which to listen, but even more, you have heart and mind with which to perceive what I speak. I will tell you of my Father's house and of the world to come. Make of it what you may, and follow as best you can."

I cannot speak for the others, but already my ears were burning. As if he knew, Jesus said, "The scriptures say that God's Promised One is to 'sit as a refiner's fire.' Fear not the flames you may feel. Gold does not resist heat but yields to it, for thus it becomes purified. You shall become as gold in the kingdom of God." He looked deeply into my eyes as he spoke those words.

"Now we begin," he continued. "You know that Abraham sought a city whose builder and maker is God. He sojourned in many places until he learned that wherever he was, God was there also. He learned that the Almighty, though unseen, would go before him to lead and instruct and save.

"Later, much later, Moses took the children of God away from the people in Egypt who worshipped many deities," Jesus said. "Tell me what more you know of Moses." No one ventured a word. "Come now," he urged. "When I ask, you must respond."

My brother, ever eager—sometimes rashly so—answered, "He saved our forefathers and brought them out of Egypt through miracles."

"He talked with God," I answered simply.

Cautiously, Philip asked, "Did he not set forth traditions and laws we keep even today?"

"All that," Jesus replied, "and so much more. With one insight, God gave Moses the key to open every man's mind to know Deity. It was not a restriction. It was a revelation. It was a prophecy, more than a command: 'You shall have no God but me.'"

"But, Master, I have always thought it was an order, a charge that we *must* obey," my brother ventured.

"True, Simon. It is a directive. But even more, it is a promise to know and *understand* because there is no other than our God. Though there be gods and lords many, there is only one God.

"Think this through with me: God spoke these words to the children who came out of Egypt. They had not known one God because of a multitude of figures worshipped as deities in Goshen in the land of Egypt.

"Moses had been out of Egypt long before God called him to free the children of Israel. He sat for tens of years in the foothill region of Sinai as a shepherd, tending the flocks of the priest of Midian.

"Midianites were descended from a son of Abraham by his second wife, Ketura. She had six sons, who fathered six desert tribes. Abraham sent these sons away with gifts to dwell in the stillness of the desert and the meager pasturelands of Sinai. And here, Moses loosed his thoughts from the courts of Pharaoh and the many gods of Egypt.

"Here, for the first time, Moses heard the voice of the one true God and saw in a burning bush substance which could not be destroyed, even by fire. He glimpsed the true nature of God: that God is never material, destructible, nor destructive. That God is not cruel but strangely ever present, all-powerful, and knowable.

"But most of all, that God was mindful of the people He had chosen to call His own. The children of Israel are descendants of Abraham, the first man who sought to know the Almighty, the maker of all that endures.

"God sent Moses back to Egypt to bring forth the children of Abraham to be God's own. And though they knew it not, God told Moses to reassure the people that they would see proof that God was with them. They did see this when the sea opened for their escape from Egypt. If they could understand this unseen Deity, they would neither need nor want any god other than the Almighty God who guided Abraham all the days of his life."

Jesus studied each of our faces. Had we understood?

Philip inquired, "How did you learn all this?"

Jesus answered, "I have spent more than half of my days in study and prayer, waiting for God to call me forth. It could not happen until I understood Him in every way. God opened heaven to me, and now I come to gather into His kingdom all who can understand. You are my first planting in this new order of life in God, good."

"We are simple men, Lord . . . ," said Philip.

"Perhaps," he replied, "but if you *can* understand and follow me, no one else can give excuse for not doing so. The kingdom is for all. Everyone, of low estate or high, must be willing to lose self in order to find and know God."

"Where is this God?" I asked. "When we see Him, how shall we know it is Him?"

Jesus answered, "God is not a man to appear like men, yet He can be seen in all men." When Jesus said this, I wondered if his teaching would be in riddles.

"I do not understand," my brother protested. "How shall we see Him if He is in all? Has God a form that men may bow before Him and bring Him tribute and offerings?"

Jesus smiled. "You ask a good question," he said. Then he grew sober. "I never had to ask this of any teacher. It was always in me to know that God could never be limited. It was given to me to know Him and understand Him to be the One conscious of all that is. He is the Mind of the universe. The thoughts of God become the Holy Spirit when perceived by man, God's image and likeness."

I reeled before these words! How could this be? How could one worship a *mind* with gifts in hand, a wave offering or meal offering or a sweet sacrifice, a lamb or a dove?

Only God as Spirit can we understand Him to be everywhere at once, and knowing all that can be known, I reasoned, Could God have recruited me to know Him by knowing already what was in my heart? I felt joy thrill my body. *The refiner's fire*, I thought. This is enough to know. I can take no more.

I looked at Jesus. He was looking into my eyes. He seemed to be looking into the eyes of each one of us at once. We were connected to him and to each other. *This is the very presence of God*, I thought. *It is bliss.*

From the shadow of the outcropping rock Jesus now led us back to the road.

We walked on toward Cana, where Nathanael lived and where Jesus's mother, Mary, widow of Joseph the carpenter of Nazareth, now lived with one of her daughters, whose name was Shiphrah.

Earlier, Jesus had been invited to the wedding of his younger sister, Abigail. Friends traveling with him were also welcome to attend. So when we arrived, they greeted all warmly. We met his mother; his brothers Simon, Judas, Joses, and James; his two sisters; and Geber, the husband of Shiphrah.

Twelve months before, Jesus had presided at Abigail's betrothal ceremony and received for her the bride-price he'd negotiated with the groom. This is the custom of our people.

Now the harvest was in, and the wedding date had arrived. Food was being prepared, musicians were hired, the wine was brought in and made ready to be served, and the governor of the feast was engaged. It was to be a festive and joyous time with neighbors, relatives, and friends bidden to attend the wedding procession and a late supper. Thus preparations for the marriage the next evening were well underway.

That night we slept in the garden, and in the morning the bride wakened us from our sleep. Her wedding day had arrived, and we all were put to work.

I recall Abigail's radiant face and gentle manner. She was betrothed to a young shepherd, Timon by name, and was to move at the end of the marriage celebration to the hut her husband had built for her on the hillside where he tended the gathered flocks of the villagers.

After the courtyard was swept, we helped set up trestles and laid planks for tables. We carried water and poured it in some of the jars hidden from heat of the sun in the loggia.

It was early evening when the house was finally ready to receive guests. We had a light supper; then Simon, Nathanael, Philip, and I walked with Jesus and his brothers up to the home prepared by the bridegroom.

As we climbed, we heard singing. Other friends had already arrived and were celebrating. Jesus greeted everyone in the house. Then he went out to climb higher into the foothills. He motioned for me to walk with him. Soon we reached the top of the hill. Cana lay beneath us, golden in the rich sunshine of the closing day.

We sat on a rock ledge and watched the sun disappear. For the longest time we were silent. Then Jesus spoke. "Do you like weddings?" he asked me.

"I do," I replied. "Like the birth of a baby, it is a time of shared happiness. I have attended many weddings. Have you?" I asked.

"Several," he answered.

"You sound sad, Master," I said gently.

"I am not in this dream of life," he said. "Nor will I ever be."

"Why?" I asked.

"It is not the will of my Father in heaven," he answered, "and I have molded my will to His."

"Then you will no doubt be given greater joy," I said, hoping it would cheer him a bit.

"I have no greater joy than to do His will," he replied, brightening and breaking out of the gloom of sadness.

"Your family is pleased with the bridegroom?" I asked.

"Yes, and also for Abigail." We sat there quietly for a while.

I was imagining the activity at the house where the bride was being readied for her nuptials. I knew her friends would be dressing her in an elaborately embroidered gown, placing jewels in her hair.

Jesus told me the gold coins, which were her dowry gift given at the time of betrothal, had been woven into a necklace, fashioned with chains and modest rounded gemstones.

Her maidens would now be fussing, as close friends are wont to, fixing her necklace just so around her neck. They would make ready small clay lamps, filling them with oil, and providing vials of extra oil to hang on cords from their fingers. They would carry these as the bridegroom came, and they went forth to greet him.

I could almost see the excitement our traditions demand, as young friends, wearing their own embroidered dresses, flutter around the bride in her finery. They would place a veil over her face and a wreath of meadow flowers upon her head, then don floral wreathlets on their own brows and wrists.

At length I suggested, "They are now in their wedding garments, awaiting the arrival of the bridegroom. Shall we put on our tunics and light our torches? It will soon be time to go down."

As soon as we were prepared for the ceremony, Jesus left us and walked alone back to the village, for he was to ascertain if his mother and the maidens were ready to receive the bridegroom, who was coming to claim his bride. Jesus found everything in readiness, except for the lighting of the lamps.

Then, from the hilltop, the bridegroom and his friends started downward, carrying burning torches. We who were friends of Jesus walked behind the groomsmen.

Before we reached the house, the cry went out, "The bridegroom comes!" And at that, the door opened, and Abigail's maidens danced into the street, carrying the little lighted lamps in their hands so that flickering light illumined the house where the bride was waiting.

When the groom arrived at the door, he asked to see his bride. From where I stood, I saw her appear in her swathed beauty, her face hidden from sight. "May I see the one I've chosen to be my wife?" he asked according to tradition. With that, he lifted her veil and cried out in joy for the treasure he was acquiring.

The groomsmen took up the cry as the groom led Jesus's sweet young sister into the street. The handmaidens followed, and the bridal couple led the wedding party in a joyful procession. The torches and handheld lamps lighted the path for the couple, and their musicians piped the villagers to wakefulness. There was no oath or promise given. The contract had been signed long before. Now it was all joy.

The groom's family lived a great distance away from Cana, and so the couple was escorted back to the home of the bride with music and song and joyous dancing.

There was a late supper of bread dipped in honeyed butter and cheese curds with dates, figs, and fresh grapes, also pistachio nuts and almond kernels and walnuts; and must of unfermented grapes was served so the guests would not become drunken and rowdy. There was minced lamb rolled into vine leaves and aubergines roasted with peppers, chilies, and onions. There was bulgur wheat with mint and other herbs, as well as cucumbers dressed with oil and lemon.

At the conclusion of the supper, Jesus and his mother escorted the newly wedded couple to the nuptial chamber.

I was waiting at the gate of the court when Jesus came forth into the darkness, having completed his duties as eldest brother, in the absence of Joseph, the long-deceased head of Mary's family. I reached out to Jesus. He took my hand,

and I reached over it with my other one in a gesture of comfort. Jesus smiled, wanly I think, though I could not see through the darkness if this was so.

"My meat and my marriage is to do the will of my Heavenly Father," he said.

We all slept that night beneath a tall locust tree, but Jesus did not sleep. Each time I wakened, I heard him praying, for he was sitting close by me against the tree. I could almost hear his whispered words as he talked with his dear Heavenly Father.

After the midnight wedding, we slept until the celebration began early the next day. It soon became joyous and festive. But wine was in short supply. When the guests called for more, there was none to bring forth.

I noticed Jesus talking with his mother. She seemed distressed, and Jesus shook his head as she spoke with him.

Later he told me, "She said, 'We have no wine.' I replied that I could do nothing to save the hour. 'Woman, what have I to do with you? Is this the hour to begin to work the miracles of the One who sent me?' I asked."

"'Every hour is His hour. This I well know,' she said to me. Then she turned to the household servant. 'Do whatever he tells you to do.'"

Jesus shrugged his shoulders when he told me this. I had seen Mary smile at Jesus. She touched his arm and walked away.

I then watched as Jesus went to the loggia. The six stone jars used for purifying water were there, each half full. I knew this because Simon, the others, and I had earlier gone to the village well to fill pots, which we then emptied into the water jars.

Jesus said to the servants, "*Fill* them all." And the servants obeyed, hurrying to the well, which was not far off. Soon each jar was full to the brim.

Then Jesus did an amazing thing. He said to a servant, "Now draw from the first vessel and bear it to the governor of the wedding."

The servant obeyed.

I watched as the ruler of the feast tasted the liquid which was brought forth. He seemed surprised, and pleased.

"Call the bridegroom to me," he said. "I must praise this wine for it is very good."

Timon, the young shepherd, came shyly to stand before the wedding guests.

"Well now," the ruler of the feast began to say, "the wine served at the start of your celebration was good. We have all drunk of it and crave more. Customarily the best wine is set forth when the tongue can appreciate its fullness. Then when appetite and taste are dulled, a lesser vintage is brought out. But this, this is better than good wine; it is the best that heaven can steep from fruit of the vine. I say, may the days of your marriage be this good—at its finest as each year ends—through all the years of your life."

The guests were then served the strange wine. No one became inebriated, for it was the first fruit—not of the vineyard—but of the kingdom of God now coming to man.

After several more days, the wedding celebration ended.

We left Cana, walking toward Capernaum. As we journeyed on, we talked among ourselves for we were amazed at having witnessed water made into wine. None of us dared question Jesus. How could anyone expect to learn the working of a miracle such as this?

But I was burning with curiosity. Water made into fine wine had happened before our eyes. I drank that which was not from fruit of the vine yet was full of flavor, sweet with aging, a treat to the tongue, and calm in my belly. Dare I ask him how?

I did not need to. Instead, Nathanael bar Tolmai of Cana, with forthrightness of character, simply said, "Will you teach us the secret of the wine?"

"Of course, I will," Jesus said. "Did I not say you may ask anything of me? I will tell you many things hard to understand. But always I will answer you. First you must learn this: with God all things are possible."

We stopped to rest and listen under a coppice of oleanders.

Jesus continued, "A miracle is simply fact and proof of the ever-presence and power of the Almighty. Write this upon your hearts. Every miracle begins with this thought: With God all things are possible. What cannot God do? All things are, everything is, possible for God to accomplish and for men to achieve with God.

"Does not the scripture say, 'Do not I fill heaven and earth. I have made the earth and created man upon it?' Has not God said, 'There is none else but I'? Reason with me then. God revealed Himself to Moses: I AM THAT I AM. I am that which is. I am all-in-all."

"If this is so, Master," I interrupted, "that God is all, then the tree is God; the blossom, the rock, sand, water, stars, wind, children, men, women, everything, and everyone that exists is God. Is this wisdom?"

The Master shook his head. "No! Do not err, my children. If this were the true statement of God's being, Andrew, every object would be a god. But God is One. A stone cannot show the creative power and presence of the All-mighty. Nor can a fish, a tree, a flower, or any created thing. Were it otherwise, there would be a multitude of gods, as the heathen believe.

"But the scripture says, 'God has spoken once; twice have I heard this: power belongs to God.' You must hold this perception of God's power in your mind. *Remember*, I say to you, with God all things are possible."

Jesus paused then continued, "God commands us to have no gods besides Him. Nothing is God but God. In Him all good things have existence. It is written,

I am the Lord, there is none else; there is no God besides me. I have made the earth and created man upon it; I, even my hands, have stretched out the heavens, and all their host have I commanded.

O Lord, how manifold are Your works; in wisdom have You made them all; the earth is full of Your riches. You send forth Your spirit, they are created. Your glory, O Lord, shall endure forever; You shall rejoice in Your works.

"I say to you, do not think 'All is God' for that would make a multitude of gods. Say rather that God is All. Did He not, in the time of Noah, say, 'My spirit shall not always strive with man, who in error considers his substance to be flesh?' The tree is not God, for God is the creator, and His intelligence is the real, spiritual, eternal substance and manifestation of all that is good."

Jesus continued, "I told you to remember certain things, which I tell you when I said, 'Only that which is real endures.' Spirit, not flesh, is that which endures. Spirit alone has reality, for Spirit is God. Miracles are natural; they are ever-present proofs that God is at hand and not far off. Again I say all things are possible to God.

"Observe what I now say. I dwell constantly conscious of Spirit. I abide in God and God in me. I endeavor to do always those things that are pleasing in His sight. For I, his Son, love the Father, and the Father loves me and shows me all that He does. Because I am His image, I must do always what God does. All that I see Him do I do likewise.

"As for the miracle of the wine, I will tell you what you wish to know. At the wedding feast, while the water pots were being filled, I went in thought to my Father. I beheld His love filling the universe, resting on field and flower, city and citizen, home and every heart dwelling therein. Though there was no wine at hand, I turned to God as both source and substance of all that is needed.

"Knowing God to be of one mind filled me with assurance that God is, in truth, the source always at hand. There is and can be no lack in God's all-knowing mind or in man. Further, I affirmed that the presence of the One who is all-in-all is practically able to manifest provision for every human need. What cannot God do? I knew, without question, that my Father thus supplies all that is rightfully needed. My Father fills heaven and earth, and even water jars.

"His thoughts can transmute water into wine even as He holds stars in their courses in the heavens above. Why do you marvel and wonder? What cannot God do? All that is has always been, will ever be, and now is. The allness of God exists in infinitesimals unseen until called forth and formed for good purpose.

God speaks, and it is done. From His infinite power and presence comes the form. Things are thought made manifest. My Father is infinitely All, and, from God's omniscience comes things most desired and needed for the welfare of mankind.

"'Do not I fill heaven and earth?' saith the Lord. All things are possible to God.

"His love will supply every honest need. Of that I have no doubt. I have full faith. God gives me such thoughts and will always prove them, for God loves His creation. I thank God for such goodness. He answers me in ways wonderful to man but natural to Him. That is how the water became wine. Such things are possible to God, especially that which seems impossible to man."

Jesus continued, "Moses, in the ministration of death in Egypt, turned water into blood. And when out of Egypt, when he was come into Canaan, he then turned bitter water into sweet refreshment at Marah. By the Spirit of God ministering unto life, I have shown that water can be made wine for the glory of God. This is the true wine as spoken by the psalmist,

> He causeth grass to grow for cattle and herb for the service of man
> that He may bring forth food out of the earth and wine that maketh
> glad the heart of man.

"I have brought to the world the new life of regeneration. Each life becomes life in God. I do this not of myself, but for the Father. It is He who has planted the grape for man, who nurtures the vine to fruitage. The fruit is swollen to sweetness for the harvest, and after the harvest it is confined for slow process to become wine, according to the thought of man.

"Now God has shown you that the process for perfection need not require time, but only faith expectant of good. So this wine, made in an instant from water wherein no grapes have bathed, gives you inspiration that it is possible to make things whole and good in an instant. It is God who does all these wonders.

"Obediently I do that which He commands, but it is He who shows forth things real and wonderful, like water becoming wine. This is the first miracle, a lesson of the new life I am to bring to the world. As man thinks, so is he. All things are done through God. Without God, I can do nothing. But I am never without God. Nor are you. Do you understand this?"

No one answered the question. Jesus was obviously disappointed.

"Rest now. I will teach again tomorrow."

Simon raised his hand to speak. "How did you come to understand all this?"

"Abide with me, and you shall learn the answer to that question. I shall teach you for many days. It is enough that you think now only on what I taught this day. Do not the scriptures say, 'Line upon line, line upon line. Here a little. There a little'?

He walked back to the road, and we followed him. We did not talk among ourselves about the wine. There was much I did not understand.

Chapter 3

That evening we supped at a quiet place along Lake Gennesaret. We were very near Capernaum. Shorebirds flew above or ran among us, seeking food washed up from the deep.

Jesus said, "It has been a long day.

"Before you sleep, I will tell you something that you must understand before I further teach you. One of you asked me, 'What is real?' I will tell you. Write these words upon your heart that they may come forth instantly and constantly.

"As I said to you this morning, again I say, only that which is real endures. And that which endures is Spirit, not flesh or things which are destructible or destructive. Now take your rest," he said. He arose and walked apart from us a bit. He sat down against a boulder, and the moonlight shone upon his face.

We quickly fell asleep. Several times I awakened in the night and rose up on my elbows to see if our Master was still near us. Each time I looked across to where he sat, his eyes, with great peace in them, met mine. He seemed not to sleep at all that night.

The next day we walked slowly south along the lake, stopping now and then to listen to Jesus. My brother, ever eager to learn more, asked, "What is the most important thing you have learned of God?"

Jesus answered, "Discernment of what is divine, and therefore real, and what is merely earthly knowledge and subject to opinion and change and variance."

"And how did you learn this, Master?" Simon asked.

"From the scriptures. All my days I have been learning from the scriptures. How I should speak. How I should judge. How I might best serve the One who fills both heaven and earth. One day the task of learning seemed to weigh me down. I pondered the words of Job, who uttered similar pain and confusion:

> Oh, that I knew where I might find Him! That I might come even to His seat! I would order my cause of righteousness before Him and fill my mouth with arguments.

I would know the words with which He would answer me, and understand what He would say unto me. I go forward but He is not there, and backward but I cannot perceive Him. But He knows the way that I take. When He has tried me, I shall come forth as gold.

My foot has kept His steps. His way have I kept and not declined. Neither have I gone back from the commandment of His lips. I have esteemed the words of His mouth more than my necessary food.

But He is in one Mind and who can turn Him. What His soul desireth, even that He doeth. He performeth the thing that is appointed for me, and many such things are with Him.

"Light from heaven fell upon me as I pondered these words. That which puzzled me grew into understanding. I saw God in true light. I saw that, indeed, His ways are not our ways. Neither are our thoughts His thoughts. His ways and thoughts are higher than ours, and I knew I must learn the higher way and not decline therefrom."

"Tell us more," Nathanael urged.

Jesus continued, "I read in the scriptures in the Book of Job the words of Elihu: 'Touching the Almighty, we cannot find Him out.' Elihu begged Job to listen to what he had to say. He said he was speaking to Job in God's stead, chastising Job for justifying innocence and denying guilt.

"Imagine Elihu offering his youthful wisdom to justify what seemed to be God's punishment of Job, who lost all he possessed yet maintained that he had not sinned against God! But the Lord answered Job, condemning the punitive comforters, and asking, 'Who are these that darkeneth counsel by words wherein knowledge is lacking?'

"God then poured forth questions, testing Job, who had simply wanted to reason with God. God spoke then of His great creation, from the balancing of the clouds to the uniqueness of all things made and the purposes thereof. When Job beheld the mind of God shown in infinite wisdom and order through all of creation, he answered God, saying,

I know that You do everything and that no thought of man can be withheld from You. Before I had heard of Your power, but now I see it in all goodness.

Thereby have I learned to seek and find You in thought. I understand that You know the way I am to take and will perform the thing appointed for me. It is You alone who comprehends and creates; it is You whom man is made to be like and to image forth.

"I gained a higher understanding from these scriptures, and great peace. Do you understand?" Jesus asked.

We nodded dumbly and said, "Yes, Master."

Jesus continued, "It is written in Esaias,

> Who directs the Spirit of the Lord, or being His counselor, teaches Him?

> Who measures the waters in the hollow of his hand, and metes out heaven with the span of his fingers, and comprehends the dust of the earth in a measuring cup, and weighs mountains in scales and hills in a balance?

> With whom takes God counsel? Who instructs Him? Who reveals to Him the path of judgment, and teaches Him knowledge, and shows Him the way of understanding?

> To whom will you liken God, or what likeness will you compare unto Him? God is not like man in form, to be worshipped in graven images made of clay.

> Have you not known or heard and been told from the very beginning that from the foundations of the earth God sits upon the circle of the earth, and the inhabitants therein cannot be numbered for they are like a multitude of grasshoppers?

> He has stretched out the heavens as a curtain and spreads them like a tent for His own dwelling. To whom then can He be compared? Nothing can equal God's being.

> Lift your eyes and behold who has created these things, who counts all His works, calling each by name. He knows them all as His own, His very Being imaged, His allness displayed in each of the many; none shall ever fail.

"Remembering all this, I asked myself, can a god of human form compass and sit upon the circle of the earth? Is a man-god able to perform such wonders and comprehend such numbers? Can the work of men's hands equal the manifest majesty of the One who is the Mind of all? Moses heard the command that there should be no graven image, no man-formed likeness, for who can fashion or limit in form the infinite God?

"Not one of us is like Him in body, for He has no finite form. Our likeness must be in heart and mind. Who can form or control Him? Do you understand this?" Jesus asked. "I say unto you, never think God to be manlike. Perceive Him rightly, and you become like Him. Andrew, have you something to say?" he asked me.

I was fidgety with joy. Obviously Jesus had read my thoughts for I was fairly bursting with enlightenment.

My words poured forth. "Yes, Master! Then we must not say, 'The tree, the blossom, the rock, man, everything, is God, for there is one alone who is God.' We may say, 'God is manifest in rock and cloud and sky and all creation because God is all and in all. God is the substance of everything, but no one thing is God.' Am I right?"

"True," Jesus said, "but all *things* are *thoughts* to God. So your thought about everything must be good. All evil thoughts and things are unknown to God. Do not the scriptures say, 'He is of purer eyes than to behold evil, and cannot look upon iniquity'?

My heart was beating so fast, and my thoughts were like sparks flying upward—too fragile to be alive long, much less apt to be wholly understood in a single moment.

Very quietly Jesus reminded us, "God saw everything He had made and observed it to be very good. If anything is not good, it is not of God. It has no enduring existence. This is the dominion which God gives to man—ability to know good as the reality and evil as always unreal. One thus finds the kingdom of God within." Jesus smiled. "Let us find a place to rest," he said.

But I could take no more. Instead, I left the group and walked away into the night toward Capernaum. Dawn found me peacefully asleep in my own bed, in my earthly father's house.

Upon waking the very first thought I had was this: "With God all things are possible," and I hastened to return to the side of the Master.

Soon I was back to the place where they had slept. They were awake, preparing to walk the last distance to town.

Simon told me, "You should have stayed, Andrew. Last evening, after we had eaten, Jesus asked us, 'Have you no curiosity? Or are you sated with these unusual truths and find them difficult to understand?'

"Then Nathanael answered him, 'Master, I have thought of little else. I scarcely heard many of the words you spoke along the way. For that I am both ashamed and sorrowful. But I did take much to my heart.' Jesus said to us, 'Ask and you shall receive, each of you who would be my disciples. Always ask to understand.'

"Philip answered him in a voice almost too small to be heard, 'Then tell us again, Master, for we are eager to learn from you. Tell us, that our hearts may understand things as you do.' Jesus smiled. 'I too had to learn the power of thought which comes from God, and that which I have learned of Him I give to you.' We stretched forth our hands, palms up, as if ready to accept with our hearts all that he might impart," explained my brother to me.

"Jesus went on, 'I have learned to see, to hear, to feel not with my eyes, my ears, my fingers, nor to taste with my tongue, nor smell with my nose. All these abilities I have in common with you. But they do not tell me of my Heavenly Father because these fleshly senses may work two ways, for good or for evil. It is not so with the gifts from heaven. I see, hear, feel, taste, and smell through mind. I take as real only thoughts worthy of God's goodness.'"

"'Master,' asked Nathanael, 'what *is* good? And what is evil?'

"Again Jesus smiled," Simon said as he continued to tell me what I missed.

"'That is just what you must know in order to understand me,' said Jesus. 'Ask again till you understand. I may need to repeat truth many times before you grasp the meaning. Now, listen closely. Evil is that which tends to destroy. It is that which is wicked, mischievous, fraudulent, malign, and not good.

"'Good,' he explained, 'is that which has a lasting quality and value. Goodness is excellence in every way. It is also kind, benevolent, benign of heart. Charitable. Merciful. Goodness in every thought produces peace and perfection. To be good is to be strong, free, firm, having worth, having virtue, being effective. That is good which is useful, complete, wanting or needing nothing to be added.

"'Goodness is virtuous, pious. Never evil, vicious, or wicked. There are many words which mean "good." But this is a start. As you have discerned, goodness is not something you can pluck up or consume or wear out or store away with hands. Goodness exists only in thought, as thought about anything. Fruit upon the table does not taste good as it lies there. But when we partake of it, the tongue may taste it as good or not good. But it is as thought that one considers fruit to be sweet or sour, pleasing or unpleasant. In the kingdom of God there are no thoughts which are not good.'"

Simon then quietly said to me, "I am sorry you missed this teaching last night, Andrew."

I too was sorry. Sorry to not have heard it from the mouth of Jesus. But the great lesson was over. We were about to enter Capernaum.

We arrived there, a ragtag bunch, some of us well known to the villagers as fishermen. We were called to and laughed at, but it did not matter. Soon enough our friends would know with whom we walked.

I offered Jesus a place in my father's home where he might find food, rest, and quiet for the night.

He declined. "I have kinfolk here," he said. "They will take me in. But I thank you for your kindness."

"Who are they?" I asked.

"One Zebedee whose wife, Salome, is my mother's sister."

"I know them," I said.

"We know them," Simon echoed. "We fish with James and John."

"Then you already know my kinfolk," Jesus said. "They are my cousins."

We walked along the sea. The fleet was in, and the fishers were at the shore mending nets.

Simon, Philip, and I encountered many of our friends and introduced them to Jesus. We did not identify him as the Savior but as a new acquaintance. I would have thought someone might recognize him from his childhood visits to the house of Zebedee, but no one did.

Jesus obviously felt comfortable amongst our townspeople for we often stopped to talk. Once he called to him the children playing nearby. He asked about their fathers and mothers, and if they were learning the law of Moses.

We found Zebedee on the quay. His sons were there too, working with him to repair nets, tightening the skeins and knots. We hailed them with loud greetings. The cousins recognized each other with great joy.

After the small conversation which followed, Jesus addressed James and John.

"My time is come. Follow me."

The two men looked to their father. Zebedee nodded his head toward Jesus. "Go!" he simply said. Immediately they left their work and joined us.

Later we escorted the Master to the house of Zebedee, where we had been invited to share the evening meal.

We ate fish fresh from the lake. Fish baked with oil, dill, and lemon served with grains and sweet melon from the garden. Flat loaves of bread, still warm from the oven, and soft sheep's-milk cheese eaten with cucumbers, onions, and small tender seeds of cumin. Fresh figs and sweet wine completed the feast.

Later, in the merriment of the evening, I sought James and John. We walked into a garden bathed in soft light from a three-quarter moon.

"You never told us you had kinfolk in Nazareth. Why? Did you know the son of the carpenter was more than a woodworker?" I asked.

"We knew," John answered.

"Why did you not shout to the skies that the Promised One was amongst us?"

"It was not ours to tell," John answered. "Besides this, we have not seen Jesus for several years. We had no notion of when his work would begin."

"Or what course it would take," James added.

"But you knew? When did you learn?" I asked.

"We were just children when we were told that Jesus was of God.

"Then about six years after he first went, at age twelve, to the temple in Jerusalem, Joseph, the carpenter of Nazareth, died. Our kinswoman Mary had borne to her husband five sons and two daughters.

"Before he died, while he was still active in his shop, Joseph and Mary gathered the children together and told them the story of strange and wonderful happenings at Jesus's birth.

"Later we cousins were told, 'Sometime you might ask Jesus about it.' Now I say the same to you. Sometime ask him."

"I will," I answered, wondering what Jesus would say when I asked.

It was very late that evening when Simon returned to his home and I to my father's house. The next day we were to begin the journey to Jerusalem, for it was again time to celebrate the Passover.

As we left Capernaum, our group spread out. The wives of Zebedee and Simon Peter and a couple of other women formed a knot to visit together while walking. The youngsters among us scrambled over rocks and into bushes along the road.

Younger men set the pace ahead of all of us, keeping their eyes on the company, coming back now to carry a weary child and then to lend an arm to one of the elders. John and I dropped back to walk beside Mary, who was accompanied by Jesus and his brother, James.

John suggested this. Mary was his mother's sister. The two families, Joseph's and Zebedee's, had visited yearly when the children were young. John had long known that Jesus was different. Even in play, as a child, Jesus had said and done strange things. I wanted to learn more.

"Forgive me, Mary, but I am curious. When did you know your son would be the Savior?" I asked.

She smiled sweetly. Patiently. Had she been asked this question countless times?

"From the moment the angel announced to me that I would bear a son," she replied.

"An angel? Were you frightened?"

"At first . . . yes. But when I opened my mouth to speak, humble words were given to me, and I accepted the angel's salutation and his message. The difficult time came later when my father and mother heard about these strange things. And also Joseph—my beloved Joseph—such a good man . . . ," she mused.

"Did you tell him what had happened to you—this angel visitation?"

"No . . . no," she said thoughtfully. "No, my parents' and my first concern was to certify the message. That meant my going at once to visit my kinswoman Elizabeth. For the angel told me that she too was with child—though she was far past the age when a woman could bear. When I entered her courtyard, Elizabeth greeted me in the full bloom of her own miracle of motherhood. The child within her immediately leaped with joy for my coming. It seemed Elizabeth already knew that the promised Deliverer of Israel would be born soon. That *I* was to be mother of the Savior outweighed the promise that her son would be the voice heralding the One to come.

"When my parents returned home to Sepphoris, they went first to Nazareth. There they found Joseph deeply concerned about my welfare. He told them of a strange dream he'd had. They assured him that his vision, a message from the same angel that visited me, could be trusted. 'In that case,' he said, 'I must go at once to Mary and complete the betrothal and take her to be my wife.'

"So Joseph came to me, my parents with him. With Elizabeth's voiceless husband, Zacharias, at hand, a temple priest confirmed our union. I was already aware of the child within my womb. So Joseph held me tenderly in his arms through the first nights of our marriage. We whispered in wonder at the great grace given us to be the ones to care for and instruct in the ways of God this promised Redeemer of the world. Thus Joseph sanctified my condition.

"A few days later they left Ein Karem and returned home, Joseph to Nazareth and my parents to their home in Sepphoris."

"And you?" I asked.

"I remained with Elizabeth and Zacharias until her child was born. Then Joseph came and escorted me to my new home in Nazareth. There it was already known that I was his wife and was with child. And so it was that the Almighty delivered me from Joseph's fear that I might be regarded as wanton and subjected to the harsh law which Moses decreed in order that the women of Israel remain pure in bringing forth offspring.

"Therein I have much to be grateful for, and the devotion of my husband is not the least among many other things. Indeed, it is the greatest, for from his love has come forth food and shelter and guidance for my firstborn—the one for whom the angel said to me, 'All women shall call you blessed.'"

We walked in silence then. My thoughts were very deep.

"And the birth?" I asked after we had covered a fair distance.

"I was large with child," she answered. "And the time to deliver was soon. But a census required that we travel to Bethlehem in Judea, for both Joseph and I descended from the house of David.

"We journeyed slowly, in company with others. The child within me had brought to my spirit a quiet holiness, and I knew little sorrow or pain. But the trip was wearisome. When at last we arrived, we halted at a caravansary outside the town of Bethlehem. There many pilgrims had already taken every room and space.

"But the innkeeper directed Joseph to a nearby place, a sheepcote or cave shelter for animals in winter—a place where we might bed down on soft grasses which had been gathered and dried for winter feed for the sheep. Gratefully, Joseph took me there, even as the throes of birth began to be felt. Did I suffer? Not that I can recall. Joseph said, 'Sing in your heart the words the angel spake to you of this hour.' I did just that, adding my own words of acceptance.

"I felt no fear. This was God's hour—did I dare think this, that His only Son, begotten of a woman, was enduring birth? Could I then not endure the birthing? And so it was that in a few hours that seemed like seconds to me, Joseph received this precious child. In awe he welcomed the Son of God.

"Joseph received the baby into a cloth of soft linen and wiped from my child all traces of having been in my body. Then he wrapped the baby in a swaddling cloth, one of several we had packed in a basket while preparing for this birth. He placed the child in my arms, his eyes alight with love and tenderness for both of us, and then he curled himself around us to give added warmth.

"Near dawn he stuffed sweet dried grass into a manger and laid the child there, covering the babe with his cloak. Then he tended to my needs. And after, we heard sounds of approaching voices. A clutch of men, shepherds, appeared in the entrance to the sheepfold. It seemed they were bathed in light—and they were—light brighter than starlight, brighter even than the light a full moon gives.

"Joseph put his finger to his lips and pointed to me, then to the manger where the child was sleeping. The shepherds came forward. They whispered, telling us that they'd been tending sheep in the nearby hills. Suddenly, they said it seemed that the stars were singing. When they looked up, the night sky was filled with a multitude of guests from heaven. It was they who were singing—a throng of angels with voices saying in harmony the melody of two words, 'Alleluia, glory, glory, glory, Alleluia.'

"'We fell on our knees,' the shepherds told us. 'We could not believe our ears nor our eyes. Was this the end of the world? But then, a voice from heaven—for the glory was suddenly all around us; and in the strange and wondrous light we saw an angel.'

"'Do not be afraid,' he said to us. 'There is nothing to fear. I am here to tell you the good news which will give you and all people much joy. This day is born for you in David's city, the Savior—Christ, the Messiah, the Anointed of the Lord. This will be shown to you as proof; you will find the baby swaddled and lying in a manger in the place where you shelter your flocks in winter.'

"'There stood the angel, telling us this good news—and all at once there was a great multitude of angels present. We heard again their song:

Praise God
We praise you, God.
Praise God for He is glorious, glorious in the heights of heaven.
And now on earth His peace—
God's kindness, beneficence, goodness, and love toward all men.

"'Then they moved away from us into heaven above,' the shepherds said. 'We decided to come to Bethlehem to see what God made known to us by the angels.' Shepherds beheld my babe," Mary said. "And with tears they cried, 'It is true!' Then they headed into the village to tell others.

"We later learned that all who heard the shepherds' story wondered if what they told really happened. But I knew it had, and I kept all these things in my heart, pondering what it would mean to me and this precious infant," Mary recalled.

"Later the shepherds stopped by again as they returned to tell the good news to those who remained in the fields to keep the flocks safe. They lingered with us, these shepherds, marveling at all they had heard and seen, thanking God and celebrating God's power and goodness, even as the angels had."

Jesus smiled at his mother when she finished telling me of his birth.

We stopped to rest in a grove of olive trees in a small valley threaded by a languid stream. Even the young people were quiet as Mary sat with her eyes closed, resting in the arms of her dear son, with a gentle smile tracing her lips.

All I could think of was this: "With God all things indeed are possible."

On our first day in Jerusalem, Simon and I and James and John walked with Jesus into the outer court of the temple. A great hubbub came from the market in one corner. There, mixed with the uproar of men's voices, were bleatings of sheep and lowing of oxen. Soft cooing dove sounds came from a raft of highly stacked birdcages.

At one side, there were money-changing tables. Behind them sat men trading shekels for foreign coins, for the temple priests would accept shekels and no other coins in payment of tribute.

I could see that Jesus was disturbed by so many voices raised in shouting, in din, clamor, and confusion. He was dismayed by the haggling and bickering taking place.

"Quickly," he said, "give me what ties or cords of rope you may be carrying."

I fished out the strand which hitched my sleeping roll to my shoulders and a braided leather strap which secured my waterskin and purse in the same manner. Each of us produced something which Jesus grabbed and used to fashion a small scourge.

Suddenly he strode fearlessly through the area, flicking and brandishing the cords. He tipped over the tables of the money changers and the sellers of sacrificial animals. There was great confusion as coins rolled across the courtyard, with many men scrambling to pick them up.

Turning to the penned sheep and oxen, he loosed them, driving them into the melee. When he reached the cages of doves, he broke stride and yelled to the sellers, "Free these creatures from this place. My Father's house is not a marketplace, a stable, or a dovecote."

He unclasped a crate. The birds flew free, mounting high above the spires of the temple. Jesus defiantly stood there in the temple court. "It is written," he shouted, "'the zeal of thine house has consumed me.'"

And again, "'I will bring to my holy mount and make them joyful in my house of prayer; their burnt offerings and their sacrifices shall be accepted upon mine altar, for my house shall be called an house of prayer for all people.'"

"Where is your joy? Where is your prayer? Commerce at the Lord's house?" he called loudly again and again.

He was suddenly confronted by a contingent of angry priests and other Jews, mainly those who were sellers and money changers.

"Who are you?" they snarled. "Why have you interrupted our lawful activity which benefits the holy temple? How is your anger justified?"

Jesus answered, somewhat scornfully, "Destroy this temple! In three days I will raise it again."

The crowd laughed. "It took forty years to build this temple! And you claim ability to raise it anew in three days?"

Without another word, Jesus turned quickly and left the Temple Mount.

We did not understand our Master's words until much later, because he was not speaking of this temple of stone, but of his own flesh.

We did not see Jesus again until that evening. It was at the Passover meal. We who had traveled with Jesus, as well as his kinfolk and ours, were gathered in the upper city in the home of my father's brother, who had invited us and our friends to dine at his table.

Never had a sacrificial lamb been prepared in such an atmosphere of hope and dread. The roasted flesh of the lamb—the age-old symbol of purification and atonement, not only of appeasement to lessen the wrath of the Almighty, but also to procure personal forgiveness—was served in thankful remembrance of the first paschal meal eaten after the journey out of Egypt into the wilderness beyond the Red Sea.

We supped in silence, except for the voices of those who recited the ancient story. As unleavened bread and bitter herbs were passed among us, I sensed stronger meaning than the familiar words had ever before held for me. The bread spoke of purity, the need of sincerity and truth. The herbs recalled the bitterness of bondage in Egypt. Remembrance of the blood of the sacrificed lamb reminded us of afflictions overcome and the necessity that wickedness must be forsaken by each one of us.

We ate the mush of vinegary fruit softened to become symbol of the unstrengthened mortar, which the Jews in ancient Egypt were forced to shape impossibly into bricks. We drank wine that was more water than juice of the vineyard.

Throughout the first evening of Passover, Jesus spoke not a single word. The next day he asked to go about the city unaccompanied by anyone.

For seven days the city hummed with accounts of the cleansing of the temple done by one Jesus, a mere carpenter from Nazareth. I followed some distance behind him for two days. He was aware of my unobtrusive presence.

Jesus did not surrender himself to anyone. Not to us who were his students. He refused to contest for acceptance. He knew that men were thinking, *Who is this man who dares to purge the temple?*

He remained aloof. He didn't need testimony of others about what was being thought of him for good or evil. He already knew. He was a threat to all unrighteousness of heart and deed. Others were beginning to know this, even as we had learned it in his presence.

For seven days our minds were bidden to feast on the goodness of God as shown in the original deliverance of Israel. We ate unleavened bread and recalled that Passover had been celebrated only five times at the base of Mount Sinai—once in the days of Moses and since then by Kings Hezekiah, Solomon, and Josiah during their reigns in Israel. Later it was observed once more in the days of Ezra when the law of Moses again became law to the people of the covenant.

On the last day of Passover, we disciples left the city at sundown and camped only a short distance beyond the walls, for we were all very weary.

Never had we been so mindful of all that Passover stood for.

Not one of us had even an inkling of what it would further come to mean to us.

Chapter 4

Our family members returned home. Jesus and we, who were his disciples, left Jerusalem but remained in Judea. Sometimes we slept in olive groves and wandered through vineyards. Landowners were kind and often asked us to share their meals. We had few thoughts of this world. To walk with Jesus was my only ambition. It was shared by each of us attached to him.

To our surprise, he did not speak of Rome, of Israel under oppression, or of need for liberation. Instead he talked about the rule of God, of man's God-given dominion, and of spiritual freedom. To our surprise, he saw himself a teacher of scripture only.

The third night after leaving Jerusalem, we were in a grove beneath date palms, around a small fire in nearby Bethlehem. Night had fallen, and firelight played upon our faces as we sat listening to Jesus. Out of the dark came a man, dressed in flowing robes over a bordered tunic. We knew at once that he was a Pharisee.

Jesus arose and drew him into our circle. I could see that our visitor was proud and cultured and obviously wealthy.

"I am Nicodemus of Jerusalem," he explained to Jesus. "I have come at night with twofold motive. First, there are no people thronging you. Second, I was in the temple market when you challenged the commerce. Many in Israel have felt this must be done. Therefore, I am here to inquire. Are you revolutionaries? Just who are you, Jesus of Nazareth?"

"Are you a master in Israel and yet know not what is real?" Jesus answered.

"You are a new master in Israel," Nicodemus explained, "for you dare to challenge that which should be forsaken. We know that you have come from God."

Jesus smiled. "Truly, truly I tell you this. Except one be born again, one cannot behold the sovereign authority of God as given to man," he said.

"How can a man be born when he is old?" Nicodemus asked. "Can one enter a second time into his mother's womb to be born again? I think not."

Jesus said, "That is true, but this also is true: except one is born of water and of Spirit, one can't enter under the rule of God. Let me explain. That born of flesh is flesh. That born of Spirit is spiritual. Don't wonder at this. You hear the wind blowing and see its effect, but you can't tell what causes it to come or where it goes and how it finally yields to stillness. But you recognize the motion of wind. Honestly, I speak what I know and tell what I see of God . . . but few believe my testimony.

"Thus it is that one need be newly born of water and of Spirit. You are born again when cleansed of sin and understand the Spirit of God to be Mind, not flesh. To be born of Spirit is to understand. That is, to have God's idea of all that is. To know the things of God is to have exact comprehension."

Nicodemus said, "How can this be?"

Jesus said, "If I tell you of the wind and you do not understand, how will you understand when I tell you of the truths of heaven? Your thoughts cannot rise higher unless you understand that you have come from heaven. Even I, a child of man, dwell yet in heaven.

"Moses led the children of Israel into Arabia from out of Egypt. Along the way there were serpents whose bite left fiery suffering and death. Moses made of bronze a figure of such a serpent and raised it on a pole. Any man bitten had only to lift his eyes and behold the brazen serpent in order to live and not die.

"Moses hereby taught Israel to overcome fear, for Moses knew they would not fear a serpent of brass. He also lifted the thought of God's people to see serpents as God beholds them—subtle, wise to move into their holes where they cannot be caught by the tail and so subdued.

"Now I, a son of man, am raised a standard that whosoever believes in *God's Son* shall not perish but live forever. God loves the world. He sent me as one begotten of flesh in order that whoever is persuaded of the truth I teach will not be destroyed unto nothing but dust. His being will live and endure forever.

"God did not send me to condemn the world, but those who choose not to believe are already condemned because I bring new light into the world. If a man loves darkness rather than light, it is because his deeds are evil.

"Those who do evil turn from the light and never receive it as you have, because their achievements will be censured and disapproved. But one who seeks truth comes to the light that his achievements may be seen to be worked through godliness."

Nicodemus had listened intently. "Master," he said, "may I join your company?"

Jesus rose, lifted up Nicodemus, and held the man to his heart. "No, dear seeker after light, you have other work to do. Henceforth, you will walk in light and reason from the allness of God's grace and goodness. You will shine light among the Pharisees and in the Sanhedrin.

"You will hear of my words and understand increasingly that the allness of Spirit—the Mind of God—is a consciousness of good alone. This night you have been born anew. Henceforth, the things of God will become apparent to you. Go now, return to the city. You believe that God is the beginning. Now believe that God is the All—the only reality—in all."

As quietly as he came, Nicodemus disappeared into the night. Jesus turned to us and said, "Already I have a disciple in high places. How happy is my Father."

The next day we went to the Jordan, to a place near Salim, where John was baptizing at Aenon. People now swarmed to the Baptist. The road was thronged with men, and women too, from beyond Jerusalem to Jericho and the villages betwixt.

When we saw the crowds, we went to Jesus and said, "Master, we also would like to baptize." Jesus gave his consent, and we went down a short distance beyond John's site and found a small beach where pilgrims could easily enter and leave the baptismal stream. Soon pilgrims were forsaking John and coming to us.

John's disciples were displeased. It was rumored that John's baptism appealed less because it required more fasting and strict observance of Judaism in daily life. It was the Pharisees who pointed out to John's helpers that we, Jesus's disciples, were attracting many more people to baptism than they were.

We later learned that John, who was content with the work appointed him, consoled his disciples by saying, "I came only to prepare his way—if they are baptizing more than we, it must surely be the will of God."

One day soon after, John raised his voice in condemnation of Herod Antipas, the tetrarch of Galilee. On a trip to Rome, Antipas had stayed with his brother Herod Philip. He fell in love with Philip's wife, Herodias; encouraged her to divorce Philip; and then took her away with him. When Antipas's legal wife—the daughter of Aretas, king of Arabia—heard of the new marriage, she returned to her father's home.

Herodias was the daughter of Aristobulas, who also was a brother of Herod Antipas. So she was not only Antipas's wife; she was, in fact, also his niece.

John knew of this scandalous behavior and began to speak out, condemning Antipas for marrying his brother's wife. He spoke fearlessly, condemning Antipas for his sensual immorality, his crimes, and all the evils which he had done.

Soon thereafter, Herod Antipas had John arrested and cast into prison, but he inflicted no further punishment. He feared a revolution by the many hundreds baptized by John—people now cleansed of sin, who were striving to lead good and pure lives.

While we, his six disciples, had been busy with our baptism, Jesus was teaching in the region round about. When word came that John was in prison, Jesus withdrew into the wilderness. When he came to us again, he said, "Baptize no more. Come, let us return to Galilee."

With John in prison, Jesus wondered whether Judea was a safe place for him to teach; so when he decided to return to Galilee, it was by the shortest route.

Samaria lies directly north of Jerusalem with mountains at the head of a valley leading from Judea toward the Galilee. The city of Sychar lies there below Mount Gerizim. We walked at a steady, quick pace. Jesus never stopped to teach, and we reached Sychar about noon.

Sychar, where ancient Shechem once was, is now little more than a village. Jacob's well used to be in a bustling part of the old city, but now it is outside the walls, in the midst of a grove of trees. We stopped at the well to rest.

The Samaritans are a strange people. They do not worship God in Jerusalem but long ago built a temple on Mount Gerizim wherein to worship Him. They do not connect with the Jews in any way, or the Jews with them. There has always been hatred between the Jews and the Samaritans. Jesus had mentioned this as we made haste from Jerusalem, deciding to travel through Samaria.

In contrast, Jesus was teaching us that the kingdom of God would come when mankind learned to love all people. He sent us into the city to buy food for our journey, so we left him at the well, where he wished to rest quietly and be alone. A woman, whom we met coming our way, was apparently approaching the well where he sat. She carried a vessel for water.

Jesus later told us that he asked for a drink.

The woman from Sychar immediately recognized him as a Jew. She must have been both amazed and frightened.

"Why are you asking me for water? A Jew would never take a vessel from the hands of one who is both a Samaritan and a woman," she said.

Jesus said he answered her, "'If you knew who is asking drink of you, you would have asked of me. I would have given you living water.'

"She replied, 'You can't draw from this well. It is very deep, and you have nothing to let down to be filled. How could you *give me* living water? Our father, Jacob, gave us this well. Are you greater than him?' 'I refer not to water from this well,' I replied. 'If I drink of it, I will thirst again. But the water that I offer you will never fail, for it will be in you a well of water ever coming, as from a spring, and you will never thirst in the life that has no end.'

"The woman said to me, 'Sir, give me this water, that I thirst not nor have need to come here to draw.' I said to her, 'Go first to call your husband then come back.'

"She said to me, 'I have no husband.'

"I replied, 'True, you have no husband, but you have had five husbands, and the one you are now with is not your husband.'

"She looked at me. 'I see you are a prophet! Do you also know that we worship on yonder mountain?' she asked. 'For two hundred years our temple stood there upon Mount Gerizim until it was destroyed by your people. You worship in Jerusalem, but it is here that we feel closest to God.'"

Jesus told us, "I was surprised when she mentioned Jerusalem. Then she told me, 'Here there will be battle between the people of Samaria and of Jerusalem, for this is where someday God is to be found by all the world.'

"'You worship God yet know nothing of Him,' I replied. 'Woman, trust my words, the time is coming when neither in this mountain nor in Jerusalem will one find and worship the Father. God is Spirit, and they who worship Him must worship Him in spirit and in truth. To worship Him in spirit is to respect and revere Him as the one perfect Mind filling heaven and earth. God can thus be worshipped everywhere at anytime by anyone.'"

Jesus continued, "I could see that she began to understand! She said to me, 'Is it this Mind which has brought me here at noonday to fetch water? There are deep and flowing springs in Sychar, yet I came to draw from Jacob's well. Sir, I know that Messiah, who is called Christ—the Anointed—is coming. When he has come, he will tell us all things.'"

We were almost breathless, waiting for Jesus to tell us what happened next. His countenance grew tender.

"I told her, 'I that speak with you am He!'"

Just then, we disciples returned to the well from Sychar. From afar we had seen him talking with a woman, yet none of us dared to ask her "What are you seeking?" or him, "Why do you talk with her?"

The woman left her water pot on the stone seat near the well and hastened away into the city. To everyone she met, she said, "Come to Jacob's well; there rests a man who told me everything I've ever done. Is this not the Christ?"

While she was gone, we urged Jesus to eat. But he said, "I have meat to eat that you know not of."

We asked each other, "Has someone brought him food?"

Jesus answered our question, "My meat is to do the will of God. He sends me to harvest what He has planted. I *was* hungry and weary. Yet I am now filled and refreshed after sharing God's love and truth with this outcast woman of Samaria. This is my Heavenly Father's work, given me to accomplish on earth: Is not this the fast that I have chosen? to loose the bands of wickedness? to undo the heavy burdens? to let the oppressed go free and that ye break every yoke?

"God sowed an opportunity," Jesus told us. "And I have reaped the blessing of joy and satisfaction in fasting." He continued, "My need has been supplied by God's love. I do always that which is pleasing to Him, and now I no longer hunger. To love means to be pleased with another."

To the six of us at the well, he then instructed, "You say in four months we will begin the harvest. I say, lift your eyes and see that the fields are ready for harvesting. If you reap, you will be well paid now and will later find you have earned much fruitage for the life to come. There will be rejoicing for both the

Sower and the reaper. This saying is true, 'one sows and then others reap.' Enter with me into these labors. With God, all good things are attainable."

Suddenly we heard and saw many coming from Sychar to the well. Upon arrival, they begged Jesus, "Stay with us." So we went into the city, staying for two days while Jesus taught the people many new truths.

They believed when he told them that God is the Spirit and the Mind of the universe in the vault of heaven and in the span of earth beneath and in all that they contain.

The woman who talked with Jesus at the well later came to him, telling of many who said to her, "We believe you now. Not because you told us, but because we ourselves have listened to his words. We know that this is indeed the Christ, who shall save the world."

Two days later we left Samaria to go into Galilee.

On the way, Jesus marveled at the receptivity of the Samaritans. As we walked, he referred again and again to the hospitality shown to us at Sychar.

We were no less amazed, but what we most talked about among ourselves was his contact with an obviously immoral woman and her openness to learn of the Christ. For when Jesus answered with such sincere simplicity her statement about the coming Christ, she literally dropped her water jar and ran toward the city to share the good news.

Whenever we got on the subject, however, Jesus either strode ahead of us or lagged behind. We wondered why but later realized he was not impressed that an outcast—and a woman at that—from the half-breed Samaritan offshoot of the Jews had responded to his words, for he knew he was sent to comfort the brokenhearted and those impoverished in spirit wherever he found them.

When we passed through very small villages, Jesus would often pause at the town well and talk with anyone who came to draw water. He told them of the kingdom of God and repeated the very words John had used when calling people to baptism: "The time is fulfilled, and the kingdom of God is at hand; repent. Have a new mind, and believe this good news."

We journeyed leisurely. People crowded around us when Jesus preached, quoting the prophets and psalms, always concluding with the same good news: "The kingdom of God is at hand."

Some asked what the kingdom would do for them. He said that God would be revealed to them as the one Mind. "That Mind," he would say, "is Spirit, not flesh. Things of the flesh are not real things to the intelligence which is God. Such things fall short of the perfect creation of the Creator. If you like the treasure you have in earthen vessels, you will love the reality of their eternal beauty when found in Mind, in the glory of the kingdom prepared for you."

Often, when we stopped at marketplaces in these small towns, Jesus was recognized as the one responsible for the ruckus in the temple in Jerusalem, for many men were in the temple for Passover when the tables of the money changers were overturned. Most felt the deed was overdue, and they were glad to listen to what Jesus had to say about the kingdom of God and the need for all to repent.

We journeyed on and arrived at last in Cana of Galilee, en route to Capernaum. "I will abide here for a time," he said to us. "Go home to your families and to your fishing until I come and call you to me again."

So Nathanael went to his house in Cana, while Simon and I and James and John went on to Capernaum, and Philip went farther along the lakeshore to Bethsaida.

Jesus was always welcome in the home of his first-married sister, where the miracle of the wine took place. His mother lived there, and I suppose they spent many hours in quiet conversation.

He also spent time at the home in the foothills of Cana, where his younger sister's husband kept sheep. Some nights Jesus slept under the stars, and, as he told us later, he listened to the music of the skies and stars and of human hearts everywhere as they entered into rest, praying even in their dreams that Messiah would soon come to the earth.

We learned later that he came down from the sheep pasture when an officer from the court of Herod Antipas came seeking him. The man's son lay at the point of death in Capernaum. He begged Jesus to come to the boy and heal him, but Jesus said, "You would first want a sign from me in order to believe. Have you not heard the scriptures which say, 'I AM the Lord that healeth you?' God is the one physician who is everywhere. Even now He is with your son."

The nobleman begged Jesus, "Sir, come down before my son dies."

Jesus knew the man did not have a spiritual understanding of the words of Moses, who did understand and therefore prophesied, "You shall serve the Lord your God and He shall bless your bread and your water, and will take sickness away from the midst of you."

But the nobleman *was* willing to ponder one thought Jesus gave him: "Your son lives!"

Jesus knew, as the scriptures proclaim, that God is one's life and the length of one's days, and he knew the child's thought would respond to the voice of God's truth and love, which declares, "You shall not die, but live," for the psalmist said, "They cry unto the Lord in their trouble, and He saves them out of their distresses. He sends His Word and heals them and delivers them from their destruction."

"Go back to your son," Jesus urged. "He lives."

"I believe you," said the child's father. "I believe the words you have spoken, and I am grateful."

So saying, he left, hurrying home to Capernaum. On the way he saw men coming toward him, servants from his own household. "Rejoice," they called loudly to him. "Your son lives! Rejoice!"

When the nobleman and his servants met, they paused for a few minutes under a date palm tree. "Tell me, what hour did he begin to recover?" the child's father asked.

"Yesterday, about one in the afternoon, the seventh hour of the day, the fever left him!"

"Praise God for the miracle," the father declared. "That is the exact time when Jesus said to me, 'Your son lives.'" Then he hurried on homeward, almost running the miles to where he lived. When he arrived, there was his son, playing at the doorstep.

He gathered his family and his servants into the courtyard and told them all about his trip to the holy man, the words they had spoken to one another, and the fact that from the moment Jesus said "Thy son lives," he knew his son would be all right.

He wept with joy and asked his servants to prepare a special meal for thanksgiving, and after that event was over, no one in the household had to labor for two days.

The next day the father of the little boy carried him on his shoulders and took him to the fish market. We had just come to shore. We heard the father tell of this miracle and saw the child.

I thought of Nathanael. Would those in Cana now wonder if anything good could come forth from Nazareth? For Jesus performed in Cana his first miracle—wine made from water in an instant; and now, again in Cana, he had brought a child from the shadow of death to immediate fullness of life.

We caught no fish that night. So we unloaded the nets and spread them to dry. "Let us go to him," I suggested to Simon. We found John and James, and they decided to come with us. But first we all bathed in the sea to refresh our bodies, then went home to change into clean garments.

We set out on the road to Cana, discussing among ourselves this miracle wrought in the name of God. We had walked only an hour when we saw Jesus coming toward us. We hailed him with joy, and he returned glad greetings to us. "Our town is full of wonder!" Simon explained. "We could not wait to see you."

Jesus stood there, beaming in our midst. "Such is the power of the living God who dwells in our hearts. Today there is a new truth upon the earth. It is the knowledge that God is the only source of life there is," he said.

"Give us this knowledge," pleaded young John.

"It shall be yours. It is a rudiment of all I understand, and I shall teach it to you. But return now to your fishing boats for I shall come again and call you. But first I must return to the place where I was brought up." He smiled and walked away.

Turning back once, he waved to us, but we stood there in sunshine and stillness, for we were all struck by his words: "God is the only source of life there is." All of us that is, except for Simon. He broke from our group and ran after Jesus. "Master," he called, "wait for me."

Jesus turned. "What is it, Cephas?"

"Forgive me, Lord," said my brother forthrightly. "We are eager to learn. What you have done has never before been done on earth. Can you not tarry with us for an hour or two? It is so easy to marvel about such miracles. Please tell us *how* you saved the child from death."

Jesus beckoned us to come to where he and Simon stood. Then he led us aside to a place of shade and bade us sit down.

"What do you think? *How* was the child saved? Have any of you an inkling?"

"Not I," we each responded as he looked from one of us to another for an answer.

"As to the miracle which you heard of from the father of the child, I will tell you my response when his plea first reached my ears, or more correctly my thought, for it is mind which hears and it is God as Mind who heals.

"The father said, 'My son is ill unto death.' My thoughts were: *You need not believe that. You cannot be made to believe or fear that your son can die. This is the tempter lying; the suggestion is false and is not truly your thought because it is not of God.* The father begged me, 'Please come.' I answered, 'You need me to come as a sign that he will be made well. Unless you see me do this, you will not believe.'

"He said, 'Sir, come down before my child dies.' The thought which I heard from my Father God was, *He surely will* not *die.* Then I cast out the demon: 'Death and fear be gone from every heart! You are no part of true thought, not of mine or of anyone else's anywhere. It is what God knows that governs all existence. God is the source of life, and there is no death. Death is false. God as Truth refutes every lie. This child's life is safe in Truth for he lives in God who is the only Life. In Life there is no death. The law of God is Life and Truth and steadfast Love. This law banishes all that is evil. This law has banished all fear of death in this father's thought. Death must disappear from every heart!'

"The father has asked, and my Father, God, has answered. 'I declare in the name of God, this child lives and is whole and well. With God all things are possible.' Then I said aloud to the man, 'Your son lives.' He answered me, 'I believe the word you have spoken. You need not come now.' And the man went his way in fullness of joy.

"Now observe this," Jesus continued. "I understood that good is real. Evil is not of God and is not real. I challenged in my thought the lie or falsity of what the man believed and feared: the death of his son. I refuted the fear, seeing it to be a lie about the offspring of God and about all creation which God pronounces very good. Knowing that God is ever present as the Life and Mind of each child, man, and woman, I knew that I, Jesus, need not be present to establish health and life for the child. God, who fills heaven and earth, is always present and effective at the point of need.

"I knew in the ever-presence of perfect Mind there could be no continuance of despair. The sickness would vanish from thought. There would be faith and hope and fruitage instead, destroying all and every fear. I knew and silently declared, 'He will not surely die.'

"Notice this," Jesus said, "when the child's father implored me to 'come ere my child die,' I at once refuted fear, reversing his words in my consciousness, 'He shall not surely die.' Then I cast out the suggestions: BE GONE! Depart from thought all fear and sickness and death! You have no place in the Mind that is God, hence no power in the thought of man who reflects God.'

"I defined death as false belief and affirmed God, Truth, to be that which destroys and dismisses all that is untrue. I understand Life to be God, in God, and of God. Life is never in flesh. I beheld the child living in God, the only Life of man. I mentally affirmed there is no death. Life, not flesh, evidences Mind—this Mind which never ceases being. All belief in death was brought to an end as I affirmed the power of Truth to destroy fear of sickness and death.

"Through God I then proclaimed the fact of the healing and the wholeness of the child. 'Your son lives!' I declared to the father. The man believed. He returned home. There he found the child at play, and his whole household now believes the power of God."

For a moment I wondered how Jesus knew that the nobleman found his child at play at the doorsteps.

"Do you understand this?" he asked. "Our Father has provided this lesson for you. This, your beginning lesson, will also be my life's concluding lesson. Ponder all that I have spoken. It is the beginning of wisdom. It will preserve life. Now I must journey on. Return to your homes. I will come for you again."

Jesus walked back to the road. But we sat there for a long time in silence, each of us assimilating what we had been told. Then we arose and went to our homes near the Lake of Gennesaret.

When we arrived at my house, our father welcomed Simon and me and sent us out to be fishermen again. We toiled soberly, ever mindful of the fact that the hope of being in the Messiah's army no longer obsessed our thoughts. We were content to have made our acquaintance with Jesus of Nazareth.

And so after our nets were mended late each afternoon after our nights on the sea, followed by early day rest, we sat beneath aspen trees which grew along the shore and there talked repeatedly about having found Jesus. We reviewed the things that we had learned from him.

Now and then we went to the house of Zebedee, where James and John told how, when they were lads, Joseph and Mary would come from Nazareth to visit them, bringing all their youngsters. With them came Jesus, who seemed to be always thinking, thinking, thinking.

He was not much of a competitor in footraces and the games the others played—wrestling, boxing, or hurling spears made of slender supple tree branches. Jesus enjoyed watching and even coached from time to time, sometimes playfully bestowing upon the winners wreaths of parsley or sea grass or braided *chittah* (wheat) stems.

This made an especially handsome prize, and James still kept one Jesus had placed on his head after he won a footrace when he was about fifteen years old. James showed us this trophy.

Aside from hours spent on the lake fishing, my main occupation became that of storyteller. Jona never wearied of my retelling everything. About how John invited me to work beside him as he performed baptisms, and what followed when Jesus appeared, and how he accepted the first few of us who sought him. Jona was proud of Simon and me.

A week later Jesus returned to Capernaum. He went to the house of Chuza, the nobleman whose son was healed. The Master had recognized him when he first came to Jesus in Cana. He was the steward for the household of Herod Antipas. What Jesus didn't know then was that Chuza had a wife named Joanna.

They lived on the outskirts just off the road into Capernaum, for it was only a short journey then to the site of the ancient city of Hammath, now called Tiberias, on the Sea of Galilee. Here, ten or more years before, Herod Antipas had built a new city. And it was there that Chuza oversaw the needs of the Tetrarch's household.

When Jesus healed the son of the nobleman, the man's wife, children, servants, and relatives were immediately convinced that Jesus was a man of God and worthy to be followed.

Joanna was a woman of independent wealth, and she implored her husband to allow her to provide in their grove a small residence, which Jesus might appreciate having, to call his home. "My home is in heaven," he would say, "but I am visiting here."

One evening, when a gentle breeze was blowing in from the great sea, Jesus appeared along the quay where our boats were drawn up on the shore. We greeted him with unreserved joy. Smiling, he told us of his new place and pronounced Capernaum to now be his city too.

For the next few nights he went out with us or with his cousins and helped draw nets, sometimes full, sometimes half empty. Then late one night, toward morning, as the fleet moved landward after good fishing, he asked us to remain offshore. He was in the boat with John and James and signaled us to draw closer.

"Put down the anchors," he said. "I have something to tell you." We obeyed at once.

As dawn brightened, Jesus began to speak, telling us he had gone briefly back to Nazareth.

"On the Sabbath I went into the synagogue as was my custom when I lived there. As usual, the chief seats were occupied. The elder who was chief of the synagogue recognized me as did a few relatives and friends. Perhaps they had heard of my work in Cana. At any rate, out of curiosity or courtesy, the chief of the elders invited me to read the lesson that day. I stood up to read and comment for the first time in the synagogue of my youth. I did not ask, but the clerk brought me the Book of Esaias.

"I took the roll, opened it, and the congregation stood to hear me read.

> The spirit of the Lord is upon me, because He has sent me to heal the brokenhearted, to preach salvation to the captives and recovering of sight to the blind, to set at liberty them that are bruised, to preach the acceptable year of the Lord.

"Then, closing the book, I gave it to the attendant, who returned the scroll to its closet. I sat down, prepared to discourse on the meaning of the text I'd read. To a man, all eyes were upon me, and I began by saying, "This day is this scripture fulfilled in your ears.

"Those present gave witness to my talk and wondered how I, a son of Joseph the carpenter, dared speak such gracious words of myself. They were astonished. To them I was just Joseph's son. I discerned a change in their thinking," Jesus said. "They began to murmur among themselves, rebelling at the thought that one from Nazareth could claim to fulfill the promise of Esaias that a man would come forth to heal the blind.

"I answered the noise of indignation that arose in the room. 'I know you are thinking of the proverb, Physician, heal yourself . . . what you did in Capernaum, do here at home. You doubt that I have healing ability; only God can bestow miracles.

"'Truly I tell you,' I continued, 'no prophet is recognized in his own country. When famine continued forty-two months in Israel in the time of Elijah, he was sent to Zarepath in Sidon to a Canaanite widow. And while Elisha lived, there were many lepers in Israel, but it was a Syrian, Naaman by name, who was cleansed.'

"At these words they became angry," Jesus said, "and rose up and laid hands on me, leading me by force to the top of the hill, from whence they intended to throw me down headlong onto a jagged rock ledge far below. But I had no fear. It was as though a path opened before me, and I passed through the midst of them, and no one came after me as I made my way here. Capernaum is now my city."

Jesus stood up in the boat. We saw him collected and serene and intent upon his mission.

"Come," he said. "The sun has risen, and the Sabbath will begin as it sets today. I will continue to teach, even in the synagogue here."

Nathanael had now the answer to his question—can anything good come out of Nazareth? We called him no more Jesus of Nazareth, but rather, Jesus of Galilee, as we rowed him back to shore.

A few days later, when Simon and I took the skiff out and anchored not far from shore, it was midnight and we noticed a roiling in the waters where high-finned fish were feeding in great number. Just as we were about to cast net, we saw Jesus walking on the shore.

He called to us, "Come now, if you want to follow me. Instead of fish, you will be catching men."

Jesus had previously sent us to our homes, saying, "Occupy till I come for you." We had lived each day expecting him to call us together again. Now the call came, and in response we dropped the net in the boat, pulled anchor, and rowed toward land. We could not wait to rejoin our teacher.

Jesus continued walking along the shore, coming to where Zebedee's ship floated just offshore. Apparently, James and John were there positioning their nets.

Jesus called them to follow him. They put down the dragnets from which they had been untangling wooden floats, lead weights, and the flaxen cords which webbed the whole.

They dropped the anchor into the sea and swam toward shore.

Jesus returned to where we beached our boat, and John and James, breathless and excited, caught up with us. We were a strange troop—four fishermen clothed only in loincloths—following Jesus away from the beach. No one was in sight except other fishermen in their skiffs; and we went home to get our clothes, our bedrolls, and our scrips.

Chapter 5

We slept the rest of that night in Chuza's grove and at midday went back to the shore. A few townspeople, thinking Jesus might preach, pressed around him, for they had heard of his healing the nobleman's son.

We walked to the place where two men were washing their nets in the shallows and where two ships, ours and Zebedee's, bobbed nearby.

Jesus entered our ship and said to Simon, "Thrust away a bit from the land." Then he sat down, and the gathering villagers stood on the shore listening as best they could while Jesus taught us.

As Jesus talked, I tried to hear every word as though it was new to my ears.

"God is not manlike in form or in act. He is spiritual, as the scriptures record. Only a perfect universal consciousness can fill heaven and earth, and the heaven of heavens," he explained. "Nothing of flesh and blood can do that. Nor can an image of clay.

"Therefore, think of the Almighty as infinite Spirit who knows and understands only that which is good."

The people murmured among themselves, "What strange doctrine he teaches." Others said, "Be still and listen."

Jesus continued, "Moses delivered God's law in commandment, 'You shall make no graven images to bow down to or worship.' Shaped clay cannot speak. Carved wood cannot save.

"God is never limited in form. As Mind, He is present everywhere to protect and save. Therefore, forsake your idols and amulets, your charms and superstitions. God is the creator only of good—including goodness in men.

"Return to your homes. Think about what I have taught." Simon rowed to shore.

As we started to walk away, Jesus said to us, "Remember, all things are possible to God."

Then Jesus called, "Simon, wait. Launch out into the deep and let down your nets to draw fish." I went with the two of them to our boat.

"Master, we toiled three nights ago, and there were no fish to take from these depths. Nevertheless, as you have suggested, I will drop down the net," Simon said.

We did not know we were being bidden to think deeper thoughts about source and supply. The net was trolled, and to our surprise, it was immediately filled with fish. Simon and Jesus beckoned to John and James, who approached in their vessel. Both of our nets were filled so full it seemed we might swamp beneath the waves.

Poor Simon. He was overwhelmed, even terrified. He fell at Jesus's knees. "Leave me, for I am ungodly and unrighteous. How is it that I should behold such power as yours. How can a sinner be so blessed?"

Jesus lifted Simon to his feet and held him until the frightful trembling ceased.

We were all amazed—I, and James and John too. They were nearby, still harvesting the multitude of fish.

"Do not be afraid," Jesus said loudly to all of us. "I have come to break the bond of sin, and henceforth you too will catch men from the shallows of iniquity. I will teach you this. Let's return to land."

Our boats were soon beached. When we heard the sound of small stones beneath the hulls, we leaped ashore. Leaving the catch to the servants of Zebedee, we straightway bathed.

Later, in fresh garments, we left our fishermen-selves behind to follow Jesus. Thenceforth, we were to catch men into newness of life, even as we were to learn to think in new ways about all existence.

We went to the synagogue. Most of the townspeople also went, for it was now sundown, the beginning of Sabbath, and Jesus would surely be bidden to read.

He was. He opened the scroll to the fifth book of Moses and proceeded to read.

> For Thou art an holy people unto the Lord thy God: the Lord thy God hath chosen thee to be a special people unto Himself, above all people that are upon the face of the earth.

> The Lord did not set His love upon you nor choose you because ye were more in number than any people, for ye were the fewest of all people.

> But because the Lord loved you, and because He would keep the oath which He had sworn unto your fathers, hath the Lord brought you out with a mighty hand, and redeemed you out of the house of bondmen from the hand of Pharaoh, king of Egypt.

Know, therefore, that the Lord thy God, He is God, the faithful God,
which keepeth covenant and mercy with them that love Him and keep
His commandments to a thousand generations.

He then spoke of God's love, explaining that the source of everything good is God's love, which becomes the manifestation of His presence, His power, His wisdom, and His knowledge of the needs of mankind. Love is the gift of God, the One who is supreme, unduplicated, incorporeal, infinite in nature and power and loving kindness.

From the congregation were heard voices of assent and approval, for this teaching was unlike that of the scribes, who only interpreted the law of Moses.

Jesus spoke of the law of God—loving, forbearing, giving, and forgiving. He bade each and every man to feel this love of God and share it in love to one another.

While approving, we were nonetheless astonished, for Jesus spoke with unusual authority, and all who listened were convinced of his new doctrine.

Suddenly there was a cry from the section where we men were seated. One known to be possessed of an unclean spirit rose up, crying out, "Let us alone! What mean you, Jesus of Nazareth? Are you come to destroy us? I know you are the Holy One, come from God. But leave us alone."

With that, the poor man indeed seemed possessed, for his eyes rolled up and his frame jerked and shook, and spit ran bloody and bubbly from his mouth as he fell to the floor.

But Jesus raised his right arm and pointed to where the man now lay stretched out and shaking violently. With a loud, firm voice he commanded the evil, "Hold your peace. Come out of him, and enter him never again!"

The body of the afflicted man arched in one last terrible throe, and from his lips escaped a horrible cry of agony.

Immediately after this, the man struggled to his feet clear eyed, calm, and grateful. He wiped the bloody smear from his face then pushed through the congregation of men and came to Jesus.

Everyone sat amazed, looking one to another and questioning among themselves. What is this that Jesus has brought among us? What new precept is this? Whence comes such authority that commands even unclean spirits to depart and in obedience they cease to be?

The man who was healed was thronged with men and women, who embraced him and wished him well-being. In return he repeated over and over again, "I am well, and I know it! I am healed, and I feel it in my heart and soul and mind."

In the midst of the rejoicing Jesus slipped away, and we followed him to the grove nearby where we sat in silent wonder at the feet of our teacher, who had shown again in Galilee the power God has given to man. The power to heal and bless and redeem. Indeed, with God all things are possible. We were beginning to understand this.

A week or two later, as another Sabbath ended beneath a blazing sky, we walked to Simon's house for he had invited all of us to sup with his family. Peter's wife, Adina, welcomed us, saying her provisions were ample, but would we be cautiously quiet? Her mother lay very ill with a sudden fever.

"Please help her, Master," Peter implored.

Jesus crossed the threshold and went to where the venerable elderly woman lay upon her bedroll on a raised platform in a dark corner of the second room.

She feebly opened her eyes. Jesus took her by the hand and lifted her up. At once the fever was gone, and she arose well and radiant and joyous, for she loved Jesus! She proceeded to help Adina serve the supper. We ate with wonderment and gratitude.

Would these days ever cease to be miraculous?

No! For with the setting sun, the villagers brought the sick of Capernaum to Peter's door—those who had disease and those possessed with devils.

We, his students, stood to one side, amazed. Jesus walked among the throng, the gentle smile of love upon his face. He had a few words for each sufferer, most of which we could not hear. He lightly touched each one as if to say, "You are all right."

He kneeled to those carried on stretchers and lifted them in his arms to stand, then walk, and some could even run. He firmly but gently detached crutches from those who came struggling to walk. Then they took steps, firm and free.

He embraced a few covered with sores and scabrous disease, and the ugliness vanished. He held a child whose arm hung loose, obviously dislocated, until she curled both arms around Jesus's neck and nestled lovingly into the shelter of his shoulder.

Those who cried out in pain or performed frightful antics as though possessed with devils he comforted with words which brought instant ease and permanent peace.

He silenced the involuntary awfulness of words emitted by those of fearful and disordered mind. We heard cursing lips suddenly change and speak praise to Jesus, acknowledging him to be the Son of God.

We saw being made sane, strong, and whole again those who had been distressed by demons, a few destined to die soon, others with deformity of body, and some who were severely wounded in quarrelsome conflict.

The babble of joy and the cries of freedom echoed in the gathering dusk. All who needed healing were made free. They departed to their homes, restored to wholeness by God's love and truth.

How can he do this? we asked ourselves.

We gathered in the home provided for Jesus by Joanna and Chuza, and there far into the night we heard from his lips how we too could learn to heal.

"With God all things are possible. This is the first truth to understand. We are all the children of God," Jesus explained. "I came directly from Him. You have come in bondage to the misbelief of birth. But you have begun your journey from flesh to the reality of God's creation, in which there is no night, no sickness, no sin, no death.

"You have seen this evening how in godliness there can be no evil, for evil is the opposite of good. God did not make evil. It is without origin other than false belief, and it cannot control anyone or anything.

"Beholding yourself in the still waters of a lake, what do you see? The image of your face and body. You move, your reflection moves. Just so, man is the image of God, not in body, but in mind.

"God is the ever-presence, expressing good. This nearness is wholly spiritual. God has no body, as mortals have bodies of flesh."

There was a shifting among us, as though some were uncomfortable.

"Do you question this within yourselves?" Jesus asked.

James, who was fidgeting the most, asked Jesus, "I know what flesh is, but what is Spirit?"

"Let me ask you, Cousin," he replied. "Do things you see and touch remain unchanged? Does not an earthen pitcher shatter into many shards? Does a wineskin remain tight and never rupture into uselessness? Does not flesh corrupt when dead?

"From this you well know that destruction and decay await all earthly objects. But it is not so with the things of Spirit, God. It takes spiritual understanding to behold the spiritual creation, wherein exist forever the things of God.

"That which is flesh is flesh. But consciousness is spiritual. Mind is the substance of Spirit. Do you understand this?"

We nodded that we were beginning to understand.

"Earlier when I taught by the seaside, I touched upon the nature of God which holds in itself all power to manifest only goodness.

"When nets were dropped into the depths and pulled forth overflowing, it was to teach you to obey and go beyond thinking real that which is temporal. Instead of the emptiness you had experienced, you then harvested an abundance of fish. To me, the fish leaped into your nets with joy."

We sat in stillness with shining eyes, and our ears—no, our *mind*—grasping new thoughts as he taught.

"In the synagogue I spoke of God's love. It stirred one man who was in bondage to fear that God did not love him because he experienced such terror through his affliction. But I heeded not his upset. I beheld God's thought, lifting him out of his fear. I held to this, and the demon was banished from this sufferer's consciousness. The afflicted one rose up, clear and free, evidencing the reality of his being the child of God."

"How did you do this?" asked my brother.

"I knew, as always, that with God all things are possible. I cast out of thought all fear and doubt. I denied that there could be an effect of some transgression for which the man was being punished.

"I saw man as God's likeness. God's love cast out the belief that this man was a helpless victim of evil. At once evil was proven powerless. The man was healed.

"At Peter's house, when I was bidden to attend to the illness of his wife's mother, I renounced fear as cause. I replaced that falsity with awareness of the love God holds for everyone. God will have all mankind waken to the perfection with which He has endowed the children of men. To be like God is to be free from all that is unlike God.

"That is what I was knowing. I knew Adina's mother to be the expression of that harmony which is God's power and presence, that she too knew what God was imparting mentally to her about herself. She responded to this power of thought. The fever was banished, and then she came forth at once to help serve our supper."

Jesus paused. Love flowed to us like a flame of fire from his eyes. In our hearts, we began to trust and understand God.

Then for what seemed to be minutes—but actually was over an hour—we asked for more, and Jesus taught us how every thought must be prayerful. How his Heavenly Father heard and answered every righteous, unselfish prayer.

About the time of false cockcrow, which is the third hour after midnight, we settled down to rest, while Jesus watched over us as he communed with God.

After this remarkable day in Capernaum and the night of teaching, Jesus went alone into a solitary place where even we could not find him, for he wished to be alone while praying to his Father God.

When Simon, the sons of Zebedee, and I finally found him in the hills the next day, we told him many people were looking for him in Capernaum.

But Jesus departed a few hours later to visit other cities of Galilee, and we went with him. Word of his marvelous works were on the lips of people everywhere, and everywhere he went there was welcome.

He preached the good news of God's presence. He taught from the scriptures in the synagogues. He healed sickness and every kind of disease wherever he found people suffering.

Even to Syria, north and eastward from the Sea of Galilee, and across the Jordan River, the news spread, and from thence came diseased and paralyzed people, some under demon possession, others insane or deformed.

They all returned home healed.

They begged Jesus to reside in every town and city he entered, but he simply responded by saying kindly, "I must preach the kingdom of God in every place where there is need to know God, for thereto am I sent."

One day, a leper, Simon by name, came to him crying for help. The man was full of leprosy, an abject and loathsome sight. From his knees he fell prostrate at Jesus's feet, crying pathetically, "If you will, you can make me clean."

To our horror, Jesus stretched forth his hands and, *touching him*, lifted him from the ground to stand upright. Jesus was now ceremonially impure for he had touched a leprous man. We, who were his followers, fell back a pace or two.

The man wore tattered garments, rags which hid most of his tortured body. Only his hands and arms were visible, and there stood Jesus with his arms stretched out in close embrace with the ugly flesh, which made everyone else who saw it flee instinctively.

Jesus wasn't afraid of the Jewish law which condemned those so afflicted to live apart from healthy people. Nor was Jesus afraid of the terrible skin condition. He knew that God created neither the disease nor a diseased person who is impossible to redeem from certain death.

"I will heal you," Jesus said quite plainly; and, continuing to touch the man, he said, "Be clean!"

Immediately the leprosy vanished! The man's skin was natural and smooth, as fresh and sweet as a child's.

Later Jesus told us how he looked upon the one in need of healing, but not with bodily eyes which told him, as well as each of us, that the man was dreadfully leprous. He chose instead to see through the disease with clear and perfect awareness in thought that this man was created to be God's image and God's likeness.

Jesus said he dismissed from consciousness every temptation to think of imperfection and contamination as real in the body or mind of the man who stood before him.

We could scarcely believe what we saw: one minute a man deservedly outcast, and in the very next the same man, radiant with joy and healthy flesh.

Jesus instructed the man to go but to tell nobody about the healing, to say nothing to any man but to straightway show himself to the priest to give evidence of his healing. The priest would then instruct how he was to be tested seven times before he was pronounced clean. Then he would be required to give offerings on the eighth day in order that the priest might make atonement for him in testimony to his cleansing.

The man was overjoyed. But he could not keep the healing secret! Why need one hide when his leprosy is gone? Instead, he spread his good news to everyone who saw him, and Jesus had to leave the village and take refuge in the desert area across the Jordan River. This man went home to be with his family in Bethany in Judea.

But there were always many people who sought Jesus for healing. So in peace and prayer he continued to heal. He could bear witness to no person being other than perfect, evidencing the presence of the perfection of God's children, who therefore are pure and sound in body and being.

We must have been a strange sight as we traveled throughout Galilee. The original followers of Jesus were now joined day after day by a growing company. Some were merely curious. Others were clearly devoted to the idea that perhaps, at last, the promised Savior had come to earth.

The entourage was mostly friendly, though now and then a doubter appeared among us and ceaselessly asked questions about such things as the law of Moses, or, if Jesus was only to heal, how could Israel be saved from Rome? And why had God not sent a man of war, like Naaman of long ago, who was good enough to be healed of leprosy and also to command an army.

To such questions Jesus always announced, "The kingdom of God is within each of you. It is here that the warfare with evil must be waged. The hearts of men are already a battlefield. Henceforth, your war will be with evil thoughts and with the actions that spring therefrom.

"On this battleground you will find that God's truth and love will gain everlasting victory over all that is unlike good. Understanding this, you can have the consciousness of wholeness, health, and harmony."

Some persons left us then, returning home, refusing to become involved, for only disbelief and earthly cares were their bedfellows.

Others would walk with us a few more days, share our communal meals, and sleep on grass or bare ground until they could take it no more. When homesickness set in, they disappeared from Jesus's infant spiritual army.

Now and again we went home to Capernaum, where we would tell our households what great things Jesus had said and done. Our family and friends always listened closely.

We would refresh our garments and bedrolls, and take long cleansing baths in the lake. Then after a day or two, we would roll up a change of clothing in our bed, fill our purses (for our boats were still taken out each night, and the gain from the harvest of fish went to each man's household), and then we were once again with Jesus as he walked the roads of Galilee.

Going from Capernaum toward Nazareth, we could take the road turning southwest toward Magdala, going along the lakeshore to where the road from Tiberias crossed the great highway to Ptolemais then toward the Jerusalem road, running from Damascus southward along the Sea of Galilee.

Or at the juncture of the Ptolemais highway we might walk west a few furlongs to where a new road led south through Cana to Nazareth, then traverse the Esdraelon Valley toward Gaza and Egypt.

Nazareth is a very small village, yet five trade routes lead through, and so we often passed that way. Some of the townspeople remembered Jesus and hailed him, but most would spit and turn away. This would amuse rather than annoy Jesus.

With frequent passage through the town, we came to identify the well where his mother once drew water and what houses and which courtyards were built when he and his younger brothers worked with their carpenter father.

Indeed, we even grew to recognize which roof beams Jesus had helped put in place and which doors were hung with his own hands. But we never lingered to rest in Nazareth. We only passed through.

A road led directly west from Nazareth through Sepphoris, the birth town of Jesus's mother, Mary. It was here that bold revolutionaries plotted rebellion against Rome. It was thought that here, release from all evil oppression would come, when God's Anointed One appeared to miraculously overthrow the enemy.

Once, while walking through Sepphoris, Simon asked, "Will you ever raise men to fight with you as an army against Rome?"

Jesus replied, "The army I am to gather will never harm or kill."

"Must we then submit to the legions of Rome?" I asked.

"There is a greater oppressor than Rome. It is sin and death," Jesus answered. "I am not sent to wage warfare on earth. My Father's kingdom is not of this world. It is enough that I am sent to fight with no weapons other than Truth and Love."

"But I am willing and ready to fight any enemy which oppresses our people," I exclaimed.

"My warfare is to stand fast in the power of God and not yield to the tyranny of flesh and the sin which leads to death," said Jesus.

"Will you ever arm with swords and knives? horses and chariots? legions and generals on land, and warships and rowers at sea?" I persisted.

"None of these," Jesus replied simply. "It is the power of God which is wholly good, with which we shall fight against evil."

"Where then is the place of Satan, that we may quickly bring it down?" Philip asked.

"Satan has no place and no power," Jesus explained. "Satan is of fear, not of God, nor to be feared by man. Satan is adversarial *thought*, hostile to all that is good. God grants no adversary either power or presence.

"Evil thought is the enemy I am sent to overpower and cast out. The attempt of evil is to oppose God. The people of earth must learn to subdue every such attempt. Satan must be stripped of every claim to power.

"Evil must no longer borrow the creation of God to war against the Creator. Therefore I come to destroy the works of the devil and the fear that evil is as real as the goodness and love of God." We pondered this lesson, and walked on.

We never lingered in Sepphoris. Jesus preferred that we travel straight through mingling in the wake of travelers who followed the caravans of merchantmen. He knew his presence might foment controversy.

Chapter 6

We returned to Capernaum. The news spread quickly when we reached Peter's house. Soon the main room was filled, and Jesus spoke loudly so those gathered in the courtyard might also hear.

Suddenly there was a commotion. Four friends of a man who was paralyzed brought him on a stretcher and tried vainly to penetrate the throng outside the door. No one would move or give way. So the friends carefully carried the stretcher up the outside stairs which led to the roof.

Without permission or even the awareness of Peter, they broke through the mud tiling over the roof of thatched palm laid on strong beams. Separating the fronds they then, by means of heavy rope, lowered the man on his stretcher right into the midst of those surrounding Jesus.

Our Master stood there, amazed at the faith of the four friends who laid this man at his feet. Grateful for such receptivity and aware of what the man must have endured in this effort to have him healed, Jesus said to him, "My son, your sins are forgiven."

Sitting near Jesus, observing his speech and acts, were scribes, doctors of the law, and Pharisees. When they heard these words, they began to ask each other, "Who is this man who speaks blasphemies? Who can forgive sin but God alone?"

Jesus knew what they were thinking and spoke directly to them, "Why are you reasoning about this? Are you wondering what is correct, to say 'Your sins are forgiven?' Or should I have simply said, 'Rise, take up the couch whereon you lie, and return home?'

"I want you to know that the Son of man has power on earth to forgive sins, to love the man made by God so completely that sin no longer binds sinners to their mistakes and temptation, and they then stop sinning. Suffering for sin ceases when one ceases sinning."

Jesus turned to the man sick of the palsy, who was indeed weary with both the paralysis and the incapacitated living from which he needed to be made free.

Jesus said, "I say to you, arise! Go home now, and take with you the bed upon which you feel so helpless."

Immediately, right before us, his limbs lost the rigidity of palsy, and flexed—enabling the man to grasp another's hand and raise himself from his pallet, standing free and suddenly active. He shouldered the stretcher, and as those around him parted, he walked upright, freely, through the assembly, out into the sunshine and sweet air.

The neighborhood knew something wonderful had taken place when they saw this fellow townsman walking and shouting, "Glory to God! I am free! I am whole! I am forgiven! Jesus has cast away from me all shame and fear. Praise to God who has forgiven my sins through His Anointed. Would that all men could know what Jesus knows!"

His four friends then hoisted the man upon their shoulders and, leaving the stretcher behind, carried the jubilant man to his house. All who witnessed this miracle were amazed, saying, "We have seen strange things today."

Jesus continued his sermon, and when the crowd dispersed, many people went their way sensing that their hidden transgressions were also forgiven.

The peace which inhabited their hearts was so profound they knew old sins would no longer be found tempting. Jesus could have told them, "Sin forsaken is sin forgiven. It needs no further forgiveness."

After another of Adina's generous suppers, we escorted Jesus to his house in Chuza's olive grove. He bade us to sit with him for a while, for he wished to teach us further.

"You have seen me prove the power of God who is ever present as Spirit. What questions do you now have to ask of me?"

Philip was the first to respond. "Why am I here if God's kingdom is not of this world?"

"You are here because mankind believes that God commanded them to multiply and replenish the earth through flesh. In truth, here and now, each one of you, women and children, as well as men, may choose how to live. It is in godly ways that one prepares oneself worthy to continue living in the Life which unfolds forever."

We were silent, each of us pondering these words.

When, at length, we raised our eyes to Jesus, he asked, "Do you understand this? It is a simple lesson, but it underlies all life."

Nathanael raised his hand to question. "From where comes evil if God is the all and only of existence?"

"Evil is mistaken thought which comes through ignorance, and it appears as either fear or evil," Jesus explained. Let me show you," he said and bent to pick up a few olives. He dropped several but held two in each palm. "Count these. How many do I hold in each hand, and what is the sum of them all?"

We each in turn answered, "Two in each, four in all."

"Were I to show these to a child who had not yet learned numbers, his answer might be anything but two and four. Two and two to him might make five or three. That is ignorance. We could correct him and teach by counting the olives—'one, two, and three, four—the sum is four.'

"So this is how one learns to heal. First, one must detect evil resulting from ignorance, fear, or sin, as mistaken thought. It is a mistaken thought leading to disobedience and fear in wrong actions. Body becomes sick, diseased, deformed, depraved, or insane because it believes evil is real.

"Do not blame the body. It is righteous or unrighteous *thought* which governs the flesh. If you would heal the body, first heal thought. Replace mistaken thought—ungodly, unloving, hateful, fearful, and harmful thought—with true thoughts which flow from the mind of God.

"God binds no one in chains to evil, sinful, or fearful thought. He releases one and all who yield wrong to right, ignorance to understanding, and fear to faith in goodness. Think about these things. Continue to learn. But go now. Take your rest. I must visit my Father in heaven through prayer, for I feel His thoughts as angels coming to my mind."

None of us said another word as we walked to our homes. Nathanael and Philip did not go to Cana but went to sleep under the stars in the pile of nets heaped in one of Zebedee's boats. The next morning we walked northward from town, with Jesus leading us and many others.

We all knew Matthew, the tax collector, and we despised him. His advantage was great, for in receipt of custom, he worked out of the customhouse on the northern edge of Capernaum where the caravans traveling the great Damascus road from or into Syria were required to stop.

It is here that merchantmen are expected to display completely the contents of every shipment. All commerce and travel halt for inspection. If contents and bills of lading do not match, or permits of passage are not fully stamped, each custom agent is free to levy a new tax.

Only exorbitant bribery can send onward the camels and carts laden with goods coming into or leaving the Galilee. Even foot travelers are subject to long delay.

And worse, Matthew, a Jew, was commissioned and paid by Caesar. For this he was despised by everyone.

Strange as this may seem, his father, Alphaeus, was a man as fully respected as his son was despised. Simon Peter and I knew the family well, for as children we played together with Matthew and his brother, James, whom we called the Little, and sometimes the Less. They were so close in age and visage that they were sometimes considered twins.

Matthew did not like the sea, but he was bright at numbers and meticulous with details so work as a publican suited him well.

On the other hand, James the Little was joined with his father in local commerce. They scrupulously ran the fish guild upon which fleet owners depended for sale of the various salted and dried fish taken to markets in Jerusalem and as far away as Damascus and Babylon. Alphaeus permitted no extortion levied on the local fishermen's produce being sent for export and subject to custom inspection.

The brothers, Matthew (also called Levi) and James the Little, were aware when Zebedee's two sons and we, the sons of Jona, left the fishing fleet to follow Jesus. Secretly they envied us, especially when Jesus began to heal and the populace of Syria, Galilee, and Judea increasingly spoke of Jesus of Galilee as the Anointed One of God.

I am convinced that Jesus not only read thought but could also discern what was in the heart of a man. Why else would he bother leading us northward to where Matthew sat at receipt of custom?

I knew that James the Little was among the multitude who attached themselves to Jesus and followed him, bearing witness in many places of all that Jesus said and did as we traveled through the province. But it was plain that this James was shocked, as I and the other students were, when we heard Jesus say to Matthew, "Follow me."

We were even more surprised when Matthew enclosed his papers and seals in a small chest, handed it to another official, and walked out. He saluted Jesus then came forward humbly.

He reached out his hand to a couple of people he knew, and then took his place in the rear of the retinue beside his brother, James the Little.

Jesus looked back, smiled, and nodded to James, as if to say, "You too." Now there were eight of us who would follow the Master constantly.

A few days later, Matthew told Jesus that he was planning a feast to celebrate his freedom from working at customs. Would Jesus and his companions accept his invitation? Jesus said, "Yes, and twelve or fifteen others will come with me."

Matthew was a wealthy man, albeit from the illicit revenues that he levied. Nevertheless, his money was well spent for he lived splendidly, though alone, on his pleasant estate in an isolated area along the seashore.

We followed a stony path which led us away from the main road into Capernaum. The path led up a knoll. When we had gained the rise and started to descend, there below us lay a grove of trees and a garden enclosed in a hedge, and within the hedge a long low house among palm and fig trees and a small vineyard. Beyond the house and garden stretched the Sea of Gennesaret, the Galilean sea.

The hedge surrounding Levi's house was a thick planting of *chadek*, an evergreen shrub which grows like a thicket. Running parallel thereto was a double row of camel thorn growing half as high as the *chadek*. It was a forbidding wall of protection for the house. Both plantings were covered with sharp, spiny thorns that neither man nor animal would venture to break through.

Seeing this, Jesus said, "Hosea writes thus in scripture, 'Therefore, behold, I will hedge up thy way with thorns!'"

We all laughed with him.

A tall door, more like a gate, led through the hedge directly into an anteroom of the house. In the anteroom, Matthew stood by as his servants washed our feet and hands. Then he kissed our cheeks and welcomed each of us by name, even those from other places who on this day walked with Jesus and were invited to come along to the feast. Many, even some who had not yet been introduced to him, were already known to the tax collector.

Matthew presented us, one by one, to his guests who were there. We knew some of them. They were his fellow publicans with whom we villagers had little contact. And there were other guests equally despised. Some had fallen afoul of the law, civil and religious. Some were known to be renegade Jews.

We could hear the soft voices of women, secluded in an area sectioned off with an elaborate pierced screen of wood inlaid with ivory.

"You are my honored guests," said Matthew. "Feel free to enjoy this house. The shore is sharp with broken shells, but the view toward the village and the ships anchored at the quay is splendid at this hour of evening."

First we mingled and gawked. Few of us had ever been inside the home of one so wealthy. We went into every room permitted and then out through the loggia into the yard. The hedge extending at either side of the house was squared to turn toward the beach. A splendid garden spread out around us.

The air was fragrant with odor of the lake mingling with the spicy ground cover, the breath of mint and a marjoram called *ezab* or hyssop. Bay trees, evergreen and bushy, were covered with creamy white flowers which gave off a faint sweet scent similar to the fragrance which is more fulsome when bay leaves are crushed. And there were carob trees in bloom, and cone-pine giving shade, and bushy castor oil shrubs, and wildflowers in the grass.

We could hear other guests being greeted—Alphaeus, Matthew's father; Mary, his mother; and James the Less. We knew them all. We went back into the house and greeted them, hailing each with sincere joy.

The women went to an inner room, and we men were bidden to the table, to recline on couches around the long three-sided banquet board.

Servants brought a stream of elegant trays laden with fish grilled with citrus; a stew, chunky and spicy; cold crisp raw and steamed vegetables dressed with oil and herbs and sweet vinegar. There were buns and loaves; and braided rings of various bread stuffs; and finally trays of fruits, fresh and dried; and a porridge of rice and yogurt sweetened with bits of honeyed melon. And there were cakes and sweets of several kinds.

I had never eaten such a meal, and neither had Peter, who sat far down the table from Jesus but close enough to be heard by me. Matthew had placed us along the left length of the table, with Jesus at the center, while Alphaeus, Matthew, and his brother, James the Little sat opposite. Friends were ranged closely along the table and across the shorter ends.

There was much bantering about how the wealthy lived, and much laughter as his friends teased Matthew for his willingness to forsake it all to walk with Jesus.

As we ate, we noticed two robed Pharisees standing within the shadow of the loggia inside the courtyard. Matthew invited them to come in, saying he would have servants set another table for them quite apart. They refused, explaining that they were not permitted to eat with publicans and sinners who departed from the laws of Moses.

They hissed protest to the servants passing to and fro while serving, and they raised uplifted palms in gestures of disapproval of what they saw.

When Jesus saw this, he called to them to enter. Again they would not, saying they could not. Jesus rose and rebuked them.

"You wonder that I dine with publicans and laugh with those you despise. Have you no understanding? The healthy do not need a doctor, but those who are ill do! Depart from this house! Go! Learn what it means which was spoken by the prophet: 'I will have mercy not sacrifice.'

"I would have you know God aright and honor him with love instead of with burnt offerings. Don't you realize that I am sent to call sinners to goodness, and need not to call the righteous? Depart now! Seek to understand the scriptures. The holy words of God are meant to be made practical!"

The Pharisees departed without another word. The feast continued a while longer, with unabated joy. Then the guests began to depart. Matthew bid his old friends good night and good-bye with an embrace and a kiss. To each he quietly whispered, "Tonight I say farewell to the life I've lived as a publican."

Aloud he explained, "Tomorrow I offer this place for a hostel for travelers on the Damascus Road. Henceforth, I will travel with the companions of God's Anointed. I have yearned to do this from the first time I heard of his miracles in Galilee, and now he has called me to follow."

From that moment, we realized what Jesus had discerned—the desire in Matthew's heart. Jesus meant for us to know we were to love our fellows as God has loved us. All men were welcome to follow Jesus.

When we were finally parting from Matthew at the gate, I quietly said to him, "I welcome you with love, dear new/old friend."

Tears fell from his eyes. "I am coming with you," he said. "Now this very night."

He turned away from his home, leaving the gate open, for he no longer needed to close it for protection. There really was no parting on our part. From that very moment, our lives were blended. We were all followers of Jesus.

We learned new things every day, some hard to understand, others easier to grasp and carry in thought.

One day John Baptist's disciples came to Jesus. "How is it," they asked, "that both we and the Pharisees often fast, but your students do *not* fast?"

Jesus answered, "Why need one give up the joy of life? We go through Galilee preaching and teaching. Should we not feast together in gladness? Moses fasted on the mount but did not prescribe it for the children who came forth from Egypt. David fasted when he prayed for his child's life. True fasting is to refrain from iniquity and in choosing to know and do good alone.

"I have chosen to promote the kingdom of God within the heart of man. This is gladness, and with joy we rejoice in all good things. Can the children of the bridechamber fast while the bridegroom is present? The days will come when the bridegroom will be taken from them. They will fast then in those days. Even then they will choose to do good rather than return evil for evil.

"Hear this," Jesus said to them, "no man puts new cloth into an old garment. The new is not faded as is the old, and the garment would not be as seemly. The old will not secure the new, for the old is weak and will easily tear away from the new.

"Would you put new wine into old skins? If so, as it further ferments, new wine will burst the bottles and spill, and both the bottles and the wine will be ruined. But new wine poured into new bottles is held by new strength, and both wine and the container will endure for good and long use.

"Some men are accustomed to the old wine and have no desire for the new, saying the old wine is better.

"That is what they are saying against the new doctrine of love which I preach. The Pharisees fast ritually twice in the week. These men who have tasted the old wine will not at once desire the new. They will think the old is better.

"My companions know the new way is to be preferred. Therefore, we do not need to fast for we have great joy in that which is now made new."

Jesus decided to return to Jerusalem for a few days.

Outside of the city wall on the north side of the Kidron Valley, between the temple hill and the main plateau of the city, quite near the sheep gate entrance, there is a spring and pool of water called the Pool of Bethesda. Bethesda means "house of grace and loving kindness." The pool has many levels or steps called porches, where pilgrims might rest.

It is believed that the water of the pool has healing qualities when it bubbles up. Though the agitated water probably has a natural reason for moving—such as an earthquake tremor—the superstitious say that an angel descends and stirs the water.

People long afflicted gather and camp in the five levels around the pool. They hope that if one is able to be first to get into the water while it is moving, such a one will immediately be healed.

We were there one day. Many, many sick people were waiting for the water to move. Amongst them was a man who had been paralyzed for thirty-eight years.

Jesus must have known this. How, I do not know. I saw him step carefully over and around many people lying or sitting closely until he came to this man whose limbs were cruelly useless, stiffened into rigidity, rendering bodily comfort impossible.

Jesus asked him, "Do you expect to be healed?"

Startled, the man looked up. Why else would anyone be there among such pitiful people? Of course, he wanted to be healed. All at once, he must have thought of Jesus's words in a new, hopeful way. Perhaps this stranger would help him, and that is why he was asked if he expected to be healed.

"I have no one to help me get to the water," he answered eagerly, for his hope now was that the strong young man beside him would carry him to the edge of the pool. When the moment came, his helpless body, with his shrunken arms and legs, could then be thrust into the depths. It also occurred to the paralytic man that he might sink helplessly and be drowned. But no, *this time* could bring healing to him.

Without further question Jesus commanded, "Rise, take up that on which you lie, and walk freely."

Immediately the man was made flexible and strong; and in this new condition of wholeness of body, he rose, picked up his pallet bed, and walked unhesitatingly in a perfectly normal way, threading his way out of those gathered on his level.

A priest standing nearby cried, "Blasphemy! This man heals on the Sabbath! He tells a man to take up his bed! On the Sabbath! It is not lawful for one to carry his bed. The Sabbath has just begun."

Thus the Jews from the temple railed against Jesus and accused the man as he climbed up the porches out of the pool area.

Jesus vanished into the crowd. Afterward he sought the man in the temple! It had been thirty-eight years since he had been able to be *in* the temple, and there he was found.

Jesus quietly whispered to him, "You are healed and made able again. It is through the ever-presence and power of God that you have been made whole. Sin no more, lest something worse befall you." Then Jesus moved away into the multitude.

"Who was that man?" the man asked those around him.

He was told, "Jesus, the healer from Nazareth who now lives in Capernaum."

The healed man, as he departed from the temple precincts said to one of the priests, "It is a man called Jesus who made me whole at the pool by the sheep market."

The priests scoured the temple. At last, they found Jesus and repeated their accusation that he had broken Sabbath law.

Jesus answered quietly, "My Father works every day in every place. Therefore, I too must work even as God who is my Father works."

The accusers were enraged! Now the offense was threefold, for he also said that God was his father and thus made himself equal with God. Again and again, they pointed a finger accusing him of blasphemy.

"Listen!" Jesus commanded. "I tell you truly, a son does nothing of himself but what he sees the father do. What a man does, a son will likewise try to do. God is my Father. He is the Father of all who are pure and righteous. Because I love God as a son loves his father, my Father loves His Son and shows me all that He Himself does. Even greater things than this man's recovery will be shown to you, and you will indeed marvel.

"God quickens and raises men from death. So shall the Son also quicken whom he will. God judges no man. He has committed all judgment unto his Son, that every man should honor the Son even as honor is given to God, the Father of us all. If you do not honor the Son, you refuse to honor the Father who has sent him to you.

"Truly, truly I say to you, listen to what I speak and hear what I say. Everyone who believes in me and in God who sends me is given life everlasting. There will be no condemnation. He will be passed from death unto life unending. Of a truth I tell you, the hour is coming, indeed now is, when those near death shall hear the voice of the Son of God. All who hear and believe shall live. For as God the Father is Life, so has He given the Son to have Life in himself.

"Don't think this is too marvelous to be true. The hour comes when all who are grave-bound will hear the voice of the Son of man who is also the Son of God, and they who are in the grave will already have come forth. All those who have done good shall rise in resurrection into the continuity of being. They will live forevermore. Those who have done evil will be resurrected to damnation, self-punished, denounced, condemned, sentenced to further discipline, and reviled.

"Take note and remember this: of my own self, I do nothing. As I hear, I judge. My judgment is just because I seek not my own will but the will of God who has sent me. If I bear witness of myself, my witness is false. There is another—God—who bears witness of me. I know the witness He bears of me is true. You went to hear the Baptist. He bare witness unto my coming after him.

"It is not the testimony of man that saves, but what I *declare*. That is what shall save you. It has saved many who have already been resurrected into continuity of being unseen by those who buried them. John was a burning and shining light. For a while, you were willing to rejoice in his light. But now I have greater witness even than John—the works which the Father has given me to finish.

"The works that I do bear witness that God has sent me. Thus the Father Himself bears witness of the Son. You have at no time heard His voice nor seen His form. God has not form, as has man. But He is the source, origin, and the substance of all that endures, for God is Spirit, not flesh. Even His Word does not live in you. You don't believe.

"Search the scriptures. You agree that in them is the promise of eternal life. The scriptures bear witness of me and testify to my work. Yet you come not to me that you might have the life everlasting promised in scripture. In the Book of Daniel, the angel Michael says, 'Many of them that sleep in the dust of the earth shall awake, some to everlasting life and some to shame and everlasting contempt. They that be wise shall shine as the brightness of the firmament, and they that turn many to righteousness as the stars forever and ever.'

"Also David, the beloved of God, sang of brethren dwelling in unity, being like the dew of heaven that descended upon the mountains of Zion, for it was there that the Lord commanded blessings of goodness for hearts united to serve God, even the blessing of life forevermore.

"Did not King Solomon leave us these words of wisdom?

> He that keepeth the commandment keepeth his own soul; but he that despiseth his ways shall die. The fear of the Lord tendeth toward life, and he that has it shall dwell in satisfaction; for he shall not be visited with evil.

"I say, search the scriptures. In them, you have eternal life promised in words that testify of me. But you do not come to me that you might have endless life.

"I don't want you to honor me. I need not honor from men. I know you have not even love for God in you.

"I come in my Father's name, and you do not receive me. Yet if someone comes in his own name, you *will* receive him and fuss over him with honor and much ado. You receive honor one of another but don't recognize or seek that honor which only God can bestow. Honor the works I've done in the name of the Father.

"Don't fear that I will accuse you to the Father. There is one who will accuse you, even Moses, in whom you do put your trust. If you had understood him, you would have believed and obeyed him. If you had believed Moses, you would have believed me.

"Moses wrote of me, 'The Lord thy God will raise up unto thee a prophet from the midst of thee, of thy brethren, like unto me; you shall listen to his words.' But if you believe not the Word Moses has written, how shall you believe my Word?"

Having rebuked in this way the thinking of the temple priests in Jerusalem, Jesus decided we should return to Galilee.

The next Sabbath found us journeying homeward and getting close to our village.

A great number of people followed, including Pharisees, who always observed what Jesus said and did. As we walked, several doctors of the law followed among the people. They excused themselves in this manner: "We are not working as we walk on this Sabbath. We are defending the rule of Moses, confuting the words of this man."

Sometimes Jesus led us off the beaten roads. We went through a fertile valley where farmers grew wheat abundantly, and melons, leeks, and mint and cumin. Wheat sown in the fall would soon be harvested, around the time of the coming Passover.

We were getting hungry. Jesus stopped in the middle of a field which was starting to show ripening grain. He surveyed the throng following him then pointed us to a grove of oaks nearby. Nearing the edge of the field, he gathered a handful of grain on the stalk. Those following did the same.

Reaching the shade, he sat down to rest, prepared to eat. The grain was just beyond the milk stage, in a semihard state. There were seven ears of bearded wheat on each stalk. Separating the grains from the chaff, flicking away the almost papery shells, we ate with relish the still creamy kernels.

At once, a Pharisee standing before Jesus berated him. "Observe this," he said, "your disciples do work which is unlawful on the Sabbath."

Jesus looked up, smiling, and said, "Plucking and undressing grain is forbidden work? Do you remember in the scriptures what David did when he and those with him were hungry?

"To meet their need, he entered into the temple and ate the shewbread. It was thought unlawful for him or for his companions to eat it; it was only for the priests.

"Read further. On the Sabbath day, priests work in the temple to perform the chores of the temple, thus they also profane the Sabbath but are held blameless.

"I say unto you that here, in this place, is one greater than the temple wherein one worships God. Man in truth is God expressing Himself in all who seek to be like Him. If you knew what it means to have mercy rather than sacrifice, you would not condemn me or those with me. We are guiltless. 'The Sabbath was made for man, and not man for the Sabbath. Wherefore the Son of man is also Lord of the Sabbath.'"

The Pharisees held their tongues but increased their watchfulness and continued walking along with us.

We reached Capernaum while it was still day. Jesus sent most of the retinue away. He asked the eight of us to go into the synagogue that he might teach if he was called upon to speak.

The scribes and other Pharisees were already there in the upper seats. Several men known to be Herodians—influential Jews who supported Antipas—were also present.

We sat among the common people. A beggar sat prominently nearby. We all knew him, and Jesus watched him intently. He had been a stonemason at one time, but a severe injury had rendered him unable to work, for his right hand was wounded and became withered and shrunken. He was forced to beg for his living.

One of the Pharisees stood up. Challenging Jesus, he asked, "Is it lawful to heal such a man on a Sabbath day?"

Jesus said, "Who among you, if you have one sheep and it falls into a pit on the Sabbath day, will not take hold of it and lift it out? This poor stonemason is better than a sheep. He is worthy to be healed. Therefore, it is lawful to heal on the Sabbath day, and I shall."

He turned to the injured man, saying, "Stretch forth your hand!"

Now, I, Andrew Bar-jona, had been with Jesus long enough to know somewhat of his thoughts as he spake those words. Jesus had taught us to regard all healing as the result of God's love for man.

So I was not the least surprised when the man stretched forth his hand. It was no longer shrunken, dried, and withered but filled out, soft, and supple, as normal as his other hand.

The Pharisee rent the blasphemy seam of his robe, and we were driven from the synagogue. The man healed came with us.

Several times Jesus had impressed upon us that man, as God's image, is never less than perfect. Never subject to fleshly harm, weakness, and debility. He would say, "Man is as spiritual as God, who is Spirit. He is as perfect as the Mind from which he is made. There is really no other man. Mortal man is not God's image and likeness. My work is to reveal to mortals their true selfhood—the perfect man made by God."

We had argued endlessly among ourselves, "How can man be flesh and yet be spiritual and perfect at the same time?"

Time and again, we put the question to Jesus, "Are there two of us, one of flesh, the other of God? One perfect, the other to be made perfect? One eternal, the other here for few days and much trouble?"

Patiently the Master would explain, "There is, in reality, only one man. There is only one Mind who holds one true concept of man. Man is created by Mind to image God in every way, including an eternal length of life.

"Acquaint yourself with God, and you will thenceforth think of man in terms of perfection.

"That man is seen through spiritual thought. Think spiritually about the one you see, and the one you see will be found whole and healthy. This also is the man you will be.

"It takes much effort to resist what your eyes and ears tell you.

"Healing results from understanding man as spiritual. That which is not of God disappears when spiritual reality appears to one's consciousness."

For the first time I understood somewhat, in a very small way, how Jesus healed. I no longer wondered at the miracles. I saw them as something which, though produced by God, could be learned and proven by man.

A few days later, we were walking through Galilee, wondering about a report that the scribes and Pharisees were still irate because Jesus healed the man with a withered hand on the Sabbath day. It seemed that they were simply filled with hatred, talking among themselves what they might do to stop Jesus. The Pharisees were even meeting in council to discuss how they might destroy our Master.

As Jesus became aware of the anger and plotting, he withdrew from Capernaum. A great multitude followed us into the countryside where Jesus was to heal anyone in need among those who came to hear him preach.

After speaking to the multitude, he was so thronged that he could barely make it through the crowds. Nevertheless, he responded, healing all who had plagues and unclean spirits, especially those who fell down before Jesus, acknowledging, "You are the Son of God."

Jesus always tried to hush them, knowing that it caused the scribes and Pharisees to despise him even more. Eventually we left the area and sailed south of Capernaum, landing beyond Tiberias.

We traveled again through the Galilee, with Jesus telling the people that the kingdom of God is at hand, to be held in the hearts of good people. It brought peace to many households.

We passed through Magdala, where a certain wool merchant always welcomed us to his house for supper and the night's rest. As we travel to and fro, here where the hills slope from the plain of Gennesaret to the sea, we often stop at this peaceful home.

All sorts of food—bread and fruit, vegetables and nuts—are prepared and served to us with such generosity and variety because this family deeply loves the Master and those of us who travel with him.

And why not? On our very first day working in Magdala, the delicate young daughter of the house, Mary by name, was healed of a terrible torment; and thus she and her parents became grateful above all others.

It happened this way: It seems that Mary had been fragile and fearful from birth, and grew to womanhood scarcely able to care for her own needs. She was obsessed that she was unlovely, unworthy, and indeed we learned later that she even lacked the ability to enter into play with children.

As she became a woman, she seemed to lack sympathy, had no tendency to comfort others, not even a wailing child. She deliberately hurt no one but simply avoided everyone.

She was tormented with fear, lacked confidence, and doubted that she was in any way a good person. The demons of such fear and uncertainty haunted her until she felt that death alone could bring peace to her troubled soul.

The first time we were in Magdala, as we walked along the thoroughfare, the quiet afternoon was pierced with a wail of sorrow. Hearing this, Jesus ran down an alley toward the sound of anguish. We followed closely.

Around the corner of a rear building, we beheld in the street a distraught young woman beating her head against a stone gatepost. She tore at the flesh of her arms and legs, determined to injure herself.

Jesus rushed to her. Enduring her flailing arms and kicking feet, he pinned her in his grasp until her agony passed. He held her in his arms when she fainted. He held her with his eyes closed and his chin as though fastened to the top of her head. He continued to hold her gently while his lips moved in silent words, dismissing the evil which often reduced her to a living death.

Blood oozed from her scratched arms and legs, staining the Master's tunic. But he held her until she regained consciousness. Tone returned to her form, and she looked up with tear-filled eyes into the face of our Master. He continued to hold her tenderly.

The panic on her face, the tenseness of her limbs, the wildness of her tresses which in the frenzy had escaped from the shell comb which held her long hair in coils—everything about her calmed before our eyes.

"Master?" she asked rationally.

"Yes, dear child," he responded.

"I feel so loved," she said with her head nestled into Jesus's shoulder, her eyes looking toward all of us.

"God's love enfolds you," Jesus said.

"I *feel* great peace," she replied.

"God's love has banished the demons of your fear, your hopelessness, confusion, uncertainty, doubt, distress, and all of your inner disturbance."

A sweet smile blossomed on her face.

"Seven demons have departed from your mind. Only God's love remains now to guard, guide, and glorify your life," he said.

Mary closed her eyes to stop her tears. Jesus smiled at all of us who were watching.

I shall never forget that moment. I knew that in it I had witnessed the power of God's love to heal, the very love that Jesus wanted us to feel, understand, and express to all, friend and foe alike.

A minute or so later Mary roused from the bliss which had destroyed her long siege of mental pain.

She withdrew from Jesus's sheltering embrace. "Come," she said. "My home is near." We followed her. At the door of the house where she lived, she lifted the latchstring and bade us enter.

Servants scurried out of sight and returned in a moment with Mary's mother and father. One glance told them that their deeply troubled daughter was now sane and peaceful.

What followed was the sharing of our Master's thoughts as he told Mary's parents how he rebuked the evil suggestions which flooded her mind, tormenting her.

Hours later, after supper was served to all of us, we left the house to go into a rear garden and olive grove where we quickly fell into an exceedingly restful sleep, for we had been invited to stay there that night.

Jesus, as usual, prayed rather than slept. Every time I roused to check our welfare, I glanced his way. He rested there in a reverie, with a gentle smile upon his face.

The next morning Mary came freshly bathed, with her long hair plaited and wrapped in a coronet around her head. She wore a modest tunic, with a sleeveless outer layer of sheer white wool cloth.

"The morning meal is being served," she said. "Come. Dine again with my family."

After we refreshed our hands and faces and smoothed our clothes, we sat on the terrace in the garden beneath a grape arbor and broke the night's fast with yogurt and fruit and fresh, warm loaves of flatbread.

Mary's father thanked Jesus for restoring his daughter to her right mind and then said, "All of you now belong to us, and all we possess is yours. Use it as you will."

And so we were once again provided with more good than we would ever need. Mary and her family considered themselves indebted to Jesus yet had no desire, need, or hope for anything except to serve us in any possible way.

We all loved Mary—purely—but none more tenderly and openly than Jesus, our dear elder brother, our Master, our Lord.

We were silently thoughtful as we walked straight back to Capernaum after that morning meal.

Chapter 7

Several days after this, Nathanael came early to Capernaum. He stopped at my father's house, leaving a message that Simon and I were to meet the troop on Mount Hattin. Then he was on his way to call Philip to the meeting. But Philip was in town, and Nathanael came back with him in tow. "Do not delay," he said, "the Master wants his regular followers to meet him on the Horns of Hattin."

Soon we were hurrying along the west shore of Gennesaret, heading southwest toward Magdala, then westward up the slope of the saddle-shaped hill, where twin peaks rose above a depression now long quiet but where there was once a smoking mountain. The lake shimmered below us as the morning sun slowly traced its path across the waters and up the slope.

Jesus greeted us warmly. "I have spent the night in prayer. Soon I will choose from among my followers—who are many—twelve who will be called apostles. You shall be given the power to heal and will continue to learn spiritual truths from me, and in time you too will heal by teaching and teach by healing.

"Let's go down to the shore now for a while and see who has come to be healed."

One man, much given to wine, was sobered in an instant as he stumbled into the arms of Jesus. His drunkenness simply disappeared. The multitude murmured approval when they saw him stand tall, clear-eyed, and humbled.

A child whose back was twisted grew straight before our eyes.

An old woman, weeping, led her blind husband till she reached the Master's side. A moment later her husband saw clearly to wipe away her tears. Then *he* led *her* home, seeing and walking freely along the shore of the luminous lake. His wife looked back many times, her arms upraised in gratitude to God.

When the sun was almost at our backs, Jesus gathered us again into the higher arms of the hill. We were scattered at his feet upon a grassy slope, and he sat on a large rock. The late morning sun reflected off his face. It seemed to me the very light was enhanced as he spoke words which burned into our hearts as he now gave us a special sermon here on the mount.

A small remnant of the multitude gathered also on the hillside—respectfully distant but close enough to hear. Jesus smiled at them then began to speak, first holding his hands in benediction upon all gathered there.

"Yours is the kingdom of heaven, you who are proving receptive in heart and eager to understand better the things of God. You are happy, for being poor in spirit, you receive the divine consciousness or kingdom of heaven as your own.

"You who grieve and weep also are blessed, for you shall be comforted when you understand that there is never a loss of life, of continued existence, or of God's ceaseless love.

"Happy are you who are gentle, humble, and submissive to the divine will, for you shall possess the good things of this earth.

"Blessed are all of you who hunger and thirst after holiness; your hearts and lives conform to my Father's law and prove true to His will; you are now filled with righteousness.

"And you who have compassion, forgiving when pity is needed, and are not cruel toward those who offend you, happily you will enjoy forgiveness should ever you give offense.

"All who are pure in heart, morally undefiled, innocent, and chaste will be happy and see in their hearts the perfect Holy One who is our God.

"You who make tranquil those brethren disturbed and quarrelsome, or who free from tumult some who would be violent, and reconcile others who are at variance, you shall be called a child of God and dwell happily at peace with all others.

"When unjustly harassed, injured, or despised because of your holiness, be happy, for yours is the consciousness of the harmony which is heaven.

"Even if men speak contemptuously of you; and provoke you; and cause pain and anguish, vexation and misery—yes, if they proclaim all kinds of wickedness about you falsely *but on my account*, be happy! Even more, rejoice greatly and be glad! In heaven you will be recompensed for the good you have given in return for evil. Those before you who were inspired and instructed by my Father and foretold things which did come to pass were also shamefully treated, but today are accounted honorable. Therein you too are to be made happy."

The lake below us was riffled with whitecaps, but where we sat listening, it was as if no one even breathed—it was so still. Even the songbirds were silent. No shadow of the wind moved across the green hills, no flower bent before a breeze. It seemed as if the words we just heard had fallen from above and entered each mind to encourage there the spiritual understanding being taught by Jesus. No one stirred—we were all deep in thought. *Is this peace holiness?* I wondered.

Jesus continued,

> "You are becoming like salt of the earth. But if salt loses its strength, how shall it be used for savor? It is no good. It is cast out, and men walk on it, not even knowing that it is salt.

> "You are the light of the world. A city set on a hill cannot remain unseen. Men do not light a candle then put a measuring basket over it, but place it on a candlestand to give light to everyone present.

> "Let your light shine and be seen of men. They will notice the good you do and glorify God *your* Heavenly Father.

> "Now, I am not come to destroy the law of Moses or the works of the prophets. I shall fulfill, not destroy. As long as heaven and earth abide, not the smallest jot or iota, not one dot or line of the alphabet shall pass from the words of this law until it is completely fulfilled.

> "So whoever breaks even the least commandment in the law and teaches others that this is permitted will be considered the least in the dominion of heaven. But if one teaches the importance of observing and himself observes the commands of the law, he shall be called eminent in the kingdom of heaven.

> "But I must tell you this, your holiness must be more in evidence than the holiness of scribes and Pharisees or you won't go into the kingdom of God's harmony, peace, and power.

> "Long ago our elders were taught, "You shall not kill; whoever kills shall be in peril of punishment." But hear what I say: Whoever is angry with his brother without cause shall be punished. Whoever says

to his fellow man 'you are a good for nothing and vain fellow' shall be in danger of being brought before the governing council. But if you call him "fool" you shall be in danger of eternal punishment. For you do not behold man as God sees man in His own likeness.

"If you bring your tribute to the altar and there remember that your brother has something against you, leave your gift; go and be reconciled, then return and offer your tribute.

"If you are opposed by someone, agree with him peaceably; settle the dispute and don't indulge in further contention. Otherwise, your adversary may force you to court, and the judge may decide against you and order his officer to take you to prison. Then you will have to pay dearly for all the trouble caused in disagreement.

"You have heard it said from Moses' time, "You shall not commit adultery." But I tell you this: whoever looks upon a woman with carnal desire has already committed adultery with her in his heart.

"If your right eye tempts you toward sin, tear it out and throw it far from you. It is better to lose your eye than to be thrown into hell. If your right hand tempts you, sever it from your arm and throw it away—this is better than having your whole body cast into perdition.

"Likewise, it has been said, "Whosoever shall put away his wife, let him give her a paper of divorce." But I say, divorce for fornication only; otherwise, she and anyone who marries the woman who is divorced, commits adultery.

"Again, you have heard from the elders, "You shall not swear falsely but only in oath to the Lord as duty requires." But I say, don't swear at all, neither by heaven, God's throne, nor by the earth, His footstool. Nor by Jerusalem, the city of our King. Above all, don't swear by your head because you can't make a single hair white or black.

"When you converse, your yes must mean yes, and your no, simply no. Anything more comes from the devil.

"You have heard, take an eye for an eye, and a tooth for a tooth. But I say, don't resist the evil doer. If he strikes your right jaw, then turn to him your left.

"If one sues you for your tunic, give him your outer garment too.

"If someone compels you to go a mile, be willing to go even two.

"Give to those who ask of you, and if one would borrow, turn him not away empty-handed.

"Love your enemies. Bless those who curse you. Do good to those who hate you. Pray for those who despitefully use and persecute you. This makes you your Heavenly Father's child indeed. Does not God's sun shine on those who do evil? Does not His rain fall on the just *and* the unjust?

"Loving only those who love you brings no benefit. The tax officers do the same. If you greet no other than your friends, what goodness do you do? The heathen do even that much.

"Be perfect in every way, for your Heavenly Father is perfect."

There was a murmur in the crowd. A man in the midst called out, "We are all sinners after Adam. How can we be perfect?"

Jesus answered him, "I repeat, be perfect! None can keep you from your godliness. Jared, a man born five generations after Adam, had a son named Enoch, who walked righteously with God. God took him that he might not taste death.

"The perfect man of God walks with God in all his ways. Be the perfect man. Be not like one who transgresses and disobeys. Be perfect before God. Keep His commandments; Do only that which is good."

A few minutes later the murmurs of approval ceased, and Jesus continued,

"Do not amass treasures on earth. Moth and rust corrupt such things in time, or thieves break in and steal them. Lay up treasures in heaven that don't corrupt and where thieves can gain no access. Heavenly treasures will lift high your heart. Earthly treasure will bind you to earth.

"The light of your body is your thought about what you see. If what you see is good, your body will be radiant with light. If your seeing is evil, your body is opaque, for darkness is in you, a great darkness where great light should be.

"Not one of you can serve two masters. You will either hate one and love the other, or hold to the one and despise the other. You can't serve God and riches.

"Why? I say to you: Take no thought for your life your need of nourishment or refreshment, or for your body what you need in garments. Your life is more than meat, your body more than fashion.

"Observe the fowls flying. Birds do not sow or reap or store what they need. Yet God sustains them. Are you not equally as worthy of care as they?   .

"Tell me, which of you can grow taller by taking thought? Why be concerned about how you look? Consider the flowers in the fields. Solomon with all his wealth was not more beautifully arrayed than these. Yet they bloom for a day or two then they are cut to fuel the ovens. God will much more clothe you in garments of His glory.

"Therefore, don't worry about such things and wonder aloud, what will we eat and drink? Where will we obtain our clothing? People unsure of God keep looking for all these things.

"I tell you, your Father in heaven knows what you need. Seek to be governed by God, for He will increase your possession of what is needed. And take no thought for the day ahead. Tomorrow will supply that which is needed for that day. Sufficient each day is the uncertainty thereof; surely God will provide.

"Another thing. Don't be judgmental. As you judge others, you in turn will be judged. As you measure another's worth, so will you be assessed, and you both shall receive accordingly.

"And why behold the flaw in your brother's opinion but then not consider the inadequacy in the way you may regard things? Dare you say, "Let me change your viewpoint," when a darker outlook is in your own thought? See things in righteousness, then you will know how to better guide your brother's vision.

"Don't share the treasures of your thought with those who will dispute with you over them like dogs quarrel over a bone. Don't cast the pearls of your mind before those who disdain your ideas and trample them with their lack of understanding, stealing your *good* thoughts, belittling you.

"Ask for wisdom and guidance, because all who ask, receive. The one who seeks, finds. To one who welcomes openly a sincere heart, the door is opened for both him and you.

"What man hungering for bread will be given a stone? Or if he asks for fish, will he be given a reptile?

"If you, being limited, know how to give good gifts to your children, how much more will your Heavenly Father give good things to all who ask Him?

"Mark these words for they are important: All things whatsoever you want men to do unto you, do you to them likewise. This is the law of all prophets.

"Two paths lie before you in this life. And two gates, one narrow, the other wide; the wide opens to a broad path leading to destruction. Many choose to go that way. The straight gate opens upon a narrow path; yet it is the narrow way, guarded with good thoughts, that leads to eternal life. Few find it. The narrow gate is chosen only by wise men.

"Beware! Some pretend prophets come in sheep's clothing but inwardly they tend to destroy the good in the lives of others. The way to discern the false prophets is to check their fulfillment. Men can't gather grapes from thorn wood nor figs from thistle plants. Good trees bring to harvest good fruit. Corrupt trees bring forth miserable fruit, and are hewn down and burned. Therefore, judge prophets as you judge trees by their fruit.

"Not everyone who says to me "Lord! Lord!" gains entrance into the kingdom of heaven, but only those who do the will of my Father, who is in heaven.

"When hoping to enter the kingdom many will say, "Lord! Lord! We prophesied in your name. In your name we cast out devils. In your name we've done many wonders." But I will have to deny them, saying, "I never knew you. Go away. You work iniquity, not righteousness."

"But whoever hears the things I have spoken to you this day and continually puts them into practice, he will be like the wise man who built his house upon a rock. When the rain came in floods and the wind blew and beat upon the house, it stood the storm, not falling when flooded, because it was built upon a rock.

"If you have heard me but do not heed and you obey not things I've said, you shall be like the foolish man who built upon the sand. His

house fell when the floods and wind came—and it was a great loss
for that man to endure."

"I have told you these things," Jesus said. "Be faithful and do according
to all I have taught."

The people were astonished at his strict doctrine, and the authority with
which he taught was so unlike the teaching of the scribes.

Not a word was spoken as we walked back to town with Jesus. What could
we possibly question or have added?

We entered Capernaum, but before we reached Chuza's grove, an officer
in the Roman army accosted Jesus, entreating him, saying, "Lord, my servant
is at home, sick and paralyzed, unable to function." Jesus felt the urgency in
his voice.

"I will come at once and heal him," he said.

To our surprise, the centurion answered, "Lord, I am not deserving that you
should enter my home. Speak the word only, and my servant will be healed.

"Like you I am under authority, having a hundred soldiers under me. I say
to this man 'Go,' and he at once leaves to do my bidding; to another 'Come,'
and he directly comes to my side. When I tell my servant to do something, he
does it without hesitation."

Jesus, turning to face those following him, said, "I've never found such
faith—no, not even in Israel. Truly I tell you, many shall come from elsewhere,
from east and west, and shall sit in company with Abraham, Isaac, and Jacob
in the kingdom of heaven.

"The children of Israel are likely to be cast into outer darkness, and what
will be heard of them is weeping and gnashing of their teeth—in anger, rage,
and pain—for they neglect their salvation when it is just at hand."

Jesus gave a slight salute to the centurion, a worthy man who loves the
Jewish people and even built the synagogue in our town. "Go your way. As you
have believed, it shall be done unto you," Jesus told him.

The centurion departed. Upon arriving at his home his servant indeed was
healed, for he greeted him by opening the door even before the outside latch
was lifted.

The next day Jesus suggested, "Let us go down to Nain."

Why Nain? We couldn't speculate, except that there are small towns along
the way. We had not journeyed this far south before. So we followed to be witness
and to learn from our Master as he preached and performed miracles here and
there in central Galilee.

Nain ranges up a small mount, and is quite lovely to see. When we
approached the city gate, we saw tombs hewn in the hillsides along the road.

As we walked along, a dolorous sound greeted us. A multitude of townspeople came slowly down the road—a long procession of mourners following the funeral bier of a young man. There was a great lamentation—women crying and men playing funeral trumpets and cymbals, and piping reeds.

We asked why and were told that a widow's only son had died that morning. She was bereft and desolate. The whole village had come out to help bear her sorrow as she buried her son.

Jesus stopped.

I crowded close to hear what he might say and see what he might do. He bent over the mother. She could hardly stand, even with two friends walking beside her, their arms holding her steady.

"Don't weep," Jesus said gently to the woman.

Then he walked a few steps to the bier. He touched it, and the bearers stood still. "Young man, I say to you, arise!" Jesus's command startled even us.

Immediately the young man sat up. "What did you say?" he asked. "Where am I? What happened?"

The bearers lowered the bier. He swung his legs to one side. Jesus put forth his hands; the young man grasped them and stood upright.

Jesus led him to his mother, saying to him, "Nothing has happened to you. You are all right. Nothing can happen to you. There's no place to go but to your home, with your mother."

His mother gasped as her son reached out to her, and she took him in her arms.

The mournful music ceased, and the pipers and trumpeters began to play a lightsome tune. The women danced to the sound of their cymbals, and menfolk gave voice to their joy as they welcomed the young man back to life in their midst.

We began to chant in song, "God is glorified! God is man's life! Glorify God and live in His name!"

Villagers responded with chants of their own.

One said, "God has visited His people! We glory in His name!" Another, "A great prophet has risen up! In His presence we are made to know God anew!" And another responded, "God has visited His people! And His people we are!"

The bier was folded. The procession turned around and went back through the city gate, escorting the mother and son homeward. The air was filled with sounds of joy, and words of comfort and wonder and gratitude.

Jesus declined an invitation to join the throng. "Forgive me," he said graciously. "I have work to do. My Father who led me here now calls me elsewhere."

With that he waved, beckoning us to him. He turned and led us back the way we came.

Later we sat beneath a wild date palm for rest. It was then that Jesus told us that it was just over the hill, in the village known long ago as Shunem, that Elisha restored to life the only son of a Shunammite woman. And across the Valley of Jezreel, northward, was the ancient village of Sarepta, where Elijah brought back to life the son of a widow woman.

"In time I will tell you more," Jesus said. "But for now, think of this. There is no death. Bodily death, like birth, is an illusion."

The next day back in Capernaum, I saw two strangers on the quay. They recognized me, and waved. Then I recalled that they were disciples of the Baptist. We had worked together with John when I first came to Bethabara to watch and wait for signs of the Messiah's coming.

I introduced them to Jesus. "We have brought you a message from John," they said. "All of Palestine has heard of you. John sent us to ask, 'Are you the Promised One, or should we be looking for another?'"

"John has no need of my answer," Jesus replied, "but you do. He knew from his youth what we were to do in this world."

The two men looked down at their feet. They wanted Jesus to use his power, if indeed he had any, to free the Baptist.

"Abide with us today, and you shall answer the question for yourselves," Jesus said.

Already people were gathering to be healed. Some with horrible skin eruptions. Others so lame they could barely hobble. A few were drawn up in crude handcarts. Some were being led by others because they were without sight. A few acted strangely. One man babbled ceaselessly, and another could not still his shaking arms. As always, scribes and Pharisees were among the crowd, watching as Jesus healed each one.

"Gather around me now," Jesus said to the throng. "You people who come to me . . . what did you follow me into the wilderness to see, you who were baptized by John? John was not a showman, a reed shaking in the wind! Nor a man clothed in soft garments! He was more than a performer. He was a prophet. Yes! A prophet. And even more; he was preparer of the way for the One promised of God.

"Among those brought forth from woman, no one is greater than John. But the least in the kingdom of God is greater even than the Baptist. Common people and tax collectors justify God because they were baptized by John. But some of you Pharisees and you doctors of the law who are present, you do not take counsel of God for you are not yet baptized.

"This generation is like children in the marketplace who call to each other, saying, 'We play the pipes, but you do not dance. Just so, now we mourn for you, but you have not wept. The Baptist came, neither eating bread nor drinking wine, and you said he had a devil. The Son of man comes; he eats and drinks, and you call him gluttonous and a wine bibber, friendly to publicans and sinners. Such is your faulty wisdom.'

"Thus Wisdom shows wisdom only to her wise children."

Not one of the Pharisees spoke a word, and none of the lawyers present challenged his testimony. Jesus simply continued his work. His fame grew. But there were many who doubted.

If John, the one prophesied to prepare his way, was in bonds in prison, then could not Jesus of Nazareth use his power to rescue his benefactor? That was the question which rumbled in the minds of all people zealous for relief from the tyranny of Rome.

Early on a bright morning soon after, sorrow surfaced. Jesus seemed disappointed. While many witnessed his healings and heard his parables, few men seemed to repent, or show interest in learning more that they also might free the sin-laden and those with infirm bodies. Jesus knew just what to do.

Of a sudden, with no provocation, he raised his voice and began to warn the populace. "Chorazin! Bethsaida! You have seen mighty works of God in your streets, yet you do not repent. The cities of Tyre in Phoenicia and Sidon too will fare better than you in the time of judgment. And Capernaum! You have heaven in your present state but will be brought down to hell because few people herein truly repent.

"Had these healing works been done in Sodom, the citizens there would have repented, and that city would remain until today. In the judgment, Sodom will find itself more tolerable than you." Then his voice softened.

"O Father, Lord of heaven and earth, I thank you. Why? Because you hide these things from the earthly and prudent people, and show them only to babes. In your sight, this is good. Babes are receptive.

"You, Father, have delivered the truth of all things to me. No man knows the Son but God who is his Father. Nor knows anyone the Father but the Son and those to whom the Son reveals Him."

His prayer finished, he implored the people, "Come then!

"Come unto me you who labor and carry heavy burdens. Come! I will give you rest. Herein my yoke is easy; I am one with God. Learn this for yourself, from me: God is All. I am the humble servant of this perfect One. In self-worth, I am lowly. So shall you also find strength, yet rest your soul in the goodness of God!

"My yoke is easy. My burden weighs little. God *is All* there is, *in all* that is. Choose not the reluctance of those cities, Chorazin, Bethsaida, and Capernaum. Choose instead to be curious to know more of our God."

The crowd grew larger while Jesus spoke. Many were brought by family and friends who waited anxiously for Jesus to set free their afflicted members.

Jesus moved to the helpless among the people, saying a few words to each person, quieting the strange ones to normalcy, touching eyes to sight, ears to sound, and those plagued to purity.

When all were healed, Jesus answered John's disciples who were still with us. "Go your way now. Tell John all you have seen and all you have heard."

A former leper came forward and showed the men his arms and hands. The flesh was normal and alive.

A lame man danced for them.

One whose sight was restored wrote in the sand, "God is good."

Another man pushed forward. "Two days ago we saw a dead lad get off the bier and walk home with his widowed mother. *He* granted the miracle," the man said, pointing to Jesus.

"Yes," Jesus said, "the work of God is shown to you through me. Tell John, 'God's anointed is here.' With him, I need no witness. John knows! But reassure him that to the poor and the receptive, the Gospel is preached."

The men saluted the Master and left to return to Machaerus to be near John, who was held in the prison there.

The next evening we wandered down to the quay at Capernaum, about four hours before the fishermen were to leave for their night's work. As usual, the area was filled with many people, for day had given in to dusk; and after the evening meal, the final hours were usually given to visiting. The streets were thronged; some people returning home were looking forward to a time of idleness.

So it was that we met Simon the Pharisee. As always, dressed in his tasseled mantle, he was strolling the waterfront when we arrived. He hustled over to us, hailing Jesus, asking him to honor him at his late evening meal.

Now we knew that Simon was wealthy and worldly. He was intelligent enough. He knew the law of Moses and loved to expound it publicly. He enjoyed a certain position in town, and to be invited into his home conferred a quasi-social status on one.

Before, Jesus had always denied Simon's offer; but this evening to our surprise, he said, "Yes, I will come."

We followed our Master to the door and watched as the Pharisee and Jesus entered without removing their sandals. We knew we were to wait outside, though one's home is not necessarily a private place. But perhaps special festivities were to be celebrated.

We were all tired, dusty, and eager to just rest; so we waited without and only later learned what took place within that evening.

Once supper was underway, we could hear the murmur of voices.

A woman of sure reputation for harlotry, Sherah by name, suddenly passed through our midst and entered Simon's house without seeking admittance. Without leave of any, Matthew's brother, James the Less, rose to his feet from amongst us and followed her in.

It was he who told us this amazing story.

The woman went straight into the room where Simon and his guests reclined on couches around the low table.

Jesus and his host occupied the center couch, with other guests on couches set perpendicular to the table of the host and honored guest. The feast was sumptuous, and all the diners were hungry.

When the profligate woman entered, they were shocked—for she was well known, and her body had been used illicitly by many uncontrolled men in town.

She went behind Simon and his guest. Having in her hands a costly small translucent white box made of alabaster, Sherah opened the box and laid it on the floor.

She then knelt at the feet of Jesus and began to weep—silently at first, then sobbing, trembling as her tears fell upon Jesus's feet, toes, and ankles.

It was pitiful to see one so abject, so heartbroken. Her tears fell steadily; and as she knelt, her hands moved, washing the dust from his feet with her tears. She bent, and with her fragrantly fresh unbound and flowing hair, she wiped her tears from his flesh and gently kissed his feet. She dipped her fingers into the box of ointment and brought forth the fragrant unguent and generously anointed each foot, gently, lovingly, and sacredly. As she performed this tribute, her tears ceased. She completed her task and sat humbly with bowed head at Jesus's feet.

Jesus dropped the morsel of bread dipped in oil which he was about to consume. He had turned toward her as the first tears fell upon a foot. He remained still as the woman, in her sorrow, showed remorse and reverenced the one person she knew could redeem her worn and weary sin-filled heart.

Simon the Pharisee, reclining beside Jesus, watched the event startled and embarrassed.

This man, he declared contemptuously within himself, *if indeed he were a prophet, he would have despised this woman, knowing that she is loose and lewd; he would have recoiled from her touch, for she is a sinner.*

Jesus knew what he was thinking. He knew he must respond. Answering, he said, "Simon, I'd like to tell you something."

"Go ahead," the Pharisee answered derisively.

"There was a man who extended credit to those in need. Two men whom he had blessed owed him payment—one in the amount of five hundred pence, the other owed fifty. When both had nothing with which to pay their debt, he willingly forgave them. Now, tell me, which of the two will love him most?"

Simon answered quickly, "I suppose the one who was forgiven the larger debt."

"Yes," Jesus answered. "You have rightly judged."

Then Jesus turned from his host to the woman at his feet, "Simon, look at this woman. You invited me into your house yet withheld the courtesy of water to wash my feet. But now they have been refreshed. She washed them with her tears and wiped them with the hairs of her head.

"You gave me no kiss of welcome. But she covered *my feet* with kisses.

"You did not anoint my head, but she, with costly ointment, has anointed my feet. Yes, she is known among us as a wanton woman. Her sins are numerous. But now they are forgiven, for she loves much, ministering from her heart. One who needs little forgiveness loves sparingly."

To the woman he said, "Your sins are forgiven."

At that, the other guests began to wonder silently, *Who is this man who not only heals, but also forgives sins?*

Jesus continued, "Your faith has saved you from the path of sin, Sherah. Go in peace."

The woman again kissed his feet then departed quietly. We watched as she left the house of Simon the Pharisee.

Later we learned that she returned to live at her father's house and undertook the care and righteous upbringing of her sister's four children, who were orphaned when their parents drowned in a tragedy on the lake.

Jesus never spoke about the incident. He knew that James had been a witness and would tell us all what happened that evening in the house of Simon the Pharisee.

Chapter 8

Now things changed even more. When the scribes and Pharisees again took counsel against Jesus, it was evident that an official signal had been given, calling into question everything he said and did.

Jesus did not wish to bring disquiet to any place, much less to the seaside village from which six of his closest disciples came. So he withdrew into the countryside, and we went with him.

But people in the region were never content until they found him, presenting their sick and lame to him to be healed. When all were healed, Jesus pleaded that no one tell where he was or what good things he was doing.

Still the people came for help. Among them, a man whose name was Mushi was brought. He was grievously distraught. People said he was possessed with a devil, but he was really utterly broken in spirit, filled with rage and a strange brute strength.

No one could make him quiet or comfort him because he was blind and dumb—helpless to move about freely, unable to converse. He thrashed around, breaking things, harming himself, and crying out with a pathetic piercing scream. He was avoided and abandoned, for no one knew how to help him. Except Jesus.

That day everyone stood watching the tortured man fumbling around. We ranged about him, but no one offered to help. Many just gawked at him. Some men clucked tongues in pretended pity. Others would erupt into mocking laughter, as if the man was performing in an arena just for their amusement.

I watched Jesus, not the man. All of us who formed the core of his followers looked to the Master. What would he do?

Jesus stood there, heedless of the noise and unmindful even of the man whose need was obviously so great. I had seen Jesus in this state of inner stillness before. I knew his thoughts went out in prayer to God whose divine power, ever present, ever tender and loving, always healed when rightly appealed to.

Suddenly Mushi quietly sat down in the dust.

He folded his hands in his lap then raised them up to comb his fingers through his hair, trying to untangle it. He smoothed his beard and lastly, ran his hands over his garment, trying to press it into neatness of some unseen sort. Looking skyward, he inclined his head as though listening to something.

Suddenly, a smile exploded upon his face. His eyes opened wide in rapturous awe. The crowd grew silent, intent, not knowing what to expect next. In normal tone and gentle voice, he began to speak.

"Am I seeing?" he asked.

He touched his tongue. "Is this the way to talk? I have heard talk. Now I too can make words." We all marveled that somehow the man had words and knowledge to speak of things he'd never known before.

Jesus walked over to the man he'd healed. He lifted him up and, putting his arm around the man's thin shoulders, led him out of the circle of stunned witnesses.

The Pharisees scoffed and said, "This fellow doth not cast out devils but by Beelzebub, the prince of the devils." We heard these words as Jesus walked away.

We followed the two of them back into Capernaum and into Chuza's grove. Later we took Mushi down to the lake and gave him wherewith he might cleanse himself. Then he dressed in clothes borrowed from Jesus, for we had thrown his old garments into a fire.

As the sun went down across the uplands to the west, we walked away from Capernaum to a place in the wooded hills. Here Jesus gave the man a new name—"Neriah"—after one of his own ancestors; and we were asked to call him "Neri." Thereafter, Neri followed us wherever we walked with Jesus. He became a servant to us, for he had chosen this way to say thank you to our Master.

We slept in the hills that night under stars that even Neri could see clearly.

Jesus went into town early the next morning to confront the Pharisees. He knew they would be idly watching the buying and selling in the marketplace. Jesus found them there and knowing what they were thinking, he said pointedly,

> Every kingdom divided against itself is brought to emptiness; every city and house divided does not remain upright. If Satan casts out Satan, he is divided against himself. His kingdom will not stand.

> If I, by Beelzebub, cast out devils, by whom do your children cast them out? Your children will be your judges. But if you understand that it is by the power of God that I cast out the evils of blindness and dumbness, then the kingdom of God is come, even to you.

Not one of the Pharisees said a word.

Jesus remained there a long time, and eventually we joined him.

People came out of their houses into the marketplace, and Jesus began to preach. Soon a great crowd stood around him.

Someone saw Jesus's mother and brothers standing at the very edge of the throng. We told Jesus that his kin were here, wishing to speak to him.

To our surprise Jesus stretched his hand toward us, his disciples standing there at one side listening as he talked. Indicating us, he said, "Behold my mother and my brother! For whoever does the will of my Heavenly Father is in truth my brother and sister and mother."

Then he said sweetly, "But those who loved me when I was a child, I also love them dearly, and I will go to be with them."

We learned later that Jesus took his loved ones to his abode in Chuza's grove, and Joanna sent her baker to them with a wonderful midday meal of warm loaves of flat wheat bread, along with pickled fish, sheep's milk cheese, and fresh sliced figs sprinkled with pine nuts and honeyed yogurt.

Shortly after noon his mother and brethren left, going to the house of Zebedee, where his mother's sister, Salome, awaited her. Jesus accompanied them.

Later we found him deep in thought sitting by the seaside.

The day was still young. Jesus said he felt he could no longer teach in the synagogue in Capernaum. He knew the authorities there sought to trap him in his words and deeds.

When he saw a crowd gathering, he called James, asking him to bring one of Zebedee's boats and to anchor it just offshore. When this was done, he went into the ship and sat, while the multitude stood on shore.

Then he began to speak to the people in parables—his earthy way of relating the truths of heaven.

He opened his discourse, saying,

> A sower went out to sow his seed. The rains had come, and the soil was ready. The seed was clean, according to the law of Moses; and the sack from which the seed was to be cast by the sower's right hand also was free from uncleanness.

> As he sowed, some seeds fell by the wayside, and birds came and ate them.

> Some seed fell upon stony ground where there was little soil. It quickly sprung up, without putting down deep roots. Without roots, when the sun scorched the earth, the tender plants withered away.

> Some seed fell among thorns, which overgrew the ground and soon choked out all the tender new plants.

Other seed fell from the sower's hand onto good ground and brought
forth a good harvest. Some a hundredfold, some sixty, some thirty."

Jesus concluded,

Whoever has hearing ears, he will hear and understand.

We were sitting in the boat with him while Jesus talked, but now we gathered
close to him to ask why he spoke in parables.

He answered quietly, "Because if I speak of the things with which they are
familiar, they quickly learn more. You students have been told the mysteries of
the kingdom of heaven—that it is a realm of thought, that God is not simply a
person but in very truth the Mind of the universe.

"This understanding has not been given to the multitudes. You have been
told plain truth. They have not. I can give *you* much more than they can receive.
Whoever has spiritual insight can be given an abundance of truth. But these
people are not ready for so much. If I were to give as I have given to you, it
would take from them even the little spiritual understanding they have, for
without foundation, they would have confusion. So I talk in parables. They see
with eyes, but not through understanding. They hear words, but not the truth,
for they have no perception.

"Esaias, the son of Amoz, had a vision of God. Did he tell it in words which
men could understand? He spoke of seeing God upon a throne; he meant that
he understood God to have great dominion over all creation.

"And the throne was high and lifted up, giving the idea that the dominion
of God was above and far beyond the reach of those who know as real only that
which their eyes see. They were seeing injustice, sin, unrighteousness, and the
wickedness of men, instead of seeing man as the likeness of God.

"An angel touched Esaias's lips with a coal of fire, to remove from him his
iniquity and purge his sin. Then he was told to tell the people who had the
covenant with God, 'You hear indeed, but you do not perceive; and you see,
but don't understand.'

"Even to this day, some people's hearts have grown coarse and shameful,
and their ears are stupid and slow to understand. Their eyes they have closed,
lest they should see and take thought for their ways. They hear, but have only
a weak desire to learn of God and comprehend what is the truth. If they were to
see with their mind, and hear through mind, and forsake their *wrong* thinking
thereby changing, I could turn their thoughts to God and heal them.

"Now understand my parable of the sower:

I speak to the people, sowing truth about the kingdom of God. One
who hears and doesn't understand is subject to the wicked one, who

takes away what I have sown in his heart. This is the seed sown by the wayside.

Seed falling in stony places is like one who hears my words with gladness but has not that spirit within which endures, so when trouble and distress arise and when unjustly afflicted and persecuted, he becomes displeased or angry and then gives up. Having no depth for growth, such as he has no willingness to seek and serve God.

Those who receive seed among thorns are those who hear my voice, but then cares of this world and the empty pursuit of riches and fame choke the word which should be put into practice. Men such as these become fruitless.

But O, he who receives seed into good ground is one who truly sees and hears and understands and carefully brings all thought to a good harvest, honoring God. This brings forth fruit worthy of sustained effort—some a hundredfold, some sixty, some thirty times more than expected.

"The people know not what I teach, unless I speak in words they can relate to themselves. Therefore I speak in parables today, to all who have gathered to listen."

And so Jesus continued speaking to the people. "Here are a few more lessons about the kingdom of God," he said.

A man sowed good seed in his field. While he slept, an enemy came and sowed darnel among the wheat then left the field. When the wheat grew, the tares also grew. Then the man's servants said, "Didn't you sow good seed in your field? If so, where do the tares come from?"

"An enemy has done this to me," the owner of the field will say. Then the servants will offer to pull up the tares; but the wise owner will say, "No, when removing the tares you are likely to uproot the wheat at the same time.

"Let both grow together until harvest; and at that time I will say to the reapers, 'Now gather the tares first; their grains will be easily seen for they are smaller than the wheat. Bind the tares in bundles to burn, but gather the wheat into my barn."

Those present murmured approval among themselves for they knew this was a wise story, but none asked how it related to the kingdom of heaven.

Jesus continued,

> Now let me tell you about the kingdom of heaven being like a grain
> of mustard seed which a man took and sowed in his field. Is not
> the mustard seed almost the smallest of all seeds? Only that of the
> cypress is smaller. Yet it grows so high one can mount a horse and
> ride unseen through a field of mustard; and its stem and branches
> grow strong and woody, so sparrows, finches, even crows, and other
> birds can lodge there to eat the seeds.

"Yes, that is so," the people said, thinking only of the seed and not of the kingdom of heaven.

"Listen now," Jesus said, "this is an important parable, for it tells a secret, like all prophecies. Something which has been hidden from men since the foundation of the world, in the first days of creation. A true prophet knows this will indeed one day come to pass.

"I tell you,

> The kingdom of heaven is like leaven which a woman takes and hides
> in three measures of meal until all is leavened.

No one asked what this meant, how the kingdom of heaven was like a woman hiding leaven. So Jesus sent the multitude away.

"Let us go to our homes now," he said to us, departing from the ship and going to his house in the olive grove. A short time later, we followed him. He came out to where we were sitting in the shade of an olive tree.

We asked him, "Explain to us the parable of the tares."

Jesus was pleased, saying,

> I am the Son of man, who sows good seed. The field is the whole world.
> You are the good seed, children of this world seeking and finding the
> kingdom of God. The tares are the planting of the wicked one, faulty
> thinking from which comes all that opposes God. Sowing of tares is
> believing that evil is real and feared by men.

> The harvest is the end of the world. Angels, the thoughts of God, are
> the reapers counteracting all evil and ignorance. Thus, the illicit tares
> will be gathered and burned in fire. So also shall it be with sin and
> all that harms men at the end of this world.

> But fear not, for I, the Son of man which is in heaven, will then send
> forth my angel. Holy thoughts will cast out that which is not of God.

All thinking that transgresses divine law and does so wickedly will lead to affliction for which there shall be much wailing and anguish until all such wickedness and evil is forsaken. Then men will delight in the things of God, for that which is evil and hateful shall be destroyed forever. Righteousness shall shine as brightly as the sun in the kingdom of our Father.

Who has ears, let him hear in heart and mind what I am teaching.

Again, the kingdom of heaven is like treasure hidden in a field, which when a man finds, he hides. Then he goes forth with much joy to sell everything he owns in order to buy the field, and claim the treasure as his own.

You are like a merchant man seeking good pearls. He finds one of great price. He sells all he possesses to have enough to buy it.

You have left all to learn from me. You who have left all to learn of me have earned the right to know the kingdom of God.

Lastly, the kingdom of heaven is like a net cast into the sea, gathering every kind of creature. Then it is drawn to shore. The fishermen who have drawn it sit down and gather the good of the catch into baskets but throw away what is not good.

Observe this, that which is not good is not kept, nor is it returned to the sea. So it is with thinking. Let go of all that is not worthy to have come from the Mind and mouth of God.

Do not hold onto anything evil in your thought. Cast it out. Waste no thought by remembering evil, sin, unrighteousness, or hate.

"This is how it will be at the end of present existence. God's angel thoughts will enable man to discern and destroy all that is unjust and evil and wicked. All thoughts will be purified in the cleansing effected by truth. Though there be much lament and moaning, anger and anguish, before evil yields to and disappears in the allness of God, only good shall endure."

Jesus paused, asking, "Have you understood these things?"

We answered, "Yes, Lord."

"Good," said Jesus. "Henceforth, you are scribes, writing the new law I give. You are instructed into the kingdom of heaven. You are now householders. In your lives, like the householder, you must bring forth out of your treasure, things new and old."

Then Philip asked, "Tell us more! Explain about the leaven."

Jesus said, "I shall, soon. But now I go again to Nazareth where I grew up. Hopefully, I will be asked to teach again in the synagogue. While I am away, each of you go to your homes and enjoy your people. Go fishing, if you like.

"But you, Matthew and Judas Iscariot, come with me. And Nathaneal, you and Simon Zelotes, walk to your homes in Cana, along with us." The five of them started traveling south and westward. Judas and Zelotes had recently been chosen disciples from among many who always walked with Jesus.

Philip, Peter, James, John, and I trooped eastward, stopping at Capernaum where James and John and Peter quit us. Then Philip walked on toward Bethsaida, and I walked halfway with him, returning later to rest in the house of my father, Jona.

I cannot forget the day when Jesus led his closest followers off the highway into coolness along the lakeshore, a shady place where we could sit at his feet and listen. A gentle breeze blew from the east across the water, refreshing us. Gulls and shorebirds came near to scrounge for scraps of food; but finding none, they flew farther down the sands, leaving us in silence to understand what the Master would say. We were hungry hearts, waiting to be fed with more bread from heaven.

He stood. We ranged comfortably at his feet. Some of us stretched out full length on our sides, resting hand to jaw; some sat cross-legged; others with their bellies flat to the soil and two hands under their chin.

Simon Peter and I sat close to the Master, our faces turned up toward his. Jesus began to speak.

"You all know James and John are kin to me. They have asked where I was those many years when my family and theirs would come together and I was not present. They were told then that I was on a journey, and after several years they no longer asked the question.

"My journey was sometimes to far-off places. I have sailed with my mother's kin to the land of the Celts and Gaels on the Isles beyond the sea. And I have walked the shore along the grand *mare* which laps the shores of Israel.

"I have gone into Egypt and later crossed Arabia, to a place which lies far east of us beyond the land of the Medes and Persians.

"Taking shipping to a land sweet with rivers, and steamy forests, and ferocious beasts and reptiles, I met people with strange arts of the mind.

"Mostly though, I journeyed to places named in scripture—places where Abraham, Moses, David, and the prophets walked. There I listened to people who recounted traditions of their elders and remembrances from the past, telling of Israel's involvement with all who loved God.

"My feet have even walked south to the land of Sheba, whose queen came bringing great wealth in tribute to King Solomon.

"Wherever I have journeyed these many years, I've heard things which bind the children of Israel to God. Wherever I found people faithful to the law of Moses, I sojourned for a while.

"I once returned from Egypt through the barrens which lie at the feet of Musa Jebel. After two full moons at that sacred place, I continued homeward, tracing the path of Moses to the Jordan River.

"I climbed into the mountains of Abarim near Mount Nebo, where Moses looked across to the Promised Land, which he knew he would never enter. There I heard this tradition from those who heard it repeated through many generations.

"Moses, the first man who knew God as I AM, longed to see the Promised Land and the valley of the Jordan, where the Israelites camped before crossing the river,

> to possess the land "from Gilead unto Dan, and all Naphtali, and Ephraim and Manasseh, and Judah unto the great sea, and southward the valley of Jericho, the city unto Zoar." This is the land promised to Abraham and his seed, which seed we are.

"One day it is told, Moses and Eleazar his nephew, the son of Moses's brother Aaron, were there with Joshua on Mount Nebo, on the heights of the Abarim range. They were talking together.

"As Moses was about to embrace them and bid them farewell, he was suddenly compassed about with a cloud. He disappeared from their sight as the cloud lowered. When the cloud lifted, a search for Moses was made on the mount and in the valley below, but he was never seen again.

"Joshua and Eleazar could not see through the cloud which obscured Moses's departure. They could only assume that Moses had died when they could not find him.

"Moses's body could not be found, for flesh had ceased to exist for him. He had risen to understand that one's eternal selfhood is not carnal, not corporeal, but divinely mental.

"Moses had been faithful to complete the work given him by God, and his reward was that he would never suffer bodily corruption. Enoch, before Moses, had pleased God by being conscious of things spiritual.

"Like Enoch, Moses did not die. It was given him to depart from earth to the harmony and spiritual reality of eternal existence, but not through death. He simply ceased to be conscious of his flesh.

"This may be hard to understand, but I know it is true. The things of Spirit are not seen by eyes, nor heard by ears, touched by hand, nor savored by any sense. The psalmist sang, 'O taste and see that the Lord is good.'

"This is not asked of the body, but of mind. This is the lesson I teach you. I have said it before, 'You have eyes, but do not see. You have ears, but do not hear.' Now I say to you, mind alone comprehends.

"God is the perfect and only intelligence. Believe and understand my words. I have told you before and will say it again and again. It is among things most essential to know.

"The time will come when all men will learn what it means to be the image and the likeness of God. From the proverb of Solomon: 'As in water face answereth to face, so the heart of man to man.'

"It is given to you to understand that it is the *Mind of God* that mankind is to image. God is not corporeal, not flesh and blood and bones. God is Spirit, creator of the universe and everything in it."

On another day when the crowd was larger than usual, Jesus gave command that we should depart to the other side of the lake. So he sent the people to their homes; but one of the scribes came forward and in servile manner said, "Master, I will follow you wherever you go."

Jesus said, "Foxes have dens in the earth, and birds have places where they roost, but the Son of man often has no place to lay his head."

The scribe disappeared into the crowd, and we never saw him again.

Then a faithful disciple came forward and said, "My father is ill unto death. Allow me to tarry and go to prepare to bury my father."

Jesus said, "Follow me. Let the dead bury the dead. Those who learn of me shall gain everlasting life." We entered into the ship, and that man came with us. His father did not die.

Jesus went to the rear of the ship, found a comfortable place, and soon was sleeping soundly. Other little ships sailed in company with us. But later the wind came up in a tempest that raised waves higher than the ship, which began to fill with water.

We went to Jesus in fear and wakened him. "Lord, save us. We perish."

He answered, "Why are you so afraid? Is your faith so small?" Then he stood up and called loudly into the wind, "Peace." To the swamping waves he said, "Be still." At once the wind died, and the waves rippled gently against the ship. The sun came out as the squall clouds broke apart.

We were all amazed; and for the thousandth time we asked among ourselves, "What kind of man is this?" Never before had it been seen that winds and waves obeyed a man's words.

It was a long time before we dared to ask Jesus how he silenced the howling wind and how he stopped the sea flowing through the air.

It was still longer before I understood his answer: "The storm was not in me," he said, "I was at peace and there was no storm *out there*. Nor was I afraid of what others were experiencing. God has given man dominion over all the earth and its seas, and every condition therein."

Our sailing that day was calm; and except for those tending the ship, we all rested. The other little ships had peaceful sailing now too. Not one had been swamped in the storm.

We landed on the narrow shore at Gadara close to Gergesa, for we had sailed from Capernaum southeastward a little, across Gennesaret. Above and around us lay steep cliffs which were slightly terraced downward to the shore.

In the cliffs were caverns used as tombs; and from one tomb along the shore came two men, men whose actions were wild and fierce, for they were showing madness in frightening ways.

One man blocked our path. The other fled up the hill to a higher level where a herd of swine was feeding under care of several swineherds.

The air was filled with anguish as these two men screamed, one echoing the other, "What have we to do with thee, Jesus, thou Son of God? Have you come here to torment us before the time when we die?"

I saw Jesus close his eyes for just a moment. Then he quietly said, "I will cast out these devils."

Down from the hill came another voice. "If you cast us out, make us to go into the swine, feeding here." Jesus shouted in answer to the one who spoke, "Go!"

Immediately, the swine went berserk and, running wildly, funneled themselves down the steep path into the sea, where they perished in the waters.

Jesus sat silently while we murmured about the awful scene.

Then he said, "Be at peace, for God's is this volition and His will prevails. Murmur not over this sad demise of evil. Are not swine considered unclean here? The cleansing depths have consumed them in the mind of each who fear yet keep swine against the law of Moses."

The man who had blocked our path now stood beside us, sane and quiet.

"The evil spirits have gone from me," he said. "Believe me they were legion, thousands of swirling thoughts telling me to run, to scream, to cut myself with stones, to hate, and kill, and even to deny the Almighty. I have heard of you, Jesus of God, and wondered when you would come to this shore," he said.

When Jesus and the man who was no longer a house for demons sat talking to one another, the other tomb dweller rushed up.

"The swineherds have gone into the city . . . to tell what you have done to their livelihood." He too was now sane.

Shortly the whole city turned out to see Jesus. They found him with the men who were healed, sitting quietly beside him, serene, and in their right mind. Oddly, the citizens did not rejoice, but were afraid of Jesus.

When Jesus discerned their fear, he had the one man tell them how he was reluctant to care for the swine and fell ill even to the loss of his senses until Jesus healed him of his fear and fury.

In response the people said to Jesus, "Depart now. Leave us alone."

So Jesus walked to where the ship was beached. The first-healed demoniac quietly asked if he might join Jesus's entourage.

"No." I heard Jesus reply. "Go home to your friends and family and tell them the wonderful thing God has done for you. It is His compassionate mercy which has restored your heart and mind."

The man watched as we departed. Later we heard that he traveled throughout Decapolis, telling how Jesus healed him, giving back to him a normal and good life. Thus he became Jesus's first disciple unto the people eastward beyond Galilee.

We sailed across the Sea of Gennesaret back to Capernaum. Townspeople saw the ship when it was far from shore, and when we arrived home the people gladly received Jesus, for they were all waiting for him. We landed on a beach near the hamlet called Gennesaret. From there we hurried to our own places of rest.

Chapter 9

"You must understand," Jesus said forthrightly the next day as we gathered for teaching on the shore southward toward Tiberias. "My work is more than healing, and my words are more than speech. I am sent to reveal the power of God which is given to man. It is time for men to waken to what it means to be the likeness and reflection of God's being, His very image, and to behold God's power, ever present, enabling every one to know and do good.

"I teach men so, saying, 'Do you bring a lamp into the room and then put it under a bowl? Does not one place it on a candlestick so that all may see its light and even things that before were hidden in darkness? Whatever is not seen because of darkness must be shown. Whatever is concealed must be brought into the light.'"

Jesus was speaking to a very small group of people.

"Think about this," he continued. "If you have ears, listen and understand. Whatever you choose to understand will increase into more understanding. Open your hearts. Receive my words. Whoever receives will be given more. Whoever does not understand the truth I share, even the little he has will be taken from him, for he does not treasure and continue to seek the gift of his own God-given dominion over all things.

"The kingdom of God is given to you—here a little, there a little," Jesus said. "It is as if a man casts seed into the ground and after many days and nights pass, the seed springs up and grows. Man does not need to know how the earth, by itself, brings forth fruit—first the sprout, then the ear, then the full grain in the ear. But when the fruit is ready, the grain is cut because harvest time has come. So it is that the kingdom of God will be found bringing forth a fine harvest, for you are the soil in which I am sowing the seeds of truth."

We knew that Jesus had long pursued the understanding by which he could heal and save. He proved what he taught. He often quoted the scriptures which affirm, "God is *a* Spirit"—not just one of many spirits, but the one, the *only*

Spirit, from which all spiritual things must be learned and likewise proven to be the source."

To those who rejected his words, he said, "You have eyes, you have ears, but you do not see the truth of my works nor hear my words, for they must be seen and heard, not through flesh, but through the mind that is of God."

"Why then this flesh?" one of us asked later when we were resting in a grove.

Jesus said, "You *think* flesh is the necessary substance of your being. You *think* substance is a thing separate from the Mind which is God, Spirit.

"You find real only that which you can touch with your hands, taste with your tongue, observe through sight, know by odor, or hear as sound. Know this: Some things are evil—to be avoided or destroyed. Other things are good—to be desired, pursued, and possessed.

"But I say to you, I see as I think, for I see through the Mind of God. I behold things as my Father beholds things. To Him and through Him thoughts become things, the manifestation of ideas held in His Mind not found in temporal substance and not ephemeral nor illusive, but tangible and practical.

"Remember the miracle of water becoming wine when I held in thought the idea and ideal of the needed wine.

"In spiritual thought there is no process of time. Ideas do not need birth. They exist forever in the atmosphere of intelligence, in the consciousness that is God.

"Remember the draught of fish? They were there in evidence as God's provision, and the labor to harvest the catch was accomplished at once.

"This is the dominion given by God to man on the sixth day of creation when God made man in God's own image. Man can know as God knows, think what God thinks, and discern what God's mind always has at hand to bestow upon all who seek to be the image of God. Man, being like his Maker, understands that good things are prepared and ready to bless and sustain man through mind—first as thought, then in form and substance.

"Through spiritual thought man has access to the things of God, and every need is abundantly supplied.

"The flesh profits nothing. Its substance is not thought, nor from the eternal source that is God. Perishable flesh springs from the Adam dream, the false account of existence erroneously deemed real and tangible, but never actually so.

"Remember when I told you that Moses understood himself to be not flesh and blood, but the image, the mental likeness of God. He simply disappeared to mortal sight but continues to eternally exist in the realm of spiritual reality, as the perfect eternal expression of the infinite God.

"So it is, and so it will be seen as the truth about all things, when the sons of men understand God."

Jesus slipped away. We sat there a long time, pondering the truths he had just planted in the soil of our thoughts. We were still there when he returned later. We arose and journeyed back into Capernaum with him. But nobody spoke a word.

As we neared the synagogue, one of the rulers, Jairus by name, rushed up to Jesus and fell at his feet.

"I've been seeking you," he cried. "My little daughter is close to death. Please! Please come and lay your hands on her and heal her, for I know she will then live."

Jesus went with him. We disciples had to walk briskly to keep up. Because we had been away from town, many people followed us and thronged Jesus. Then suddenly, he stopped.

"Who touched me?" he asked.

We were scornful, and someone asked, "You see this multitude and ask who touched me?" But he was serious.

"Somebody has touched me. Someone in this crowd needs healing . . . is it you?" he asked a woman we all knew. For twelve years blood had issued, seeping constantly from her body. She had tried many things prescribed for the condition by many physicians but nothing had healed or even helped her. In fact, she was worse and suffered hopelessly, until . . . until she heard that Jesus was passing by. Quickly she had slipped in behind the Master. *If I can just touch the hem of his clothing*, she thought, I *will be healed.* She then reached forth her hand and touched the hem of Jesus's robe.

Instantly, the flow of blood ceased as if the fountain had dried up. She felt certain in her body that she was healed and would never again be plagued by that condition.

Jesus knew the goodness of God's healing power had gone forth from his thought, which he had been inwardly affirming. He was focused on God's power, presence, and perfection in order to bring healing to the little maiden who was dying.

The consciousness of God lifts thought to God's power, and Jesus knew healing had taken place in someone in the crowd of people, for his spiritual virtue had been touched and flowed forth mentally to meet somebody's need.

The woman came trembling, to tell how and why she touched the hem of his garment. As she kneeled before him, tears of gratitude were in her eyes.

"It is all right, woman. Your faith has made you whole. Go in peace. You are free of that plague."

She reached up to embrace Jesus, but even as he spoke these words a servant from Jairus's house came to tell him. "Your daughter has died. Why trouble the Master any further?"

When Jesus heard this, he said, "Don't fear, Jairus. Simply believe, and she shall live."

He turned to the throng of people. "I ask you to return to your homes. All except you, Peter, and you, James and John. You three shall witness this victory over death." All obeyed and returned home.

When Jesus arrived at the house of Jairus, mourners were already present. Women were weeping and wailing the dirge of death; pipers were sounding special flutes being played to signify that a death has occurred. There was great tumult because the child was the only daughter of the ruler of the synagogue.

Jesus entered the house and asked, "Why make this ado and weep? The maid is not dead, but sleeping." The servants and others present laughed scornfully. Jesus put them all out of the house. He took the parents, along with Peter, James, and John, into the room where the child was lying.

He walked over to her couch and, taking her small hand in his, said, "Talitha cumi" which, when interpreted, is "Damsel, I say to you, rise up."

And she did just that! Straightway—as though she had not even been sleeping—she arose from her bed and walked into her father's arms. Everyone, except Jesus of course, was astonished.

"Now," Jesus said to the father and mother, "tell no one anything except that the child is all right. That is all that needs to be known at this time. But first, give her something to eat, for this will prove that she has fully recovered."

Jesus and the three disciples left Jairus's family and house through a rear door. They ran down the narrow passageway at the back, skirted the nearby synagogue, and disappeared while we stood, talking with townspeople in the street in front of Jairus's home. Rejoicing, they gave credit and thanks to God. Everyone marveled when they heard the good news that the child lived and was well. When the tumult subsided a bit, we left to join Jesus at his abiding place in Chuza's grove.

When we arrived, we saw from a distance that Jesus was standing to one side in his dooryard, watching two blind men trying to find the entrance. The men cried out softly, first one, then the other, "O Son of David, have mercy on us."

Jesus put his finger to his lips and beckoned us quietly to his side. "They followed me here . . . ," he whispered.

Stretching both hands in front of themselves, the blind men moved forward. Jesus stepped quickly onto the stone doorstep. "Do you believe that I am able to do this for you?" he asked.

"Oh yes, Lord," they replied in unison, "yes!"

Jesus reached out to each man. He gently touched the lids of their sightless eyes, then withdrew his fingers. "Very well then," he said. "according to your faith, sight is now restored to you."

Suddenly, their eyes, long closed by habit, opened. The two men just looked at each other in wonderment. Then at the sky, the ground, the trees. Laughing, they turned again face to face and examined each other.

"See that no man knows what I have done for you," Jesus said.

"Surely you jest," one of the men exclaimed. "That will be hard, Master. Everyone has seen us stumbling and groping in the darkness of our lives. People will see the change in our being."

"Would you have us pretend blindness?" asked the other.

We have rarely seen Jesus laugh, but he truly was amused. "Go your way then," he said. "God will guide your thoughts and words. Live well!"

One day soon after, he was teaching at noonday on the beach, for it was a cloudy day. A great crowd, much larger than the usual multitude of people, had gathered. Someone brought to Jesus a man possessed with a devil of dumbness.

Jesus took in the sad state of that man who needed another person to speak for him. He closed his eyes in prayer for a few moments.

When he opened them, the man was opening his lips. Then his tongue moved, and words poured out in a torrent of praise to God for His healing power.

Word spread through the crowd like a breeze whispering coolness as it moves through sunlit space. The usual gathering of scribes and Pharisees who stood at the fringes of those seeking healing heard that the man who was dumb now talked freely. Two of them pushed their way through the crowd muttering. "This man casts out devils through Beelzebub, the prince of the devils."

They were about to confront Jesus with this accusation; but before they opened their mouths he, knowing their thoughts, said, "Every kingdom divided against itself is brought to destruction. Every city and house divided with people both for and against something has no basis for peace and no stability. If Satan is governor of a mind which honors the prince of evil, Beelzebub, yet also claims ability to cast out evil, Satan is divided against himself.

"But if I cast out evils through the power of God, by whom do your children cast them out? Children cast out evil as their fathers cast out devils. Even I cast out evil by the power of God, who is *my* Father.

"If you can see that it is by the Spirit of God that I cast out evil, then God's kingdom is come to you even before you expected it.

"How can one enter a stronghold of evil and spoil the influence it would have, unless one recognizes the evil and breaks its hold? If you disagree with me, disagree and leave me. If I cannot gather you in the name of God, you are indeed already scattered.

"If a tree is good, the fruit of the tree is also good. But if the fruit is unsound, the tree becomes useless, for a tree is known by and kept for the fruit it produces. O you are a generation of vipers! Being evil, you cannot speak good things; your mouth speaks that which your heart abundantly holds. A good man brings from his heart's treasure good things. An evil man brings forth from his treasure of evil, things likewise evil.

"But I say to you, watch that you speak not meaningless and useless words, for in the Day of Judgment one must account for his unfruitful words. It is by your words that you shall be justified, and by your words that you shall be condemned."

Days later, Matthew, who had gone with Jesus when he went back to Nazareth, finally told us what happened there. They had gone to the synagogue from which Jesus had been rejected a few months earlier. Again Jesus was asked to teach. Many who gathered to hear his words were astonished. They asked amongst themselves, "Where did he get this wisdom? How does he do these mighty healing works we've heard of?"

"Aren't you the carpenter's son?" one man asked. "Is not Mary your mother? We know your brothers, James, Joses, Simon, and Judas. And your sisters, we remember them also."

Others clamored to know, asking, "From what source do you get the miracles people say that you have performed?"

Matthew said it was sad to see Jesus shake his head in dismay. "Why am I an offense unto you?" he had asked. "Truly it has been said, 'A prophet is honored everywhere except in his own town and in his own house.' I cannot do mighty works and wonderful things for you because you don't believe that I am able to do such things.

"Therefore, having tried before to teach you the scriptures and you did not credit my words worthy to be heard then, now I again must shake the dust from my sandals and depart from this place."

So they left Nazareth and returned to Capernaum. Jesus called us to meet with him, and we walked far southward along the Sea of Gennesaret to where Judah takes over the land at the border of the Galilee.

It was here that we heard from two of John's disciples the sad news of the death of John the Baptist. They told Jesus that Herod was said to be sorry that he was duty-bound to give Salome her wish to have him take the Baptist's life. He had given the body at once to John's disciples, and they buried it and then hastened to find Jesus and give him the sad news.

They told him about the celebration on the birthday of Herod Antipas. Herodias, whom John Baptist had condemned when objecting to the immoral marriage of Antipas and Herodias, had arranged for her daughter to dance seductively before Antipas.

Salome had been coached by her mother to ask Herod Antipas for the head of the Baptist, who was imprisoned at Machareus, the Roman fortress east of the Dead Sea, near the river Arnon.

Added to the shock and sadness of the news of John's death was word that he was beheaded, and his head was placed upon a charger and presented to Salome.

When Jesus heard this, he went into a ship and sailed across to the eastern shore. He needed to be alone.

We remained at the lake, awaiting our Master's return. We knew that he would challenge the sadness, and from this experience he would gain new insight, strength, and courage.

From that time, John's disciples followed Jesus. Also from that time whenever a miracle of Jesus was told to Herod Antipas, he attributed these marvelous works to John the Baptist, fearing that he had risen from the dead.

We did not have to wait long for our Master to join us again. We walked northward then through the villages and cities of Galilee. Jesus preached everywhere we went. And, of course, he healed. Multitudes came, bringing their sick with them. There were so many!

Jesus said, "They are as sheep who have no shepherd to guide and care for them."

One busy day he instructed us to go apart a short distance to rest. "I will come to you soon."

We managed to secrete ourselves somewhat behind a thicket atop a small hill. There in the lengthening shade of the coppice, under the brushwood, we rested comfortably until Jesus rejoined us. He sat down for a few moments, saying, "The harvest is ready, but the laborers are few. Pray that God will send more laborers into His harvest fields.

"Tomorrow, after you have spent the night praying, I will come again at the break of day. Be faithful now. Pray as I have requested."

He left us to send the people away, for it was evening, and they needed food and shelter and quietness in their homes.

None of us talked around the fire that night. We were as silent as the stars in the heaven above us. We were being spiritually moved and inspired. I had no desire to talk; my consciousness was like a massive basket being filled. Truths poured into my thoughts. Fragments and fulsome discourses repeating the Master's words appeared in my consciousness—illumined, understood, and bound in a web of tender love.

We each prayed silently, earnestly, asking that others might be made ready and willing to glean in the harvest fields of our Lord. Not one of us slept until about the time of the cock's crowing. And then we nodded off one by one. At length I too closed my eyes, succumbing to a new inner light which kept the night at bay even as I slept.

At dawn our Master came. There was new hope in his eyes. We sat again on the dew-fragrant humus beneath the brushwood. He spoke to us one by one and with tender touch wakened us to a new day in our collective lives.

He called my name first. "Andrew, my first-called follower, I give you awareness of God's power against all unrighteousness of thought and act, against sinfulness and the regret one earns when he is defiled within because he knows what God's law requires of him yet does not obey. You shall cast out all manner of fearful thinking to heal every form of sickness and all kinds of disease for those who ask."

Quietly, lovingly, he repeated the same words to Philip and then to Bartholomew, also known as Nathanael bar Tolmai of Cana.

I watched and listened as he spoke to my brother Peter, the Rock, as Jesus was wont to call him.

He clasped his cousins James and John each by a shoulder and commissioned them. Then Matthew, as he sat with his head bowed. I thought of the great journey of the mind Matthew was experiencing—from purloined wealth to riches of the kingdom of heaven.

Thomas called Didymus—brooding, listening, ever watchful—he too then received the promise of God's power and presence in the work of healing and preaching.

So did James the Less, the son of Alphaeus and brother of Matthew sometimes called Levi. And Thaddaeus, called Lebbaeus and sometimes called Judas. They stood quietly as Jesus commissioned them with the same words and embraced them briefly.

Simon Zelotes felt the touch of our Master's hand and looked into his eyes as Jesus gave him power to heal as he himself healed; and finally, at the end of the bestowals, Jesus bent low to Judas Iscariot and almost whispered into his ear words we all heard: "You shall serve my cause faithfully." Judas, the only one of us from Judea, bowed his head, nodded, and clasped the Master's hand.

And so we twelve were now ready for special missions in his name, teaching, preaching, healing even as Jesus did in his Father's name. But we were not sent forth right then, for Jesus asked to be alone once more.

His thoughts needed to be further brought into harmony to give him peace about his cousin John. He asked for a ship to carry him again across the lake to the desert region. It was not unusual for him to take one or two of us with him when he went off alone. Jesus told us to follow in a second ship about an hour later.

But then he signaled to me, "Come," and the two of us were ferried the short distance across the lake from Capernaum to the southward region beyond Bethsaida. I wondered if perhaps Jesus intended to walk either to Bethabara where John had baptized him, or perhaps even farther south to Machaerus, the fortress near the Dead Sea where John had been imprisoned and was martyred.

But no, he simply wanted to get away from the multitudes, and we walked in the direction of Decapolis.

"I wanted you with me," he explained as we set out. "You, more than anyone, knew John, his righteousness, his courage, and his humility."

"Yes," I responded. "I remember his disciples telling us that at Aenon near Salim when you gave permission for us to baptize also, they complained to John because more people now asked purifying of you than came to them. But John answered them so selflessly. As I recall he said, 'Only that which is given from heaven can be received by any man. You all know that I am not the Christ, but I am the one sent to bear witness of his coming.'

"Then," I explained to Jesus, "John said words so beautiful I have tried to keep them in memory. He said, 'He who has the bride is the bridegroom. But the best friend of the groom, his very closest friend, rejoices greatly because the bridegroom is so happy.' Of himself John said, 'This, my joy, is also thus fulfilled.'"

I glanced at Jesus. Peace filled his eyes.

I continued, "John told his disciples, 'He must increase, but I must decrease. One coming from above is above all. I am of the earth, therefore earthy and speak things of the earth. But he'—meaning you dear Master—'he who comes from heaven is above all who come from the earth.'"

Jesus stopped walking and stood still while I said words I realized he had never heard spoken.

"John told his followers, 'What Jesus has seen, that he swears to; and no man receives his testimony. Yet *if* one receives his testimony, he has the sign that God is Truth.'"

"Did John say that?" Jesus asked.

"That and more than that," I answered. "He said further, 'He who is sent by God speaks the words of God, for God has given to him of His own Spirit—with no measure and no limitation. The Father loves His Son and has given all things into his hand, that the Son might redeem the world from things temporal and carnal.'"

Jesus looked at me, but I put up my hand to stop his words. "Let me finish," I begged. "This is what John told his disciples in words so wonderful that I recall them often, especially when you teach about the kingdom of God within. John said, 'He who believes the things taught by the Son of God has everlasting life. But he who believes not the Son shall not see enduring life, for the indignation of God abideth on him.'"

Now tears fell from Jesus's eyes. "Oh John my departed brother, you are no more on earth for you have ascended to your glory. I weep not for you but for myself. But I must not weep, for we shall meet again in our glory. Now though, I must finish the work my Father has given me to accomplish."

So saying, Jesus embraced me and said, "Thank you, Andrew. Both John and I are blessed that you came into our lives. Let us go back to Bethsaida and continue the work."

I was surprised, but Jesus didn't seem to be, when a great company of people awaited us near our ship in a desert place not far from their homes in Gadara and Gerasa.

One of the men who was often in our wake as we traveled through Galilee gave this explanation: "We saw you take the ship and the direction it went, so we decided to follow you. Footsore we are, but we hunger to hear you teach more of the kingdom."

Shortly after this, the other apostles arrived in yet another boat.

So Jesus stood there on the grassy plain beneath the eastern uprising of the Gergesa range of hills. He faced westward so the sun would not be in the eyes of those who stood around, listening to him teach the things of God. He preached for hours, and every now and again someone would come painfully forward to be healed.

Miracles abounded that afternoon; but as the sun lowered across the Sea of Galilee and cast a kind light which heated no one to exhaustion, the greatest miracle imaginable was about to happen.

The crowd started milling around, for they were getting hungry. Thaddeus came to Jesus and whispered, "Send them away. This is a desert place, and the time is now passed for their evening meal."

Other disciples joined Thaddeus. "Yes, send the multitude away so they can go into the villages and buy themselves provisions."

But Jesus said, "They need not depart. Give them food."

Our answer came quickly. "We have only five loaves and two fish among us."

"Bring them to me," Jesus said, "and command the people to sit down again on the grass."

The scant supply of food was brought to Jesus. He took the five loaves and two fish. He looked heavenward then said expectantly, "Father, bless these as I break and share them."

We stood by to receive from his hands the great increase of loaves and fish he seemed to be culling from air.

One by one he gave the multiplied loaves and fish to us, his closest disciples. We carried them to others, and the others gave to the seated multitude. Loaves and fish kept filling Jesus's hands, multiplying time after time after time into our hands, until all the people were fed.

Multiplied by the Christ, five loaves and two fish had been transformed into abundance.

All I could think of was, *This is a foretaste of heaven*. A few earthly loaves subjected to the ideal of the Christ and behold, supply is no longer limited but replaced by an abundance to meet the need. Therefore, this was truly food from heaven, multiplied by God's love to man.

"Gather up the fragments," Jesus requested; and each of us gathered a basketful.

What a lesson was given. Twelve baskets filled, to remind us of this day when heaven touched earth and proved that we need not labor bodily for that which perishes, but mentally for that which increases even unto everlasting life.

Jesus told us, "Now take your baskets and get into the ships and go ahead of me to the other side. I will send the multitude away. Then I'll go apart into the mountain and thank my Father, who today has shown His love to the children of men."

We entered the ships as he bade us, and ate our fill just as the five thousand men, besides uncounted women and youngsters, had filled their bellies just an hour or two before.

As we sailed away, we could hear the multitude praising Jesus, saying, "This is in truth that prophet which is promised to come into the world."

Then the twilight was rent with a loud cry, "Let us take him—by force if need be, and make him our king."

We were not concerned. We knew that Jesus could pass through the midst of them unnoticed, and that is exactly what he did. Departing from the multitude, he went up into the basalt mountain alone, to continue praying to his Father.

We were midsea returning to Capernaum when the wind suddenly came down from Mount Hermon, rushing and swirling from the entrance of the Jordan down the whole length of the lake—twelve and a half miles—to the point where the river exits the lake and flows southward. The wind was so contrary it was hard to set our sail, and waves were being blown ever higher. Water cascaded into the ship.

None of us slept. I was keeping the watch when an apparition, coming toward our vessel, appeared on the sea. I passed the word.

At once, the other disciples peered into the spray-filled night air. We could not guess what it was that we saw, but it was troubling to have our attention drawn from the rise and fall of the ship. Sloshing water threatened to swamp us if we moved around too much, setting the keel off center.

"It is a spirit!" someone yelled. "It is a spirit!" Fear set in for every man. But just as suddenly came the familiar voice of our Master when he called, "It is I, don't fear."

Peter, my dear, impulsive brother, broke the fear for all of us by calling back to Jesus, "Lord, if it is you, bid me come to you, as you are coming to us, walking on the water."

"Come."

That is all Jesus said. "Come."

And that is what my brother did. As the ship wallowed toward Jesus, Peter simply, calmly, and—may I say—foolishly stepped out of the boat.

Unbelievably, he walked *on* the water! Walked . . . just as Jesus continued toward us, walking atop the water.

Unaffected by the rise and fall of the waves Peter moved forward. Supported only God and Jesus knew how, he walked one, two, three, four steps. As he raised his foot to take the fifth step, the boisterous wind rose sharply. Waves dashed much higher, then fell very low.

As the spray hit our faces, we all drew in our breath and were seized with rational fear.

Peter began to sink. I prepared to launch my body into the depths to save him. I matched my fear to his as I heard him scream, "Lord! Save me . . . please save me!"

I stood transfixed, but Jesus stretched forth his hand and caught him. My knees went weak with relief.

Jesus rebuked that hulk of a brother of mine. "O Peter, so little faith," he said, "Why did you doubt? You were doing something no one of flesh has ever ventured to even try. You *walked* upon the water."

Then Peter and Jesus came into the ship. To our amazement, the wind abruptly ceased.

And then Jesus made us forget the moment of fear we felt when the waves began to swallow Peter. With a wisp of a smile he said, "What makes this moment more meaningful is this: a stone sinks, but Petros, my Rock, walked a step or two upon the angry sea."

We all broke out in laughter and then sobered when Philip said, "Truly, Lord, you are the Son of God!" Everyone voiced a heartfelt "Amen."

Then we were further amazed forever, for from midsea the ship arrived instantly at the shore near Capernaum, and we were safely home!

I, for one, did not sleep that night for I had glimpsed the power of our omnipresent God. The fact of what I'd witnessed was so distractingly awesome, I had no need to sleep.

Chapter 10

Our town on the lake is toward the northwestern curve where the shore turns southward. We are on a fertile plain watered by a spring fountain called Cepharnome, which is the old version of Capernaum. On this plain grow fruit and nut trees, grapes and grains, olives, melons, and herbs. Many people are farmers and vintners. The hamlet close by called Gennesaret is little more than a beach area, and it is there our ship drew to ground after the storm at sea that night.

Now opposite, on the eastern shore of the Sea of Galilee, live the people of Gergesa. They, the multitude who had eaten the day before of the endless supply of loaves and fish, followed Jesus by ship.

Knowing that we disciples had departed by boat, the Gergesenes wondered where Jesus was. He'd gone into the mountains to pray after sending the people to their homes. When they could not locate him, they asked men visiting from Tiberias, "Did any of you take Jesus of Capernaum to his home across the lake?" No one had. So getting into their own vessels, they came to Capernaum looking for him the next morning.

They found Jesus in town near the fish market and asked, "Rabbi, how did you get home?" He smiled as he answered, "You seek me, not because you saw the miracle, but because you liked the loaves and fish and were filled without laboring for your food.

"Don't labor for meat which does not last but must be gotten new every day. Labor for that which endures and sustains one's life everlastingly. That is the meat which I gave you last evening. My purpose? That you might know of God, that He has set His signet upon my words and my works."

Someone among the Gergesenes answered, "What must we do that we also may do the works of God?"

"This you must do," Jesus answered. "Believe on the one sent by God to show you what it means to be the image, the likeness of God. Then change yourselves."

"What is the sign that we may prove that we believe you. What will signify that we too know God?" they asked.

Jesus replied, "Your forefathers ate manna in the desert; as it is written in scripture,

He gave them bread from heaven to eat.

"*Moses* did not give that bread from *heaven*. It was God's giving, though they knew not what it was that they had been given.

"Our Father is now giving you the *true* bread from heaven. The bread of God is he who has come down from heaven and gives life unto the world."

The men from the other shore were glad. "Lord, evermore give us this bread."

Jesus said, "I am the bread of life. Whoever comes to me shall not hunger. And whoever believes all that I teach shall never thirst. But I must say this: you who have seen me but do not believe still do not yet understand my works or credit my speech.

"All whom the Heavenly Father gives me shall come to me and remain in me. I will for no reason cast away all who come. For I came from heaven, not to do what I want, but to do the will of God who sends me.

"This too is the Father's will, that of all that he has given me, in wisdom and in knowledge, I shall lose nothing, but at the last day will lift it even higher.

"It is God's will that everyone who sees me as the Son of God accepts that I am from God. He will gain assurance of life everlasting. At his last day on earth, I will raise him up. He shall surely live, he shall not be found among the dead."

This was a new thought to most of those Jews who came from Gergesa in Gaulinitus beyond Bethsaida. But they murmured against him because he said, "I am the bread of life which comes down from heaven."

They questioned, "Isn't this a man named Jesus?"

Some from Capernaum said, "Yes. We knew his father and mother. They were kin of the fisherman Zebedee and his two sons."

"How is it then he claims 'I come down from heaven?'" others asked.

Jesus answered, saying, "Don't murmur among yourselves. No one can come to me except the Father who sends me among you and brings *you to me*.

"In the scriptures the prophets have written, 'And they shall all be taught of God.' So everyone who has listened to me and has heard God's Word comes to me.

"No one has seen the Father except the man who is of God—he has seen the Father. Truly if you credit what I teach, you will have endless life, for I *am* that bread of life. In the wilderness, our forefathers ate manna, but that was not the bread of life.

"The bread of life comes living from heaven. Those who partake thereof do not die. This may help you to understand. Flesh and blood do not live forever. The fleshly man who gives life when bringing forth his offspring in time ceases to live.

"But I am the true bread of life, and it is in partaking of *this* living bread that one shall live forever. The bread that I give you is my body, which I give for the life of the world."

Did I, Andrew, hear right? My knees went weak. Was Jesus to give his flesh and blood, even as heathens sacrifice the flesh of animals on their altars? Not only was I disturbed at these words, but the Jews who wanted to hear Jesus preach, they too were disturbed and questioned among themselves, "How can this man give us his flesh to eat?"

As though he heard their disquiet, Jesus said, "Truly I tell you, except you eat the body of the Son of man and drink his blood, you have no life in which to continue. Flesh is not life. It is subject to corruption.

"My true flesh and my blood is divine Truth which sustains life. It shows forth the man created by God, not as flesh but as idea, having the true knowledge and infinite understanding of God and God's creation.

"My body is of Spirit, not flesh. To eat my flesh is to think spiritually as I think. To drink my blood is to understand as I understand. Whoever partakes of this wisdom and understands the things of God, that man truly partakes of the substance of my flesh and drinks my blood. He dwells in me and I in him.

"Flesh is not my life, but knowledge and spiritual understanding are my life. I live by the Father. He is the divine Life of all. He who perceives this dwells in me in the truth which comes from heaven. Not as the manna which sustained our ancient fathers, who are now dead. This new bread of Life once eaten, gives life forever."

Jesus spoke these words then walked to the synagogue. He repeated them as he taught that Sabbath eve in Capernaum. There were many present. Their response was, "This is a hard saying, who can really understand it?"

These were people who regularly followed Jesus and witnessed the miracles. But when they heard this teaching about the bread of life, they could not understand it. "This is a hard saying, who knows what it means?"

Jesus sensed this murmuring about his words and said to the followers, "Does this offend you? What would you think if you saw me ascend to heaven where I was before? Try to understand this important lesson. The spirit of my life quickens your hearts. The very words that I speak, they are spirit, and they are truth and life. Some won't believe this." He knew of whom he spoke. "I have told you that no man can come to me except it is my Father's plan that he come." After this, many disciples no longer walked with him.

Jesus gathered the twelve of us whom he had named apostles and asked, "Will you also go away?" Simon Peter said, "Lord, to whom would we go? You speak the words of eternal life. We believe—no, we are certain—that you are the anointed Son of the living God."

Jesus grew very sad upon hearing Peter's words and said, "I have chosen you twelve, but one of you will do an evil thing." Jesus knew the Sanhedrin were now plotting constantly how they might destroy him and his new teaching. We didn't know it then, but Jesus was speaking of Judas Iscariot, the only one of us from Judea beyond Galilee. Judas would deliver our Master to the temple authorities.

The next morning Jesus sent us out on our first healing mission. We were to go two by two with the fellow disciple we knew best. Then if any disparity in our practice came up, we could settle it reasonably.

Naturally, those of us with brothers paired up. James and John. Levi called Matthew and James the Little. Nathanael and Philip, because of their long friendship. Simon Peter and I. Thomas and Thaddaeus. Simon Zelotes and Judas Iscariot.

We were given definite instructions:

Take nothing for your journey—neither staff in hand nor purse in sleeve, nor bread nor money nor even change of clothing.

Take only your faith that all things are possible to God;

Your conviction that man is as perfect as God who makes all good things;

Your heart which loves as God loves, condemning no person;

Your willingness to endure all who persecute and misunderstand you.

And above all, for those who repent, give them the peace of God.

Abide where you are welcomed in, and depart when you have blessed them through your presence.

If any do not receive you, don't contend. Shake the dust from your feet, as testimony against their reluctance.

Do not salute strangers along the way—go to their abode and knock. If welcomed, enter in. If refused, leave in peace.

Glorify God in your every thought and in all you do.

It was Jesus's intent to follow up our work, so he sent us into cities where he knew he would soon be working himself.

Simon called Zelotes, from Cana, and Judas Iscariot, from Kerioth, went across the lake to the country of the Gaderenes. Here they met one of the men who had been healed by Jesus, the one who had ranted and raved furiously in the tombs.

They found him obedient to Jesus's request that he remain among his own people telling how he was restored to sanity. His name is Josias, and he kindly offered to travel with Simon Zelotes and Judas Iscariot while they worked in Gadara.

He watched closely as the two apostles were welcomed in the villages on the southward plain of the Jordan and in the hummocks and crags in the upthrust mountains. They engaged the interest of the people, befriending even children whose curiosity brought them forward when the men stopped in village squares.

All three were adept at bringing their conversation around to the remarkable healings Jesus accomplished. Especially Josias, who told how he had been insanely tormented but was now a living witness to the man who walked the shores of the lake, healing those who were infirm, diseased, or otherwise disquieted.

When these two apostles returned to Capernaum, they told of how the villagers responded. One lad who had fallen on a spike found the long-festering wound healed when Judas Iscariot commanded him to let the sore be closed in the name of Jesus the Christ of God.

A woman, whose heart was breaking because her husband and daughter had perished when they fell down the steep cliffs where they were rescuing a newborn lamb, was comforted when told that they still live because God is their life, indeed, the eternal life of all who believe.

A man ranting obscenely was brought to a shameless peace when Josias commanded him in the name of God to curb the cruel words, which he had too long hurled at women—young and old alike—from the time of his youth.

A farmer feverish with an infection was relieved of his fear and returned, a day and night after his family feared he was dying, in full strength to work his grain fields. He required no time for recovery of any kind.

Philip and Nathanael went to Chorazin, lying only two miles north of Capernaum. They walked up along a steep watercourse falling from the rocky summit, to where the village rises in the hills almost nine hundred feet above Capernaum. From these heights one can see the entire lake below.

The stonework in the village houses is black basalt; and the stone cutters often endure painful bruises, cuts, and injuries when stone is being harvested and used. So when many people listened raptly, the fear of injury lessened. Bad wounds closed in healing.

The two disciples told of Jesus's wondrous works, and later reported that dozens of people sat for hours, listening to them. When the villagers went home for the evening meal, they returned with their sick folk. The apostles then spoke of God's ever-presence and all-power, and with the lightest touch many who were sick with various diseases found themselves suddenly well.

Meantime, our father Jona asked Peter and me to heal his eyes which were growing progressively dimmer. We sat in the garden under the tiel tree, telling our father that it is through Mind that one truly sees and hears, and that nothing can endure that interferes with the ability which God Almighty has established. As he listened to our words, a smile spread across his face, and those proud eyes began to lose dimness. The film dissolved. He saw perfectly and broke into a doxology of praise to God. We touched other lives too, simply but directly.

Later, what was talked about most was the joy of a child whose pet bird was almost dead when brought to us where we sat on the quay. Simon said, "Life is in this creature, for God is at once the source and substance of all things that live to make happy the children of this world."

This little bird's feet had stiffened as the tiny thing shuddered violently and closed its eyes, dying. Then, suddenly, the eyes opened wide. The little bird sat up, tucked its feet beneath its breast, and rested contentedly in the hand of the lad. The smiles of those who witnessed this happy miracle knew that again the love and power of God was shown in their midst. A simple proof, maybe, but one never before seen.

We remained in Capernaum, hoping to bring to our town the proof that which Jesus knew could be learned and practiced by others, even simple fishermen such as us. All who came to us were restored to health.

James and John, sons of Zebedee, went south to Nain and called upon the widow whose son was raised from the dead.

When the young man was told who the visitors were, the mother and the lad went about the village calling to the people, "Bring your sick and helpless, the healers have come back to town." The widow's home was soon crowded by those curious as well as those hurting in some way. The two apostles satisfied each need, assuring everyone that with God all things are possible, for God loves the world and His kingdom is to be found in righteous thoughts which every person is capable of thinking. Many went home rejoicing, for they were healed.

James the Little and Matthew were in Bethsaida when a wee child, laid on the stony beach, was expiring slowly and gasping horribly, having fallen into deep water from a fishing boat. The child's father was devastated with sorrow, but the mother was nowhere to be found.

James plucked the little form from the bed of rocks. Holding her gently, he closed his eyes and prayed aloud to God a steadfast prayer that the child would surely live and glorify God in the presence of the people.

Suddenly the mother pushed screaming through the crowd, coming it seemed from nowhere. The father caught her in his arms, trying to still her desperate grief. "Listen," he said. "These men walk with Jesus who healed the child of Chuza and Joanna. These men say 'all things are possible to God.'"

As the words were spoken, the child gasped and gagged, and a flood of water poured from her nose and mouth. The child was breathing! Vomiting continued a bit longer.

The father then took the child from James's arms and gave the little girl into her mother's embrace. The child snuggled wearily after each throe until those present gave a joyful cheer, certain that she would live. Then she sat up and looked around and said, "You silly things"; and everyone laughed and agreed with James and Matthew, sons of Alphaeus, that all things are possible to God. They had just witnessed another miracle of a child's restoration to life.

Matthew told how Jesus had called him from his despicable career as custom taker and so filled his mind with a new view of God Almighty that he wanted nothing more now than to follow the healer from Galilee, as many people now called Jesus.

Thomas called Didymus and Thaddeus (also named Lebbaeus or Judas), were the last to come back with stories of success. They visited again the region which lay south of Capernaum; towns and villages such as Magdala, the Valley of Doves, and Arbela; and from the pass below Mount Tabor.

When they realized that James and John were going to Nain, they backtracked, going instead to Tiberias on the Sea of Galilee. Here they preached in the square in the shadow of the royal residence. Later they talked to the people, telling of many healings they'd witnessed and how Jesus told them time and again that with God all things are possible.

A young man on crutches had an unwieldy bandage on his left foot but sat listening intently. With one crutch, he tried to keep in place the ragged wrappings which were unraveling. Everyone knew his foot had been deformed from birth. But now the more he fiddled with the covering, the more it seemed to loosen.

Thomas told the people how they followed and worked with Jesus—healing the sick, casting out demons, and even witnessing the restoration to life of two people, a little girl and a young man. Both were restored to life by Jesus after they had died. Some people murmured "Wonderful" and stretched forth their hands, saying, "Give us this gift that we fear not the flesh."

As the people pressed close, a blind man was given sight with the lightest touch to his eyes and the words, "In the name of God, your sight is restored; no longer indulge in blind rages."

To a child whose skin was raw from ceaseless scratching, Thomas whispered, "Be at peace, God's love comforts you and makes peaceful your mind and heart. No longer will you be tormented." And her flesh was at once smooth, and the skin unbroken.

Other simple truths brought health, strength, and peace to all struggling to overcome their pains and sorrows.

The young man whose foot was uselessly deformed was healed. He cast away the bundle of rags hiding his foot. He cast away the crutches also and stood for the first time upon the soles of both feet. Someone piped a lilting tune on a reed flute, and everyone's feet were set to dancing, but none more wondrously than the feet of the young man who had been crippled since birth.

Two by two we returned to Capernaum and told Jesus the wonderful things that happened when we harnessed our thoughts to all that he had taught us and, time and again, had proven before our very eyes.

There was a fine supper and quiet rejoicing in Chuza's grove that night as we brought again figuratively the sheaves of healing which we laid at our Master's feet. We ourselves were awed by the harvest we had gathered.

The next day Jesus reviewed our work, and as we each told of our thought process which resulted in healing and blessing so many, he praised our perception of all he had given us in instruction as he did his work.

He corrected us several times, and that in itself became teaching. When the last account had been given, Jesus gave a summary and heartfelt gratitude for our willingness to work in the wide harvest field of human needs.

This is what he said:

> First you proved that with God all things are possible. You understand that God is perfect and that man finds therein all thoughts that are spiritual.

> You were told to hold your thoughts to the reality of the ever-presence of God and the power of all that is righteous, therefore true. This you did.

> You learned to discern that what appears to exist, but because it depends upon carnal substance, is always subject to change or destruction. That which seems so real always yields its substance

in thought, to spiritual consciousness which affirms the allness of perfect Mind and thereby heals.

You changed the evidence of illness to wellness through the understanding Mind of God, good.

You loved! You truly loved, as God loves, by holding man to be like God—perfect, holy, healthy, active, righteous, and loving. This always results in healing.

Very importantly, you believed every word you spoke, and spoke only words that inspire, bless, and heal. You understand that God is the source of all that resulted from your sincere effort to heal.

God is the healer. You are witness to what God does. You are the light of the world. You each have much to give. Pray to be always worthy. Rightly divide the Word of God.

Even Jesus closed his eyes and slept soundly that night, as we all rested peacefully in Chuza's grove.

After the sermon on the bread of life, when many followers of our Master turned back and walked no longer with him, the mood of the people changed perceptibly. The scribes and Pharisees encouraged the populace to consider this teaching unfaithful to traditional Jewish precepts, practices, and beliefs. Few remained trusting and devout followers.

"We'll go to Phoenicia," Jesus announced unexpectedly one evening. "Tomorrow at first light, we shake from our feet the dust of Galilee and go northwestward to the shore of the Great Sea. Perhaps we will find peace there."

We walked for hours the next days, stopping only for brief rests. At last, we reached the sea and the city of Tyre. The heathen people were curious about this young man and his companions. When told "This is Jesus, the miracle healer from Galilee," the people of Tyre brought their sick and infirm; and Jesus healed them.

We left Tyre and walked north along the sea to Sarepta. What I most loved about this journey we were on was that Jesus knew the history of the Canaanites and the coming of the Jews into the Promised Land. In Sarepta, Jesus reminded us of the prophet Elias of Gilead, whom God sent long ago to Sarepta (then called Zarephath) near Sidon.

None of us knew the details of this story. But I remembered that Jesus had mentioned Sarepta after he recalled the son of the widow at Nain to life. I asked him to tell us again.

"Elias, the ancient story goes, encountered a widow woman at the gate of the city. She was gathering wood for a fire to heat her oven, planning to use her mere handful of meal and the bit of oil in a cruse to fix a small last meal for her son and herself.

"'Make me a cake first then make yours,' Elias said. 'Have no fear, the meal in your barrel and the oil in the cruse shall not fail to provide all you will need until rain comes again and the drought is ended.'

"The woman did as Elias had asked and baked first the little cake for the prophet. Then she and her son had their meal, but it was not the last—as the widow woman feared—for she, her son, and Elias did eat again and again until rain came. The store of meal and oil was never diminished."

"Master," said James the Little, "you have shown us the fruits of understanding God's constant care and provision. You raised a widow's son, and you fed five thousand souls with but a handful of fish and bread."

"Indeed," said Jesus, "the ever-present Father, of His love and grace, has given me charge to renew the faith of the children of earth, even as Elias showed it eight hundred years in the past.

"Remember how at Nain I told you of the woman in a heathen land to whom this prophet was sent. This same woman's son fell sick and died. Elias took the lad from his mother's bosom, laid him upon his own bed in the loft of that house, and prayed, knowing God brought no *evil* to the woman by killing her son. Then he prayed, saying, 'Oh Lord, my God, I pray you, let this child's soul again be in him!' The child revived, and the prophet delivered him into his mother's arms."

We murmured among ourselves, "That is wonderful! How is death allowed when men of God can turn such sorrow into the fullness of joy?"

Jesus answered, "In time, death will have no power over the lives of men."

Leaving Sarepta, we moved on to Sidon. Now the people of the coast spread the word that a healing prophet was come out of Israel and dwelt among them.

A woman of Canaan made inquiry and, learning where we were staying, came a long distance and burst into our midst crying loudly, "Have mercy on me, O Lord, who art a man of the Jews. My daughter is distraught, troubled by a demon."

Jesus made no reply or response to the woman.

She then came to us. "Please, please help me. My daughter is so deeply troubled, and I can do nothing that gives her peace." Again and again she told her sad tale; she told it to each of us and asked that we heal her daughter.

We appealed to Jesus. "Send her away, Lord, send her away. She is begging us to do something to quiet her daughter."

Jesus shrugged his shoulders, saying, "I am sent only to the lost sheep of the house of Israel."

At that, the woman fell prostrate at his feet. "Help me," she said in a pathetically humble voice.

"It would not be right to take bread provided for children and cast it to dogs," said Jesus.

"Truth, Lord," she said, "yet the pups eat crumbs falling from the Master's table."

"O woman!" Jesus said, amazed. "Great is your faith! As you will, so it shall be!" Returning home, the woman found her daughter well and peaceful.

So much the more then, the people of Canaan sought Jesus to be healed. But the Master knew that to heal was to teach, and to teach was to understand. But it was God the Almighty who healed, not faith in the many gods which the Canaanites blindly worshipped.

Jesus was sought by crowds, but few came to hear his words; rather they came to seek relief from bodily ills and vexatious demons. So he decided to return to Galilee. It was the kingdom of God he preached, but in Canaan he found few interested in his words; they sought only his healing touch.

He had hoped to find here a place of quiet seclusion. Instead he was pressed to flee, and we departed the coasts and went inland toward the headwaters of the River Jordan, which then led us southward.

When we neared the Sea of Galilee, we skirted the valley of the lake and continued in the mountains southeastward into Decapolis. Several of the ten associated Greek cities here—Gadara and Gergesa and Gerasa among them— had already been visited by Jesus. Here, the Gadarene demonic was healed, and later in Gergesa five thousand were fed. Coming down from the north into the mountains east of the Jordan we arrived at a high place where a triangular lake lies in a basin of marshland. Here by the Waters of Merom, in heights overlooking the Sea of Galilee, Jesus bade us sit and rest.

It became quickly known that Jesus and his companions were there. Multitudes began to arrive, bringing their lame, those who were sightless, dumb, maimed, and others afflicted in some way. Patiently a great number of people waited in turn to bring their family members or friends to the feet of Jesus. Jesus rewarded their faith and healed each person.

The people were amazed, grateful beyond words, filled with wonder when the dumb began to talk, the maimed restored to wholeness, the lame walked, the sightless saw. To a man, the multitude rejoiced. In every heart, with every voice, glory, honor, and praise poured forth to acknowledge and adore the God of Israel. This caused the heart of Jesus to sing.

We assisted him by shepherding the eager crowds, urging patience, helping to bring the most infirm to Jesus's feet that they might be made whole. We were aware of the temper of the people and of the thing which pleased Jesus the most, that it was the God of Israel who was reverenced and thanked. At last we twelve realized why Jesus had been moved to forsake the crowds which came to him in the coasts of Tyre and Sidon.

The power to heal was in the presence of God. The wonder, glory, and praise belong to God and were not to be bestowed on any man. Thus, our Master taught us humility and that we should not think it was any but God who healed. How blessed we were. People in the coastal cities who worshiped many false gods had come only for healing—they did not wish to forsake their clay gods. But now we were back in Israel in the heights of Merom through which the Jordan flows. Simon Zelotes noticed in the crowd a man who was alone, talking with no one, and listening to none. He was buffeted hither and yon and never seemed to move closer to Jesus. Questioning the man, Simon got no response. He realized then that the fellow was deaf and could not speak without stuttering miserably. Another man stepped forward and verified Simon's conclusion; whereupon he was asked by Simon to assist in moving the deaf person through the multitude into the very presence of the Master.

Jesus rose from the stone whereon he was sitting and, putting his arm around the poor fellow, led him away from the crowd, aside from the tumult and the eyes of everyone there.

Then, Jesus reached forth, put his fingers in the man's ears, and touched his tongue to let the man know that he was being healed of his imperfection.

Instantly his ears were opened, and the man heard the voice of Jesus telling him that God is the One who plants the hearing ear, the seeing eye, and the vocal sounds in mind, and only the symbol of these talents were in the human form as eyes, ears, and tongue.

With that, the string of his tongue was loosened. No longer was he stuttering. He spake plainly; and his first words were, "I thank you."

"Thank God," Jesus replied," I only do what I see the Father do. It is He who has healed your ears and given you words."

Together they walked back to those waiting so patiently to be healed. To the first few people they met, Jesus said, "Tell no man, let *him* tell what God has done." But it did no good to ask such a thing.

The news of this man's healing swept through the multitude, and everyone rejoiced to hear it. Even so, the people were amazed, even overwhelmed, that Jesus was able to do this.

They agreed with one another, saying, "He does all things well; he has made a deaf man to hear and the same man able to speak clearly." Hearing this, Jesus shrugged his shoulders and reminded us that power belongs to God, and it is with God that all such things are possible.

The hours passed quickly. Nights were restful for us and for the multitude who slept on the grass, as we did. Days were filled with the arrival of many more people coming to be restored to health and usefulness.

Then late one afternoon, Jesus called us to his side. "My heart goes out to this people," he said. "Three days now they have been coming to be healed. Patiently they have endured, awaiting their turn.

"Most have had nothing to eat. I won't send them away now, for they are hungry, and I would not have them faint because they have chosen to fast."

Simon Peter spoke for us, "Where would we find in this wilderness so much bread to feed so many?"

"How much bread have we?" Jesus asked.

Judas Iscariot, who kept count of our supply, answered, "Seven loaves and a few small dried fish."

Jesus stood up. "Pass the word back through the multitude to sit down in orderly ranks upon the ground," he said.

When the multitude obeyed and had formed rows so one could pass among them without stepping on anyone, Jesus stood before them. His look of peace and love radiated outward upon them all.

He took the seven flat loaves in one hand, the meager few fish in the other, and held them high, giving thanks to God for providing food for man's use. He handed the fish and loaves to James and John to hold, then he took each one and multiplied it.

I was beginning to suspect that all space is filled with minute unseen thought-substance, and Jesus knew how to mentally bring it to form, to be seen and used.

We disciples each reached forth and filled our arms. The abundance of loaves was proven. As fast as we could, we distributed the food, beginning with those seated furthest away.

Those nearer were engrossed in watching the marvelous multiplication of seven loaves and a few small fish into a feast for four thousand hungry men and, in addition, their wives and children. Everyone ate to fullness. There remained seven baskets of fragments of the food, which we had shared with the people.

Then Jesus sent the multitude home.

We began our journey homeward the next day.

We got into a ship and sailed from the Decapolis near to the place where the Jordan flows south from the lake. Tacking diagonally, we crossed the lake to the city of Magdala in the area of Dalmanutha a few miles closer to Tiberias.

When Jesus left the ship there, a couple of Pharisees and Sadducees came to him, saying, "Give us *a sign from heaven*, Jesus, you wonder-worker."

He responded, saying, "You look at the sky and when it is red at sunset, you say tomorrow it will be fair. On a morning when it is red, you say, foul weather today for the sky is red. You are hypocrites, discerning *weather* from the sky but pretending not to know signs of the times from God.

"I remember your asking a sign of me some weeks ago. I told you then that like Jonah being alive after three days in the belly of the whale, so will I be three days in the heart of the earth. You are wicked and adulterous, yet you seek signs. No sign is to be given you other than the sign of Jonah."

So saying, he turned away and left them and went to see the wool merchant, his wife, and dear Mary, out of whom had departed seven devils.

After a few quiet days in Magdala, we took ship again and sailed across to Bethsaida. We neglected to take provision other than a single loaf of bread. This we gave to Jesus as we sailed.

Later he said to us, "Take notice and be cautious of the leaven of the Pharisees and of Herod."

Among ourselves we questioned, "Is it because we have no bread?" We asked him.

His answer: "Why do you reason my words to mean that you failed to provide yourselves bread for this journey? Haven't you learned yet? nor understood? Have you hardened your hearts? Do you have eyes but don't see? Or ears but don't hear? Don't you remember? Five loaves fed five thousand, and there were how many baskets of fragments uneaten?" We all answered at once, "Twelve."

"And then seven loaves fed four thousand, how much was left?" Again we replied, "Seven baskets full."

"Seven small loaves fed so many, and yet there remained seven basketsful. How is it, my children, that you don't understand?"

I, for one, was ashamed. That one loaf which we gave to Jesus could have amply fed the twelve of us, and even more. Thus Jesus drove home a lesson I would never forget.

I could not help thinking that this is the way the Adam curse will be set at naught. The human race will awaken from the deep sleep which had the first man created from dust and woman made from a rib of the sleeping man! We must better understand the Christ. Then the curse that man must till the earth for food, and that thorns and thistles will also be brought forth, that in sweat and sorrow man shall eat bread and the fruits of the field and earth until he return to the dust from whence he was taken, will no more be heard.

Chapter 11

We left the ship anchored in Bethsaida and walked northward. A blind man named Eliud was brought to Jesus, who was asked to touch him with his healing power.

Jesus took the arm of Eliud and led us with him apart to a quiet place. He put spit on the man's closed eyes for he could not see that Jesus was about to heal him.

Then Jesus reached forth his hands, touching the man as he had been asked. "Do you see anything?" Jesus asked.

The man looked up, his eyes open but still moist with the saliva with which Jesus anointed them.

"I see men as trees, walking." We disciples grinned at the thought of being seen as walking trees.

Jesus again put his hands on Eliud's eyes, removing the moistness. "Look up now," he said to the man. He opened his eyes and saw us clearly; and this time he was the one who laughed, saying, "Are you the trees I saw?"

Jesus laughed too. "Go home now, don't go into town, and don't tell anyone in town how you were healed. They will see soon enough that your sight has returned," he said to the man.

The man untied a sack from his waistcords and gave it to Jesus, saying, "This is all I have to give you—some fresh figs, a few nuts, and a small cake, my next meal. It is a token of my thanks. Please take it as if it were a great treasure. I must in some small way pay tribute to you, Master."

Jesus graciously accepted the offering, embraced the man, and turned him homeward. We watched Eliud go off alone, sure-footed because healed.

There were tears in my eyes, and I had to swallow hard to dislodge the lump in my throat. I don't think I was the only one close to weeping.

"Now then," said Jesus, "being already north of Bethsaida, we shall not go back into town. Let us continue in this direction and go up to Caesarea Philippi in the foothills of Mount Hermon."

So we set out on another journey, and none of us dared to ask if we should take provisions. We all knew Jesus could amply multiply the food given him by the man no longer blind.

As we walked along, Jesus explained to us what he meant when he told us to beware of the leaven of the Pharisees and of the leaven of Herod. He was talking of their corrupting influence in opposition to the teaching and miracles which Jesus was presenting to the people in a new idea of God. He was not talking about baking bread.

The walk northward from Bethsaida took us through valleys and up lower mountain slopes where herdsmen watched flocks of sheep or goats. The countryside was mostly pasture, with rock outcroppings and treed canyons, some with freshets of water, convenient to both beast and man.

We walked slowly, enjoying the breeze, birdsong, and flocks wandering freely, as they grazed on grass-covered acres spiked with meadow flowers, wild fruit trees, and berry bushes.

Our conversation involved remembering the experiences we'd had as disciples of Jesus. When we felt we needed to perceive more fully some point or spiritual basis of his teaching, we would find shade and stop for whatever time was needed to increase our understanding.

Jesus talked often about our discipline of thought needed when a request for healing was made.

He loved talking about his Father, God. He had many names for the Holy Spirit. Most often it was Father, my Father, our Father, your Father. Of course, it was natural and acceptable to refer to God as Mind, my Mind, our Mind, the Mind of everyone, everywhere, ideally every moment, all of the time.

The Spirit, the Source, the Life, the Soul, and the God who is Love all meant the same; and we used these as names of God.

"'Who is so just a god as our God?' is an unanswerable question," the Master once told us. "There is no other God. Therefore, there simply can be no comparison."

Jesus told us that God has no limited form, power, knowledge, expression, or presence.

"Moses," he said, "gave the first of God's commands—'have no other gods before me.' In plain words, no other person or thing is or can be God. Man and the universe are God's expression of God's own being. God is All—the Whole, and there is none beside Him. No man is God."

"There is a spirit in man," Jesus explained time after time, "but no man is that Spirit. That Spirit which is God has no fleshly body, no carnal consciousness, and no opposition. When man understands God, he discovers what God has made each one of us to be, to do, to know, and to prove. Knowing this, we use our unity with God to evidence God's power in every way in our individual lives."

Simon Peter and I agreed that we had a vast ignorance of God. But we were beginning to understand the unity, the oneness, and yet the distinction between God and all of God's creation.

People and all *things* are created. Creatures fly, crawl, or walk, others breathe beneath the waves of the sea. Men, women, and little children—each and every one—is created by God. What a world! It seems even more wonderful since we learned of God as the Mind responsible for bringing forth His Love in all creation.

Jesus knew we grasped the fact that man has a mind able to comprehend that Almighty God alone is responsible for the goodness and glory of all that exists.

"Each of you are tender-hearted to others," he said. "I have noticed this when pitiful persons have been brought forward to be healed. Tenderness underlies compassion, and compassion toward all men is foundation for the love of God which heals."

This was the substance of our talk as we journeyed northward along the Jordan River. We traveled on the verge of meadows and trees, and then more and more in shade as we neared the foothills of Mount Hermon. Here, in the embrace of a small plain surrounded on three sides by verdant hills, the city of Caesarea Philippi spreads out its gleaming beauty. We could see from a distance the marble temple built by Herod the Great in honor of the mythical Greek god Pan, the deity of shepherds.

We stayed in Caesarea Philippi three days, walking through the prosperous city, visiting the grotto where a likeness of the god Pan reposes in an exquisite niche amidst ferns and lush greenery. Here, waters from melting snow on Mount Hermon tumble into the city, forming pools and aqueduct diversions of water throughout every quarter, then escape into the widening Jordan as it continues to flow southward.

Jesus cautioned us, "Don't be seduced. The kingdom of God is many times more beautiful. Pray to attain the spiritual consciousness that is the kingdom of God.

"My kingdom is not of this world," he would say when we were enraptured by earth's beauty. Then he would quote the words of Esaias.

> Since the beginning of the world, men have not heard nor perceived by the ear, neither has the eye seen, O God . . . what is prepared for him that waiteth for Him.

Jesus often pointed out to us the wisdom of God's ways: That water always flows to its lowest level. That the sun rises and sets oppositely, yet travels north and returns over months toward the south. Seasons show this progression—for seedtime, growth, harvest, and the time of rest follow the sun.

There may be cause for sadness in some happenings on the earth. From clouds, rain falls and becomes floods on earth. Or sun burns away the clouds that should water the fields, and in drought the tender vine no longer grows.

In the kingdom of God—the consciousness of things spiritual—such events never occur. At God's command, the heaven and the earth of Spirit is unerringly protected and provided for. There is no curse upon man or his offspring; consequently, there is no need to till the soil or otherwise work to acquire needed possessions. Also, there is no gathering of water into seas. Water and all needed things spring from Mind as needed.

How we treasure his teaching. How we need to become aware of the reality of spirituality and become, as Jesus is, conscious of heaven and earth as spiritual.

On the third day, Jesus led us away from the grotto of Pan to a place of shade and water in the northward foothills at the foot of Mount Hermon. We were sitting where moss cushions the ground when Jesus suddenly posed a question, "Whom do men say that I the Son of man am?"

We answered variously, "Some say, as does Antipas, that you are John the Baptist . . . Some think you are Elias . . . Others speculate, 'He is Jeremias, or one of the other prophets come back to earth.' Everyone seems to have a different opinion of you."

Jesus sat there thinking about this. "But who do you say I am?" he asked. His voice was gentle, his question barely heard.

Simon, my brother, blurted out at once the conclusion we had privately reached among ourselves: "Why, you are the Christ, the Son of the living God. You are the prophesied One, anointed of God."

Jesus sat there, grateful almost to tears. "Oh, blessed are you, Simon, son of Jona. Flesh and blood have not revealed this to you. My Father which is in heaven has given you this understanding," Jesus said.

"You *understand* that I am the Christ, the Anointed One of God. This is the rock, the foundation, upon which my church shall rest.

"I shall build not a human, but a divinely instituted movement; and the gates of hell—endless human woe and death—will have no effect upon this Truth.

"Peter, you have boldly confessed that I am the Christ of God. This is the key to the kingdom of heaven. Whoever on earth knows the Christ shall be bound in heaven by the words you spoke. Whoever denies the Christ shall be unfit for heaven."

Jesus gave strict instruction that we should tell no one that he is the Christ of God.

He continued, "Soon we will go to Jerusalem. I will suffer many things at the hand of the elders, chief priests, and scribes. I will be killed, but the third day after I will be raised up from death."

At these words, my heart plummeted to the ground. I could not breathe. We all looked stricken, terribly pained.

Peter, quick to react, took Jesus by the shoulders and shook him, saying, "No! No! God forbid! It can't be true, Lord! This shall not happen to you!"

Jesus turned on Peter, saying sharply, "Get behind me! Like Satan, you are an offense to me. You don't know for what cause of God this shall be. You only think you know what it will mean to you men."

Then to the rest of us, he said, "Hear this! If any man will follow me, he must deny himself, take up the troubles and afflictions he endures because of his devotion to me, and follow me in spite of them.

"Whoever wants to save himself by forsaking me shall lose his life in Christ, but one who loses his life *for my sake* shall find it. Is anyone profited by gaining the world but losing one's own soul?

"I, the Son of man, will in time come in the glory of my Father God, with God's angels, and reward every man according to his work. Truly, some standing here will not die till they see me coming with the authority of God as life."

For three days we sat listening at Jesus's feet in our green sanctuary, wrestling with the thought that our next trip to Jerusalem might mean our Master's death. Jesus seemed reconciled to this terrible event, but I carried a cold fear in my belly and great sorrow in my heart.

He tried to reassure us that his Father would raise him from death—for I think everyone knew that none of us possessed the power or understanding that enabled Jesus to call the little maiden and the Nain widow's son from death. If not we, *who* would call him again to life?

The next morning, Jesus sought Peter, James, and John and asked them to walk with him higher up the slope of Mount Hermon. Being very high, it is snow covered all year round. From the top of its three peaks, one can see to Damascus, Tyre, and even the Sea of Galilee far to the south. They returned the next morning, telling us almost nothing about the view they must have seen. So we walked back to Caesarea Philippi, the white city, staying there a few days.

As usual, multitudes gathered when they saw Jesus. Also, as usual, scribes were there, asking the people what it was that attracted their attention.

Jesus asked the scribes, "What question have you with these people?"

Before an answer could be given, one of the multitudes came to him and knelt at his feet, saying, "Lord, my son is dumb and very disturbed. He often falls into the fire pit and often into the water."

Now this father had brought his sorely vexed son to us the previous day, asking us to heal him, but we failed; we simply could not cast out the evil spirit which caused the lad to do things harmful to himself.

Jesus sighed deeply, then said, "O faithless and perverse offspring. How long shall I be around to suffer your needs? Bring the lad to me."

Then from the midst of the crowd the little boy, Ethan by name, was brought to the Master. When the child saw Jesus, immediately an evil spirit tore him, and he fell to the ground in a seizure and lay there shaking, wallowing in foam which spewed from his mouth. Jesus reached out to the father and said, "Everything is possible to those who believe that goodness from God is also possible to man."

The father wept. "Lord, I do believe that you can heal my son. If there is a shred of unbelief, help me still!" The multitude began to crowd us; and seeing their curiosity, Jesus said to the foul spirit, "Deaf and dumb spirit, I command you to come out of this child and never again enter into him."

At that, the child was horribly shaken, and a scream that was frightening came from him. We knew the evil was destroyed, but it seemed that the child had died. In fact, many of those present said, "He is dead."

But then, Jesus bent over the child and took him by the hand and lifted him. The child was not dead. He arose, and the father and mother gathered the little boy into their arms. Their eyes filled with tears and their mouths with praise and gratitude to God. Their son was no longer dumb or epileptic.

The multitude dispersed. The happening was so profound the people went away, shaking their heads in wonder. I knew just how they felt for I too was in awe of the power of God in Jesus.

We went with Jesus to the home of the lad, and there had a fine meal. Afterward we had a moment alone with Jesus and asked, "Why could we not cast out that evil?" Jesus answered, "This kind can come forth by nothing but prayer and fasting."

"Does that mean we should not partake of food in order to become better healers?" one asked.

"No," replied Jesus, "by fasting when you are healing others, I mean you should have total disbelief of the evidence presented by the evil which needs to be destroyed.

"It seemed that the lad was miserably afflicted, and subject to great danger and distress. In such a case, one must ride hard upon one's own thinking process and deny any cause as a reality or an effect, when an alarming condition is to be healed.

"It is then that one desiring to destroy the affliction must without reservation see through the situation to the very power and presence of the Almighty. Since God, good, fills heaven and earth, there can be no reality in anything which disputes this grand fact.

"The task then becomes a necessity to bear witness to nothing but the truth of God's ever-presence and absolute power. The reality of perfection known to God becomes apparent to man in no other way. This is true fasting."

We spent the rest of the evening pondering this precept of spiritual healing. While we sat discussing this new insight, the child played happily at our feet.

His parents, having returned to the room, remained nearby, raptly interested in every word being spoken by our Master. They were very grateful.

We departed from that city, walking southward from Caesarea Philippi along the Jordan to the Galilee. We neither sought nor received much attention. Jesus did not talk much; neither did we.

Our thoughts were still struggling with sorrow, saddened by our Master's words that he would soon face death in Jerusalem.

Imagine then the depths of grief which settled on us, when, as we walked, Jesus dropped behind us a bit now and then. When any of us fell back, he slowed his pace even more. Finally he stopped, and we gathered around him to hear his words.

"Don't despair," he said. "The Son of man shall be betrayed into the hands of men. They shall kill me, but on the third day thereafter I shall rise again. Please don't despair."

What he was saying was unthinkable, yet that is all we had talked about among ourselves. Now he listened quietly to our sorrow.

"Do not tell anyone this which I have told you and now explain to comfort you," he said. "I shall rise again after three days. The days are before us when I will be delivered into the hands of men who will kill me. On the third day after I am killed, I will rise from the dead. Do you understand this?"

How *could* we understand what he was saying? My ears were offending me. Should I cut them off and throw them into the river so they would float into the briny sea after many days, and I would never hear of this evil thing happening?

We stopped walking and just stood there. No one said a word. We were afraid to ask anything of Jesus, although questions thronged my thoughts and I knew it must be the same for the others.

Who would do such a thing? Who would deliver you into the hands of those opposed to your goodness? Where? When? Why? Who of us is wise enough to waken you, even as you called the little damsel from her sleep in death? What will happen to us? Will we also be killed? Each question remained unspoken.

Then Jesus, breaking the ugly silence, said, "Let these words sink into your ears. The Son of man shall be *delivered* into the hands of hateful men." We didn't understand what he meant . . . he would be delivered . . .

It was all hidden from us, and we perceived nothing and so remained mute, not wanting to hear that dreadful events lay ahead of our Master. We didn't even say words of comfort such as, "You will prove that God is your Life" or, "We know all things are possible to those who believe."

Jesus stretched forth his arms and, like sorrowing children, we went into his embrace, not one by one but together, with Jesus in the center, we surrounding him with our arms around each other. Our hearts were in our throats, and not one of us said a word. "Let's go home," Jesus said, and we separated and walked sadly on.

Our lessons continued a few days later as though nothing threatened our Master.

We went to Jesus as he sat near the fish market, watching the people.

"Who is greatest in the kingdom of heaven?" we asked.

Jesus called a child who was playing with other little ones while their mothers gossiped. The lad leaned against Jesus's knee, happy to be near his special grown-up friend.

"Listen to what I say and change, because unless you do so, you won't even see the kingdom of heaven. Truly, I tell you, you must become as little children to enter the kingdom. Humble yourself as this child, and *you* shall be greatest in the kingdom of heaven.

"You ask how to humble yourself? Receive into your heart one such little child as this lad who came quickly when I called him, and you receive me. Anyone who offends one of these little ones who love me, it would be better for that man to have a millstone hung around his neck and he be thrown to drown in the sea.

"Grief and sorrow will come in this world. Laws will be violated, but great misery will come to the man who gives offense. Anyone whose hand does harm or his feet run to hurt a little child, it is better that such a man cut off his hand or foot to prevent harm to a child. It is better to live halt or maimed, than to have both hands and both feet yet deserve hell fire.

"Never, *never* despitefully use one of these little ones. In heaven, their angels ceaselessly look upon the face of God. Children give no offense. If one of a man's hundred sheep is lost, the shepherd leaves the flock to seek the one gone astray. Your Father in heaven is just as concerned should one of these little ones perish at the hands of an unholy man. Whoever harms on earth shall be denied heaven. Determine a man's righteousness, find him innocent, then he is as free in heaven as on earth."

My brother Simon then asked, "Lord, how many times can a brother sin against me and be forgiven? Seven times?"

With a twinkle in his eye and a glance at me, Simon's brother, Jesus answered Peter, "Not seven times but seventy times seven. Here is a lesson for all: The kingdom of heaven is like the king who was settling his accounts. One servant owed him ten thousand talents. The king had no compassion and sought to take from him all he possessed in repayment.

"The servant begged him to have patience and to give him time, for he intended to pay every cent. Now the king had compassion and loosed him by *forgiving* the debt. But that same servant was owed a hundred pence and went to his debtor, took him by the throat, and demanded payment. When asked to have patience, he refused to show the kindness the king had shown him and promptly threw his debtor into prison.

"Other servants saw this and reported it to the king. He called the wicked servant and said he should have shown his debtor pity even as he, the king, had shown pity to him. The king wanted this servant to pay immediately the ten thousand talents he owed the king. When he couldn't, the king ordered the servant delivered to debt collectors to torment him till he paid up.

"This," said Jesus to us, "is what my Heavenly Father will do: If you forgive the trespass of others against you, you will be forgiven your debts."

Knowing that we would soon be setting forth to return into Judea, Jesus sent us home for a few days. After spending those days among family members, we were eager to rejoin our Master.

Imagine our surprise, when we gathered again in Chuza's grove, and Jesus raised the question we had discussed among ourselves on the walk from Caesarea Philippi back to Capernaum.

"What was it that you disputed among yourselves along the way?"

We all held our peace, no one admitting that our question had been, "Who amongst us shall be acknowledged by him as greatest?"

Jesus went into his house and sat down, then he called the twelve of us to him. "Come in," he said, "for I have something to say to you.

"Any man who tries to be first, the same shall definitely be last and a servant to all. Do you know what I am saying to you?"

For a moment we were amazed. He knew our every thought. I, for one, felt ashamed of myself. Here was the Son of God, the Christ given to the world, and we had debated who amongst ourselves would be greatest!

Jesus called the child playing nearby to come to him. It was none other than the son of Chuza and Joanna. He had been at the point of death when his father came to Jesus in Cana at the very start of Jesus's ministry.

The lad came to Jesus, who took him into his arms and said to us, "Whoever receives one such child in my name, receives me. And whoever receives me, receives not me but God; for it is God who has sent me to show you the way to live and love, in order to experience the kingdom of heaven on earth. A little child is always greatest in my Father's kingdom." There was our answer!

To a man, we all felt our hearts burn within us. We sat in silence for a long, long time, assimilating the lesson Jesus had given us. He sat quietly, a blissful smile on his face, with the child in his arms sound asleep.

When at length the child stirred and wakened and skipped off to play, John, son of Zebedee, spoke up, saying, "Master, we saw a man yesterday who was casting out devils in your name. I didn't recognize him as one of the many who follow us. We forbade him, rebuking him because he was not one of your followers."

"Oh, John," said Jesus, "do not forbid anyone, for no one who does miracles *in my name* can lightly speak evil of me. Don't you realize that anyone not against us is for us? Learn this: whoever gives a cup of cold water to drink in my name will receive his reward, for no man can do goodness and not be rewarded.

"If your hand does intentional injury to others, cut it off. It is better to be maimed than to go into the unquenchable fire of hell. And if your eye offends, pluck it out. One can enter God's kingdom with a single eye but cannot escape hell if he leads others into paths of perdition.

"In every case of evil and injury, the corrupting worm and the consuming fire is never checked for the evil wrongdoer. He, though it is unlikely, must first cease to do evil and learn to do good. He must repent and do no wrong."

Sometimes James and John, the sons of Zebedee, and Simon Peter and I marveled that we, unlettered men lacking in wealth and status, should have been called to follow this prophet with his new and astounding spiritual message.

Now each day, Jesus seemed more restless. Simon Peter pointed out to me that his endless walking, with just the twelve of us in tow, enabled him to sort through his thoughts.

He didn't want to go into Judea too soon. He knew the Jews were seeking to kill him in order to bring a halt to his message of salvation through the perfect mind of God.

He knew that fear of death was the specter which haunted everyone. Flesh and blood is destructible, and carnal life has limits. Jesus knew that the final act of his earthly mission was to end mankind's ignorance of the fact that God is man's real life.

After several more days in and around Capernaum, Jesus told us to go ahead of him to Jerusalem to celebrate the Feast of Tabernacles.

We observe three great festivals a year, when all Israelites come to the temple sanctuary in Jerusalem. This last one, the Feast of Tabernacles at the end of the harvest season, is a feast of gathering. The people dwell eight days in temporary booths made of tree boughs, symbolizing the years in the wilderness after deliverance from Egypt.

At the morning and evening oblations each day, a priest carries into the temple a golden vessel filled with water from the pool of Siloam. It is received there with a blast from a trumpet and the words of Isaiah.

Therefore with joy shall you draw water from the well of salvation.

Jesus sent us to the feast, thinking that we might see a few people whom we healed and now considered themselves to be our own disciples.

He said, "You have done good things. Now show yourselves to the world. My time is not yet that I should be seen, but the time is always ready for you to do good works. The world cannot hate you. People seek healing, but don't follow you to hear your words. I am hated because I testify before men that the world of flesh and blood and things done by the sons of men are often more evil than good. I show them how to be children of God. Now you must go ahead of me to Jerusalem."

I was not happy with this, but I knew that he understood what was best at that time. "I won't go with you just now, my time has not arrived," he said. He urged us to go to Jerusalem, so we started off.

With heavy hearts, we arrived in time to observe the first sacrificial ceremonies. It was attended by people who took branches of palms, myrtle, and willow intertwined; and with these and fruit in their hands, men marched around the altar. It was intriguing to watch.

We did not know it, but Jesus actually followed us to Jerusalem the next day. The Jews of the temple came to us asking, "Where is he?" Other people asked the same question, and there was much talk concerning him. To some, he was a good man; to others, he was deceptive. One dared not to speak openly good things about him.

Then midway through the feast he came fearlessly into the temple, and many gathered to hear him. Some wondered aloud, "How does this man know how to teach, having never been schooled?"

Jesus explained that his doctrine was not his "but God's, for it is God who sends me. If any of you do the will of God, you will know that the doctrine is not mine, but God's. If I speak of myself, I glorify myself. But when I seek to glorify God, then I am true."

"Moses gave you the law of God," he said, "yet some don't keep the law; the temple authorities want to *kill* me."

The people were scornful of this and said, "You have a devil! Who seeks to kill you?"

Jesus answered, "If I've done one thing to help you, you believe and you marvel at healing, except when it is done on the Sabbath. But hear this: Moses gave you the rite of circumcision as our fathers had chosen it. It is performed on the Sabbath as on any other day, yet it is considered no violation of the Sabbath.

"I heal a man, making him whole in body and spirit on the Sabbath day, and it is angrily charged that I break the Sabbath. Why judge according to appearance and not make righteous judgment?"

Some in Jerusalem did know that a movement was underway to kill Jesus and were amazed that he spoke so boldly in the temple.

The temple authorities plotted how they might silence him, but no man laid a hand on Jesus because the time had not come for him to finish his work.

Many continued to believe that Jesus was the Christ promised to mankind. "When Christ comes, will he do more miracles than this Jesus of Nazareth has done?" they would ask.

Seven days of the festival passed. Now on the eighth day, a more recent tradition is observed. The last day of the Feast of Tabernacles was to be a day of solemn thought. The altar was circled by the people seven times on the seventh day, not just once as in previous days.

In the Court of the Women, the cast-off linen of the temple priests had been made into wicks for the two great lampstands there. Now the wicks were lit, and a soft glow of illumination brightened the court, the temple, and went out into nearer parts of the city of Jerusalem.

On the eighth day of the feast, Jesus stood amongst the people; and with his voice carrying far like the glow of the lamps, he said plainly, "If anyone thirsts, come to me and drink what will refresh your soul. Whoever believes the truths I speak, out of him shall flow living waters." Jesus spoke this of the Spirit, for the scriptures say, "I will pour out my spirit upon all flesh."

The people, hearing this, responded, saying, "Truly, this man is a prophet." Some said, "This is the Christ."

But others said, "Shall Christ come out of Galilee? The scriptures say that Christ comes of the seed of Jacob and from the town of Bethlehem, whence David came."

Thus, we saw that the people were divided; some would have arrested him, but no man dared touch him in any way.

Later we heard that officers sent by the council to arrest him reported back to the priests and Pharisees who asked, "Where is this man? Why have you failed to bring him to us?"

The officers answered, "Never have we heard a man speak like this man."

"Are you also deceived by him?" a Pharisee asked. "Have any of the rulers or Pharisees believed his teaching? The people who believe him don't know the law of Israel."

Then Nicodemus rose to a point of order, asking, "Does our law judge any man before it hears *from him* what he is doing?"

The Pharisees answered him, "Are you also from Galilee? Search and look into the matter yourself. No prophet has ever arisen out of Galilee." So saying, they ended the discussion, and each went to his own place to rest.

I remembered then how Nicodemus first came to Jesus in the night to inquire if he was a prophet in Israel. Now Jesus rejoiced when told that someone among those who sat in the council understood his mission. And he was glad to hear that Nicodemus had asked this important question, "Does our law judge a man before it hears from his own lips what he is doing?"

When in Jerusalem, the Mount of Olives was a favorite place of our Master. He would spend long hours there—thinking, instructing us, listening to our discussions, or answering many questions that we had about the healing work.

Sometimes we disciples slept in the olive grove on the Mount of Olives when Jesus went on to Bethany to be with his dear friends, Lazarus and Martha and Mary.

Early one morning, after the Feast of the Tabernacles, Jesus went to the temple. Many came to where he stood watching the people come and go. So he then sat down and began to teach about the kingdom of God.

Several scribes and Pharisees came to him and abruptly casting a woman down at his feet, said, "She is an adulteress; we took her in the very act!"

The scribes and Pharisees were testing Jesus that they might make an accusation against him: "In the law of Moses we are commanded to stone her. But what do you say?"

Jesus answered, "I say four words: 'Where is the man?' In the command of Moses, the man and the woman—both of them shall die."

Jesus then stooped down and wrote in the dust with his finger. The question was raised again, "We know she should be stoned to death, but what do you say?"

Jesus stood up. Looking every man straight in the eye, he said, "He who is without sin among you can cast the first stone." And again he stooped and continued writing.

Each man, hearing the Master's wise words and seeing his own sin written in the dust, felt guilt in his conscience. The accusers then went out one by one, the eldest first, until no one remained.

Jesus stood up. "Where are your accusers, woman? Has no man remained to condemn you?"

Her answer was plaintive, "No man, Lord."

Jesus said, "Nor do I condemn you. Go. Never sin again." And he sent her away, comforted with his words.

He returned to his work teaching in the temple treasury. "I am the light of the world. Follow me and walk no more in darkness, but rather in possession of the light of life," he said.

A Pharisee spoke from the fringe of the people, "You are bearing record of yourself. Your record is not true."

"Though I bear record of myself, it is true. I know whence I came and where I am going. You know nothing of this light. You judge after the flesh. I judge no man. But *if* I judge, my judgment is true, for I'm not alone. I am with the Father who sent me. Your law states that the testimony of two men is true. I bear witness of myself, and my Father who sent me bears witness of me."

They asked, "Who is your father?"

Jesus answered, "If you had known me, you would have known my Father."

No one dared to arrest him. The hour had not come when he should be subject to inquisition.

Jesus continued, "I go my way. Where I go, you cannot come. You seek me, but will perish because of your sins."

This perplexed the Pharisees. "What do you mean, we cannot come?" one asked.

Jesus said, "You cannot come because you are from beneath. I am from above. You are of this world. I am not. That is why I say you shall die in your sins. You don't believe that I am the one sent by God. That is your mistaken thought. You believe that all life is of flesh—yes, you will die because you limit life."

The Pharisee snorted. "Who are you that we should believe you?"

"I am just what you were told in the beginning. I am the one sent of God to bring new light into the world. I have many things I could say to you and about you, many things in judgment; but God has sent me to tell the world the things I have heard from Him."

They understood nothing of what he was saying.

Jesus continued, "When you have lifted up the Son of man, then you will know that I do nothing by myself; but as my Father has instructed me, I tell you things that shall shortly come to pass. The One who sent me is with me. My Father has not left me to do this work alone. I do always what pleases Him."

We listened intently to all that Jesus said in reply to those seeking to destroy him. It was plain that many present heard him speak these words and sincerely believed that God was his Father, always taking care of him. His next words were to them: "If you continue to listen and learn from my words, you are my disciples in fact. You shall know the truth, and the truth will make you free.

"Do not be afraid to hear and know that which is true. Do not be afraid of knowledge. To know is to have a clear understanding, to perceive with certainty, to learn. Again I say, you shall know the truth and the truth shall make you free."

To my surprise, the response to these words was a question from the Pharisees: "We are children from Abraham and never in bondage to anyone. What do you mean, we will be made free?"

Jesus replied, "I say, if you commit sin you are in bondage, for you have become servants to sinfulness. A servant does not remain forever in a man's house, but a son abides there all his life. If the Son of God makes you resistant to sin, then you are really free.

"I know you are Abraham's seed, but you seek to kill me because the things I say and teach are new to you. I tell you and show you what it means to be the likeness of God. What I have seen with my Heavenly Father I tell you, just as you tell me what you have seen with your earthly father."

"Oh no!" one man protested. "Not one of us is born of adultery or incest. We too have your Father, God, for we have been born of righteousness, not illicit union."

"If God were your Father in the way that He is mine, you would love me, for I proceed forth and have come from God who is Spirit, not flesh. I come not for myself. He sent me," Jesus replied.

"Why do none of you understand what I say? Because you don't hear my words. I tell new things, things kept secret from the foundation of creation. No man has reasoned out from God the things I speak of. But now is the time to speak these things. The family of men can now journey to the perfection of the Creator whom I know as my Father, my source, my origin, and my life eternal. This way has not been clearly known before now.

"You are of your father, the devil," Jesus continued. "He claims the race of man is of the dust and sentenced to death and oblivion. The devil is a murderer from the beginning. He abides not in truth because there is no truth in him. He speaks lies, his own falsity. A liar fathers only lies. He appeared first as a serpent, tempting disobedience to the Creator. He said God planted a tree bearing fruit both good and evil. The devil speaks of himself, not of God Almighty.

"My Father is Creator of only that which is good. I speak truth, but you do not believe me. You cannot convict me of sin through disobedience. I am speaking the truth. Why don't you believe me? I tell you why: Whoever is born of God, hears God's words which promote truth, goodness, and love. You don't hear these words, proving that you are not of God."

His audience did not appreciate what Jesus told them about themselves. Someone called out, "You are not a true man of Judah, but a Samaritan, and Jews have no dealings with such as you. You have a devil, not we."

Jesus answered, "I have no devil. I honor God. I don't seek my own glory. There is One who seeks the righteous and judges the unrighteous. My Father is that One. He has sent me.

"Truly I tell you, if a man keeps the things I say alive in his heart, as a guide to his thoughts and actions, he shall never see death. Before Abraham was, I AM."

At once the Jews seized the Master's words. "Aha! Now we know you have a devil. Abraham is dead. The prophets have all died. Who do you think you are?"

Jesus had a ready answer. "If I honor myself, it counts as nothing. Believe this, or don't: it is my Heavenly Father which honors me, enabling me to do miracles. When you observe His miracles you say he is your God yet it is clear that you have not known Him as I do.

"But I know Him, and if I were to say 'I don't know Him,' I would be a liar even as all of you are. But I know Him. I keep His saying and show you His power and goodness. Your father Abraham looked forward to seeing my day. He has seen it and is glad."

At that, the Jews laughed and said, "You aren't even fifty years old, and you say you've seen Abraham?"

"Truly," Jesus replied, "truly I say to you, before Abraham was, I AM. I am man created by God's divine Mind, the original spiritual man, the image and likeness of God. I am the anointed of God, the Christ. I AM He, indeed."

"Stone him, stone him" was the cry of those standing near listening to this exchange of words. Jesus hid himself in the midst of his followers. We moved protectively through the irate mob and passed through the temple precincts in stately flight from those venting their anger and hatred. Not a stone touched us.

Chapter 12

As we passed through the city en route to the Garden of Olives, Jesus saw a man we'd noticed before, a man blind from his birth, sitting, asking alms; and we all stopped.

We were curious, and someone asked, "Master, who sinned, this man or his parents, that he was found sightless at birth?"

His answer: "Neither the man nor his parents. Do not look for cause when you intend to heal. The Mind of God is, in reality, the one and only Cause.

"This man will see the glory of God, for the works of God will be displayed in him. It is the fleshly mind that wants to have a reason for the ills of the flesh. As I have told you before and now once again, the condition to be healed is never of God, but when healed it is to the glory of God.

"Sightlessness opposes the truth that God is all-seeing, all-knowing, and the fact that man is God's perfect image. The opposite of Truth is falsity, a lie, a mistake. Truth is real. Every error is unreal. That is why errors can be corrected and healed. Never seek the reason why evil appears real, producing limitation in someone.

"It is my task to undo the heavy burdens and to let the oppressed go free. This is the will of my Father. I must work the works of Him who sent me while it is day. The night will come when no man can work such blessings. As long as I am in the world, I am the light of the world."

So speaking, he spat on the ground and mixed the spittle into clay. Then he daubed the clay on the man's eyes. "Go now," Jesus ordered the man. "Wash in the pool of Siloam."

To reach the pool, the blind man had to enter an aqueduct through which water was sent to the underground pool. The pool itself is very large, hewn in rock. It is a reservoir. Water spills into it from a small basin fountain cut in the rock at the terminal end of the aqueduct.

The blind man entered, walking upright into the aqueduct at the outer border of the Valley of the Cheesemongers, the Tyropoeon. The tunnel grows smaller; and the blind man had first to bend, then drop to his knees, and finally crawl on hands and knees to reach the pool. But this he did, obeying the command of Jesus. At the pool, he dipped his cupped hands into the water of the basin. He washed from his eyes the clay still anointing his eyelids. He was soon thoroughly wet, and it was still very dark to him. When he finished this chore, he had to back away from the pool. Then turning when there was enough space, he crawled back through the stream of water, his eyes still closed.

We were waiting near the entrance and heard his call before we could see his form. Then he stood upright and walked into the daylight. We cheered. His eyes open, his face was now wreathed with the joy of sight. When he emerged from the dark, he looked around and asked, "Where is that man who touched my eyes? I don't hear his voice!"

We told him the man's name was Jesus and that he had walked on, knowing for certain that the blind man would come forth, seeing for the first time in his life.

The man departed to his house, a friend showing him the way. We followed along. When his neighbors saw him walking freely, they found it hard to believe that he could see and told us, "This fellow sat and begged." Some of the people said, "But this is he." Others said, "No it isn't, however he does resemble the man who begged."

At this, the man confessed, "I *am* he."

The neighbors wanted to know, "How were your eyes opened?"

He answered, "A man named Jesus made clay and anointed my eyes. Then he told me to go to the Siloam pool and wash. I went and I washed, and now I have my sight."

Someone in the crowd that gathered asked, "Where is this Jesus?" The healed man said, "I don't know."

A day later a few men in the group said, "Come then." And they took him to the Pharisees. Did they rejoice at the man's ability to see? No! They wanted to accuse Jesus, for he had healed on the Sabbath a man born blind. So they questioned the man again.

"He put clay on my eyes. I washed, now I see," he explained.

The Pharisees announced, as if it were decreed, "This man Jesus is not of God. He transgresses the law of Moses. He does not keep the Sabbath."

One of the neighbors spoke differently, "How can a man who is regarded to be a sinner do such miracles?"

The people were about evenly divided on the issue. Again the Pharisees questioned the man. "What do you say about the one who opened your eyes?" He answered, "He is a spiritual seer. He saw me as I am seen by God."

"Come now, confess that you weren't really blind. Let's see what your parents have to say. Call them. We want to question them."

They were brought in before the Pharisees who asked his father and mother, "Is this your son? Was he was born blind?"

"He *was* born blind."

"How was his sight restored that he can now see your faces?" was the next question.

"By what means he now sees, we don't know. Neither do we know who opened his eyes. He's not a child, but of age to be a witness. Ask him. He can speak for himself."

It was evident to those of us standing by that the father and mother of the man feared the Jews. Anyone who confessed that Jesus was the Anointed One promised by God would be put out of the synagogue. That is why the parents said, "He is old enough to answer. Ask him."

So again they called the man who used to be blind and said to him, "You should be praising God. We know that this man you claim has healed you is a sinner."

"Whether he is a sinner or not, I have no knowledge of him. The one thing I do know is that I was blind, but now I see," he replied.

So the Pharisees persisted. "What did he do to give you sight? How did he open your eyes?"

The man answered, "I've already told you. But you don't credit my words. Why do you ask me again? Do you contemplate becoming his disciples?"

The Pharisees became very angry. "We know Moses talked with God, but as for this fellow, we don't know where he is coming from and who gives him power to heal."

The man replied earnestly, "Why, this is a marvelous thing that you don't know whereof he has this power, yet you see that my eyes have been made to see. We know that God doesn't regard sinners, but if any man truly worships God and does the will of God, he does not sin. God must know this man.

"From the beginning of the world it was never heard that any man opened the eyes of one who was born blind. If the man who opened my eyes to see was not of God, he could do nothing."

The Pharisees consider all men as descended from Adam, and they said, "You, like everyone else, is born in sin, yet you presume to teach *us*? Away with you! Out! Out of this place."

Thomas and I, and Thaddeus and Nathanael bar Tolmai had remained in the throng when this questioning took place in the temple. Now we hastened to find Jesus and tell him what happened after he had slipped away. Hearing that the man had been cast out of the temple, Jesus asked us to help find him; but it was Jesus who finally found the young man.

"Do you believe that man can be the Son of God?" Jesus asked him.

The answer was sincere. "Who is he, Lord, that I might know this man?"

"You are talking with him at this very moment."

The man's face brightened with joyful recognition. "Oh, my Lord, is it you? Truly I believe! I not only hear your voice, I can see your face."

Jesus accepted his worshipful words and said, "For truth and righteous judgment I am come into the world that those who see not—that is, who do not understand the truth about God and man—might see and know; and that those who see not have been made blind through unrighteousness. But they also may learn to think as God thinks. The kingdom of God is now coming on earth."

As usual, there were Pharisees standing among the people listening to Jesus. "Are we blind?" they asked.

"If you were blind to unrighteousness, you would have no sin. But you claim to see, even though you doubt righteousness. You credit evil thoughts and deeds as real. Yet you claim to believe in God. It is sin when you challenge the works of God and deny the glory due His name."

Jesus quit the debate, ended his discourse, and walked away, leaving the people to ponder his words.

A day or two later he went again into the temple and sat down to teach. Many gathered. He began: "Hear my words. You dwell in Jerusalem. Some among you have come from the country round about and have seen shepherds tending their flocks. You know the sheepfold is where the flocks are brought to bed down and are kept safe in the enclosure for the night hours.

"The shepherd guides the sheep into the fold. They come and go by the entry. If a man seeks to enter not by the door but by climbing in some other way, he is most likely a thief. When a shepherd comes, the doorkeeper of the fold, who knows the voice of several shepherds, will open to him. The sheep hear their shepherd's voice calling them. Then they separate from the other flocks and are led in or out.

"The shepherd goes before his own sheep, and they follow for they know his voice. A stranger they won't follow. Sheep run from strangers."

Other people present were listening, and they wondered why Jesus was talking about sheep and shepherds.

"Well, then," Jesus said, mainly to his apostles but speaking loudly so all might hear. "I will speak in a parable. Let me explain what I've just said. Think of the kingdom of heaven as a place where people are kept in safety and given gentle care. I am the door through which all must enter the kingdom of God.

"Others try to enter but not the right way. They steal in and pretend to lead others to the kingdom. But I am the door. If any man enter by me, he will go in and out, and find that all his needs will be provided for. A thief comes to kill, to destroy. I am come that men may live forever, supplied abundantly with every good and needed thing.

"I shepherd my flock and am willing to give my life for those who follow me and obey my voice. A hireling will not sacrifice himself to protect his flock from wolves that kill and scatter the flocks. Because he is only a hireling, the hireling flees. The sheep do not belong to him.

"Now as to the kingdom of God, I am the shepherd of His flock, and my sheep hear me. The Father knows me, and I know the Father. I lay down my life for my sheep. Other sheep I have which are not of this fold. They rest in other places, but in time I will bring them also. They in time will hear my voice and then follow me. There will be one Shepherd and one fold for the sheep.

"My Father loves me because I am willing to lay down my life and take it up again. No man will take my life from me. I, of myself, will lay it down. I have power to take it again. My Father has commanded me to do this."

This caused a division among the Jews. Some said, "This man has a devil. He's mad. Why listen to him?"

But others said, "Can a devil open the eyes of the blind? These are not words spoken by someone who has a devil."

Jesus then led us away from Jerusalem to Bethany. We rested in the vineyard of Lazarus while Jesus spent many hours with his dear friend Lazarus and the sisters, Martha and Mary.

Winter came and with it the Festival of Lights, known also as the Feast of Dedication. It celebrates the ancient purification of the temple and continues for eight days like the Festival of Tabernacles.

It commemorates the end of Greek idolatry and the desecration of the temple by Antiochus Epiphanes, who set up a statue of Jupiter in the Holy of Holies, sacrificed swine on the altar, robbed the temple, and ordered destruction of all the sacred scrolls that could be found.

All Israel celebrates this feast. So again we went up to Jerusalem. We walked with Jesus in the porch believed to have been built by King Solomon—a magnificent colonnade on the east side of the temple, above the Kidron Valley.

Several Jews saw Jesus and came to him, saying, "Why keep us in doubt. If you are the Messiah, tell us plainly."

Jesus answered, "I've told you in many of my discourses, but you find it hard to believe. Consider this: The works I've done in the name of God, my Father in heaven, bear witness that the Father has sent me. Still you don't believe me. Why? Because you are not of my flock.

"My sheep hear my voice and follow me, and I give them eternal life. They shall never perish. No one can pluck them away from me. God, my Father, gave them to me, and I am given to them for salvation.

"God is greater than all else. No one can pluck my followers out of His hand. I and my Father are one!"

Again they sought to stone him. "I've done many good works," he said in answer to the threat. "For which of the works do you stone me? I showed them to you, as from God."

"It is not for the works that we stone you but for your blasphemy, and because you, a man, make yourself God," they answered.

"Now listen," Jesus said. "It is written in the Psalms, 'I have said, you are gods, and all of you are children of the most high.' If the psalmist called them gods unto whom the word of God came—and the scripture cannot be broken—do you say of him who is sanctified and sent into the world by the Father 'You blaspheme!' because I said 'I am the Son of God'.

"If I don't do the works of God, then don't believe me. But if I do, though you may not believe me, believe the works, so you can know and understand that the Father is in me and I in Him."

This enraged those listening, and the people tried to hold Jesus. But he struggled and escaped their clutches, and we ran from the porch into the town, then fled into the hills toward Jericho.

As soon as we could safely do so, we went into a place beyond the Jordan, beyond Bethabara, where John had first baptized, where I had worked there with him.

Many people came to Jesus in desperation, saying, "John did no miracles, but everything John said about you is true." Many in that region remembered this, and they let it be known that they believed that Jesus was truly the Messiah.

He continued to teach and to heal. The time was coming when he would be received for sacrifice, but before then, we went back again into Judea and on to Samaria. Jesus sent messengers to make ready for our arrival. But when it was learned that it was his intent to return later to Jerusalem, the Samaritans refused to receive him.

James and John were incensed at the refusal, and, going to Jesus with this message, their anger spilled out of them; and they said, "Lord, do you want us to call fire from heaven to come down and consume them as did Elias upon the prophets of Baal?"

Jesus rebuked them, saying, "You don't know what manner of evil spirit you are expressing, for as the Son of man, I came not to destroy men's lives but to save them."

So we left Samaria and went directly across Judea to where we could cross over the Jordan River to another city in Peraea.

Here only the most devout of Jesus's followers continued with us. There were about seventy who were steadfast, and they sincerely wanted to learn to do the works our Master did—works that made men sane and whole and healthy.

Jesus decided this was a good time to train them in proof that the doctrine he'd given was for all men. But first he gave them instruction, repeating what he had taught when we twelve were sent forth to heal.

> The harvest is great. The laborers are still few. Continue to pray to
> the Lord of this harvest to send forth laborers into His harvest.

When you go forth, you will be as lambs in the midst of wolves. Give no occasion for them to destroy you.

Do not contend with your opposers.

Do not argue to make them understand what you know and how you use it.

Be sure that when you intend to heal, the sick person desires your ministry. Salute one's consciousness before you enter.

Know without doubt that all things are possible to God.

Do not promiscuously spend the healing talent.

Hold fast the awareness that it is not *out there*, that your healing will be wrought. It is within you as a reflection of God and your understanding, your stillness.

God reveals the solution to every need. Then move in thought to see clearly, really, that all who are nearest the one needing healing are also aware of the grace of God and the power of His truth and love.

First banish fear, yours and of those surrounding the person needing your healing prayer.

Pray that everyone is released from anxiety, uncertainty, and doubt.

Know the ever-presence and all-power of God.

Know God to be All in the goodness of every heart and soul.

Know that nothing can interfere with your awareness of healing and your recognition of this from others.

Understand clearly that nothing can delay, destroy, deny, or divert the evidence that God, good, is ever present and all-power.

Hope is fulfilled when faith seeks healing for the glory of God. Be steadfast in your knowing, and show fearless confidence that all things are possible to God . . . that in reality, all is God's perfect creation and that with God there is nothing to fear.

Take no scrip in which to carry provisions. Have no purse in hand, no shoes on your feet.

Make no offering to those you meet along the way. Go to the home; but before you enter, pronounce peace upon the house, and if you are greeted peacefully, you will be welcome to enter. If not, let your peace remain. Be not dismayed, but don't enter that house.

Let discouragement fall to the ground; do not carry it with you.

Where you are welcome to enter, remain and partake of the food and refreshment offered to you.

You are worthy of your hire.

Do not just go from house to house. Be sure you are welcome to enter the consciousness of those who need healing and will accept your ministry.

Likewise, in every city you enter, if welcome, abide there, eat what is provided and heal the sick of that place. Say to them with conviction, "The kingdom of God has come to benefit you."

If you are not welcome in any city, be not dismayed. Leave that city, saying, "Even the dust of your city we leave with you, wiping it off as we depart. But know this: it is the kingdom of God which is being brought to you."

Understand this: If any despise you, know that they despise me. Whoever despises me, despises the One who sent me. Now, go forth to heal in the name of our Father in heaven."

Two by two the seventy new healers eventually returned to Bethabara, where we were staying. They had been sent to villages where Jesus himself intended to later preach the news of the kingdom of God within man.

Such joy! The new disciples joyfully recounted the healing success. Their voices rang with gratitude as they told of their spoken prayers, and prayers often expressed affirmatively in exquisite silence that proved the fact of God's kingdom being within each man's heart.

No one argued with the supremacy of God, of God's ever-presence and all-power, of God who creates and maintains both heaven and earth and all that they contain.

One after another, the seventy expressed amazement at the response of the people. The evils of fear and of demon possession, shown in many plagues and sicknesses, yielded to the power of knowing God in the new way taught by Jesus.

There was immediate response when people were told the truth that it was the presence of God which heals—proving that lies, ignorance, and fear have no origin, no source, no support, no substance, and that no disease can be manifested or further evidenced when one acknowledges and trusts the power of God to heal.

All that God makes is, like God, pure and perfect, enduring and real. What is not made by God is temporal, unreal, and needs to be healed through perfect mind.

How well we knew these thought processes. How easy it was to share the joy and satisfaction of the seventy. How perfect their report to our Master: "Even the devils are subject unto us through your name!"

Jesus met their success with a joy of his own. "I beheld the adversary as lightning fall from heaven. Nothing can resist the presence of God. You have also learned through my teaching that you reflect God's power and can tread even on serpents unharmed, for things subtle or evil cannot tempt or deceive you.

"No scorpion can put forth venom to sting you or cause you to suffer. You have power over every fear which causes harm, suffering, or death. Nothing can in any way hurt you.

"Despite all this, do not rejoice simply that things which are evil are healed. Rejoice also that your names are written in heaven. Through healing work, you prove that you are acquainted with God, that God hears righteous prayer and has answered."

With quiet but inspired appreciation, Jesus prayed aloud,

> I thank you, my Father, Lord of heaven and earth, that you have hidden these things from the worldly wise and cautious. Instead, you reveal them unto those who have innocent and loving hearts. Even this is good, for it is your will, and you know to whom the word of truth is sent and which, when received, will produce blessed results.

> All things are delivered from you, Father. No one recognizes you as Father but your Son. And none know me as your Son but those to whom I, your Son, reveal You.

Jesus then turned to the twelve of us and said in a voice barely heard,

> Blessed are your eyes which see what you know can be seen. I tell you, many prophets and kings desired to see the things that you behold but did not see them. They hoped to hear the things I say to you but never heard them.

From the people gathered around to hear the Master came a call from a local lawyer, who stood forth in their midst to test Jesus, saying, "Master, what must I do to possess eternal life?"

Jesus answered, "What does our law say? How do you read what is written for the instruction and guidance of every man?"

The lawyer answered, "I am to love God with all my heart, soul, and strength, and mind, and my neighbor as myself."

"Yes," Jesus said. "You have your answer. Do this and you will live."

"But who is my neighbor?" the lawyer asked, as if to show himself willing to obey the law.

Jesus replied, "Let me tell you. Once a man traveling from Jerusalem to Jericho was set upon by thieves. They took his clothing, leaving him naked. They beat him and left him half dead on the highway.

"A priest came along, saw him, and then went on, walking on the other side of the road. A Levite came along, looked the poor fellow over and continued on his way . . . again on the other side of the road.

"A Samaritan came along. When *he* saw the man, he went to him, and with pity he took care of the man, pouring in wine to cleanse, oil to comfort his wounds, and then covered them, binding flesh securely with bands. He clothed the man and, putting him on his own animal, he took him to an inn. He cared for the man that night.

"Needing to journey on the next day, he gave money to the innkeeper, asking that care be given to the man. He asked that money be spent for whatever was needed for further care, assuring the innkeeper that he would repay him when he again came that way."

The lawyer listened intently. Then Jesus asked him, "Which of these three—the priest, the Levite, or the Samaritan—was neighbor to the man who had been beaten?"

"The Samaritan who showed mercy," was his reply.

"Yes," Jesus said. "Now go, and do the same to others."

With that, we left Bethabara. Crossing the river, we traveled westward beyond Jericho, as far as to Bethany. As we had done many times before, we stopped at the house of Lazarus. While Jesus visited with Lazarus's sisters, Martha and Mary, we companions camped beneath the double row of olive trees which bordered the hillside vineyard owned by the family. Our resting place was in the corner where there was a well and a ring of stones we used for our firepit.

That evening, the two sisters came, as usual, with warm loaves, dried fruit, soft cheese, and wine. Martha was a good woman, and her sister Mary helped her. Together they maintained the comfort of their home and kept the avenue of olive trees neat and ready to welcome us. Even the path through the vineyard was free of twigs and stones sharp to one's tender feet.

We enjoyed our repast then settled around the fire to discuss the things we'd learned from Jesus that day. The next morning we helped Lazarus with some chores in the vineyard.

Martha was bustling around as usual, waving cheerily, and speaking lovingly whenever we saw or met her on the path. But Mary sat at the feet of Jesus, listening to explanations of his healing and teaching work.

I noticed that Martha seemed to grow weary, and we later learned that she needed help, for she planned to send us a substantial meal that evening.

She confessed, "I went to Jesus this morning, asking him to bid Mary to do her share of the work. I found Mary at his feet," she said, "hearing his words and learning more about his way.

"'Jesus,' I said, 'don't you care that Mary has left all the work to me? I cannot serve alone. Please bid her help me!'"

Humbly, Martha told us how Jesus responded to her plea. 'Martha, Martha,' he said kindly, 'you are considerate and careful in all that you do, but you are much troubled that things be just so. One thing is needed by all; that is, to know God. Mary has chosen to learn more of the things of God. She has chosen the better part, and I cannot take her from it. Instead, dear one, lay aside your broom and join us!'"

"And I did!" Martha assured us, saying, "Jesus was right, Mary has chosen the good part, and I am grateful my eyes have been opened to see this. My housework can wait."

It was no wonder to us why Jesus loved to visit this sweet family.

On the third day Jesus came to us in the grove. "I'll sleep here with you tonight. At daybreak we'll move on. I'll join you later this evening," he said, and he walked back to the house.

At dusk he came to us, in company with Lazarus and the sisters, all of them bearing food to be shared around our fire. It was a sumptuous meal, indeed a savory one, with roasted fowl, a good pottage, and thick bread to be used as a sop for the stew or to dip in olive oil, if one so chose. There was a mix of cold lentils, cucumber, mint, and garlic, dressed with a vinegar of wine mixed with honey. There were curds and finally chopped fresh fruit sprinkled with sweet wine and served with cakes made with fine flour, buttered wild honey, and crushed nuts.

After this we wiped our fingers and hands with wet cloths and carried the remnants of the meal back to the house, and there we bid our grateful farewell to these people.

Jesus walked back with us to our place in the grove. "I want to pray awhile," he said. "Rest now, and we will talk later."

Some of us slept, others remained silent.

I watched the Master sitting apart from us a bit as he closed his eyes and entered into that stillness which always interested me. Quite a while later he stirred, and we wakened the sleepers amongst us and gathered close to the fire, for it was very dark and the air seemed cooler.

I said, "Master, John taught his disciples, now will you too teach us once again how to pray?"

Jesus smiled, and we drew even closer to him.

"When you pray," he began, "speak understandingly, words such as these, in like manner and simply.

> Our Father, abiding in heaven,
> Sacred is your name.
> > May heaven's dominion draw near.
> And may your divine intent appear
> > As in heaven so also upon the earth.
> Supply each day our daily needs.
> > Overlook lovingly our offenses to you
> Just as we overlook the offenses of others to us.
> > Bring us to righteousness
> That we do wrong to no one else;
> > Rescue us from that which would
> destroy the harmony and perfection
> > of all we should think and do in your name.
> For you, dear Father of all, rule over all; your power is used for good
> alone, and your glory of grace and peace is forever given to all.
> > Amen.

Having given us the essence of prayer in these words, he then questioned us. "Suppose you have a friend who comes in the middle of the night, asking you to loan him three loaves of bread because a friend has unexpectedly stopped for the night at his house and he has nothing to feed him. Would you call back to him, saying, 'Do not bother me, my house is closed for the night, and the family is in bed, as I am, and I cannot get up to give you what you need'?

"I say you might not make the effort to help him simply because he is your friend, yet because of his urgent need, you *will* arise and give what he has asked. Just so, in your need ask your Heavenly Father, and it will be given you. Seek, for you will find. His love will meet your need. Knock, and you will be admitted into the kingdom of Heaven.

"If a son asks his Father for bread, will he be given a stone? Asking for a fish, will he be given a snake? Requesting an egg, will he be handed a scorpion? If you, being earthly, know how to give good gifts to your children, how much more will your Heavenly Father give the Holy Spirit to those who ask for it. The lesson is over," Jesus said. "Take your rest now, for we shall leave at first light."

I, for one, did not sleep very much. I prayed as he taught us, asking to feel forever the Father's love in answer to my prayers.

The next morning, as we walked toward the Holy City, many joined our group. Before long, a man who had a demon of dumbness was brought to Jesus.

Jesus cast out the demon by saying simply, "Come out of him, you speechless deceiver. This is a child of God; God's love, not fear, inhabits his heart and mind and tongue."

The dumbness fled from everyone's thoughts as Jesus prayed. At once the man began to speak, plainly and normally.

Some witnesses contended that Beelzebub had broken the spell. Jesus recognized their thought. He said, "A house divided cannot remain upright and serve the dwellers therein. You suggest that I cast out devils by the prince of the devils. How then can the power to cast out evil stand? But if I cast out evil by God's power, then you know the kingdom of God endures with healing effect.

"A strong man arms himself to protect his possessions. But if one stronger comes and overpowers him because the armor in which his defense is placed, fails, his possessions are plundered.

"Anyone not with me, understanding that my strength and protection are in God, is against me. Whoever does not gather goodness from my doctrine scatters abroad only his own unbelief. When a man is freed from unholiness but does not turn Godward, there is no rest for him. The unholy demon returns, completing his wickedness with added evils. God must be credited and understood as the source and power which blesses all seekers wishing freedom from that which is evil."

As Jesus was declaring these truths, a certain woman called loudly from the midst of people standing near, "Blessed is the woman who bare you, and blessed are the paps at which you nursed."

Jesus answered her, "Yes, but even more blessed are you who hear the Word of God and keep it."

All this took place as people gathered. The crowd grew thick, and Jesus wondered that so many came to hear him. "This is an evil generation," he said. "I am asked to give you a sign. No sign is to be given but the sign of Jonah who survived three days in the belly of a great fish. His sign was to the people dwelling in Nineveh. I shall give the same sign to this generation.

"I thereby shall light a candle that, when placed on a candlestick, all may see and seek to dwell in its light. The light of the body is your eye. With singleness of vision, your body will be illumined with wisdom from on high. But if your eye sees evil as reality, your body will be devoid of light and dense with darkness. If you have no part with darkness, your body will reflect the light, even as a room is transformed from darkness to light when a candle is lit and placed up high." There was a murmur of approval as Jesus finished the day's lessons.

The time for the evening meal approached, and a Pharisee living nearby invited Jesus to dine with him. They went into the house and sat down to eat. The Pharisee remarked that Jesus did not wash his hands before eating.

Jesus answered, "You Pharisees take great care to make clean the outside of a cup and all things, but inwardly you are yourselves filled with covetousness and the wickedness of unrighteousness.

"Don't you know that washing the inside of anything makes clean the outer parts also? Does not Isaiah, the son of Amos, say, 'Wash you, make you clean'?

"Does not Isaiah then tell how to be cleansed? 'Cease to do evil, learn to do well.'

"But no! You make clean the outside of the cup and the platter, but your inward part is ravening and wicked. Did not God, who made that which is without, make also that which is within?

"Behold, all things are clean in your own eyes, for you give alms from your savings and then consider yourselves altogether pure. But woe to you! You tithe with herbs but pass over righteous judgment and the love of God for man. These you ought to have done, as well as the other.

"Woe to you who love the highest place of power and authority in the synagogues and to be hailed and greeted effusively in the marketplace.

"Again, woe to you, misery and sorrow. You scribes, you Pharisees, are as graves that are invisible. Men walk on them, not aware that death is there."

One of the lawyers in the crowd answered Jesus, saying, "Master, saying all this, you reproach us too."

Jesus agreed. "Grief to you also! You lawyers load men with burdens too great to bear, while you yourselves will not observe or lighten restrictions with one finger.

"Woe to you! You build tombs and honor the prophets whom your fathers killed. You thus approve the death-dealing deeds of your fathers.

"You build memorials to those they killed, yet justify your opposition and express the same disdain and rejection of my new prophecy, just as your fathers did to the spiritual seers of their times.

"'Therefore,' saith the wisdom of God, 'I will send the people prophets and apostles. Some, like John Baptist, shall be slain; others they will persecute. Therefore, the blood of every prophet that was shed from the beginning of the world may be shed anew in this generation. Yes . . . from the blood of Abel to the blood of Zacharias, the righteous were martyred by Jews between the altar and the temple. Truly, blood shall also be commanded of this present generation.'

"'Sorrow then shall be to you lawyers! You have taken away the key of knowledge. You enter not into heavenly understanding, and those who *were* entering in, you have kept out.'"

As Jesus said these things, the scribes and the Pharisees began to criticize him urgently with great force and threats of violence, trying to provoke Jesus to speak many more such things, for they were lying in wait to catch something from his own mouth, with which they might forge a strong accusation against him.

In the meantime, so many people had gathered to hear the dispute that they trampled one upon the other. Seeing this, Jesus called together his disciples, had us turn our back to the throng, and spoke quietly to us.

"Beware," he said, "of the leaven of the Pharisees, the hypocrisy which corrupts and depraves their practice of the traditions of the elders of Israel.

"They pretend righteousness and consider themselves more faithful to the teachings than other people. They pretend to listen to my words, but they interpret them to serve their own cause. This is the hypocrisy against which I caution you.

"They seek to destroy my doctrine and also my acceptance as the Anointed of God. Beware of the flattering words of Pharisees, which engage you in response. There is nothing covered that shall not be revealed of them nor hidden that shall not be made known.

"Be aware that the words you speak in seclusion will be spread abroad in daylight. That which you share when closeted together shall be proclaimed from every housetop."

Then Jesus called us "friends," saying to us tenderly, "And I say unto you, my friends, be not afraid of them that kill the body and after that can do nothing more to you.

"But I forewarn you now, telling whom you must fear. Fear the one who after he has killed, has further power to cast into hell. I say to you, fear him.

"Why? Because you know there is no death, so killing you does not destroy your life or mind.

"How then *has* he power to cast you into hell? By suggesting and proclaiming to the world that you could save others but not yourselves.

"God knows otherwise, and at some time all must learn that my doctrine saves from eternal punishment, death, and the lower regions in finality of life in the grave."

I had never seen Jesus so intent on preparing us for opposition in this world. We all listened with open ears and undistracted minds. Was he teaching us how to stand secure in faith after he left us? We hoped so.

He continued, speaking quietly just to us, "Five sparrows of any kind of birds are sold for two farthings to be eaten. Yet I tell you this, in truth not one of them is removed from heaven, nor is one bird forgotten in the thought of God. I tell you, every bird is numbered in the allness of good that is our very God.

"But that is not to be considered marvelous. Even the very hairs of your head are numbered. You have nothing to fear. You are of more value than many sparrows. Also, I must tell you this . . . whoever acknowledges me before men, the Son of man shall acknowledge him in the presence of the angels of God.

"But whoever rejects and disowns me before men shall in turn be denied in the presence of the angels of God. Whosoever says anything against the Son of man, it will be forgiven him. But to one who speaks irreverently, reviling and speaking contemptuously against the divine Spirit which is the Holy Ghost, this will not be forgiven any man.

"So when you are brought into the synagogues or before magistrates and legal powers, don't think beforehand how you will answer or what words you will speak. Trust this: the Holy Ghost will, in that very hour, teach you what is a just claim for you to make."

Now I, Andrew, can only speak for myself. But at this point in our Master's discourse, I felt great comfort and hoped that my brother apostles shared my peace.

However, the crowd was uneasy, waiting impatiently to hear words addressed to them by the Master. From the company of the restless, a man called out to him, "Master!"

We turned to face the people.

"Master! Master!" the man continued calling.

But Jesus went on teaching us an important lesson, warning us of latent hypocrisy and fear.

"Master," the man called again. "Speak to my brother that he divide the inheritance with me."

Jesus called back, "Man! Who made me a judge or divider of you and your brother? I say to both of you, take notice and guard against greed, for a man's life is not appraised or sustained by the abundance of the things he possesses.

"Let me tell you a story," Jesus continued, speaking now to the whole assembly. "Land owned by a man already wealthy brought forth abundantly, and he wondered what he should do because he had no place to store his harvest. So he decided to pull down his barns and build larger ones to have more room to store his produce and his possessions.

"The man said, 'Then I can say to my soul, "Soul, you have much laid away for many years. Take it easy, eat, drink, and enjoy."' But God sent this message to the man, 'You are very foolish. Tonight your life on earth will end, then who will own all the things you've provided for yourself?'

"This is how it is with those who have treasure laid away but are impoverished when it comes to God."

Jesus turned back to us. "I tell *you* this now: don't worry about your life, what will you eat? Or about your body, what will you wear? Life is more than food. Body is more than raiment. I've told you this before. I repeat my words: 'Seek first the kingdom of God, and all needed things shall be added to you.'

"Be like servants who wait at the door for their lord to return from a wedding, so that when he arrives and knocks, they are there to open the door at once. Happy are servants when their lord's coming finds them on duty, watching.

"Their lord will give of himself and make the servants to sit down, for now his intent is to *serve them instead of being served*. So, coming soon or late, watch. The Son of man, likewise, shall come at the hour when you least expect him."

Jesus said, "Who is wise and faithful enough to be made ruler over their lord's house? To serve, timely or late, it is the readiness of the willing worker that is important.

"But if the authoritative servant takes advantage of a delay and becomes harsh or wanton with the lesser servants, the *unexpected* arrival of one's lord will determine that servant's unworthiness, and he shall be loosed and sent forth with nothing. Of one to whom much is given, much will be asked.

"I am come to send fire upon the earth, but if it is already kindled, what then am I to do? My fire is for baptism, which I must endure myself, and my path is narrow until my purpose is complete.

"Do you think I come to give peace on earth? No! Division rather than peace.

"Does Micah hint of this when writing, 'A man's enemies are the men of his own house'?

Jesus turned to the people and said, "You watch the sky, and you test the direction of the wind to see when it will be hot weather. You are hypocrites, assuming wisdom from the sky but look not to the signs of these times. You judge incorrectly. Take heed. There will be a time when it will cost you dearly if you do not learn from me."

Someone in the crowd raised the question about the Galileans recently slain under orders from Pontius Pilate, procurator and agent of Rome, who then mingled the blood of these slain men with the blood of animals sacrificed on the altar in the temple. "Were these unfortunate men sinners more than all other Galileans, that they suffered such a fate?" he asked.

"No," Jesus replied. "No more than the men upon whom the tower in Siloam fell. *They* were not greater sinners than any others. But I tell you, unless you repent, you will all likewise perish.

"Hear now what I say. A man had a fig tree planted in his garden. One day he told the manager of his vineyard, 'For three years I have come to gather fruit from this fig tree but have never found any. Cut it down! It takes up space and is fruitless.'

"But the gardener said, 'Lord, wait a year longer. I'll cultivate the soil and fertilize it. If it bears fruit, that is good. If not, you then can have it removed.'"

So it was that Jesus taught us, trying to lift our thought above the limits of earth to the value of his patient, kindly, and heavenly instruction.

Chapter 13

On a Sabbath day soon after, we were again in the synagogue in a small village in Peraea. Jesus was teaching.

Among those present in the women's section was a woman for whom one could not avoid feeling great sympathy. She had been infirm for eighteen years. Whatever disease had crippled her, the effect was that she was bent over and could not lift herself into a normal standing or sitting position.

When Jesus saw the woman, he called her to him, and she laboriously shuffled to where he sat in the assembly room prepared to give the lesson that day. Taking notice of her need to be healed, he simply said, "Woman, you are loosed from your infirmity." And he reached forth and touched her hand. Even as he did so, she straightened up into a natural position. She raised her voice in prayerful thanksgiving to God. This was the first time a woman was healed by Jesus in a synagogue.

But as usual, the ruler of the synagogue became indignant. It was the Sabbath. "There are six days," he said, "in which men ought to work. Come then and be healed, and not on the Sabbath."

Jesus was quick with a response: "You hypocrite! Do not each one of you on the Sabbath loose your ox and your ass from the stall and take him to a watering place? This woman, a daughter of Abraham, bound in evil condition for *eighteen years*, should she not be loosed from this bondage on a Sabbath day?"

At those words, his adversaries were ashamed. But the people in attendance rejoiced for they had heard of the wonderful things Jesus had done for those afflicted in any way, and now they too became witnesses to one of his miracles.

Then Jesus continued teaching, "What is the kingdom of God like? I'll name a good resemblance. It is like a grain of mustard seed which a man planted in his garden. It grew and grew until it became a great tree, and birds flew and lodged in the branches of the mustard tree.

"How else may I describe the kingdom of God? It is like leaven which a woman took and mixed into three measures of meal until the entire huge mass of dough was made light and ready to be baked."

After we left the synagogue and went to the place where we would rest for the night, I said to Jesus, "Master, long ago, on that day when you taught us the eight parables from the fishing boat, while your listeners stood on the shore . . ."

Jesus interrupted me, "Yes . . . yes, Andrew. I recall that on that day I promised to explain to you the parable of the leaven. This is what it means: In the fullness of God's day, when people are able to bear it and carry forth the change which will—must—come for every man to seek and use the truth I am sent to reveal, a woman known to God from the foundation of the earth will dwell among men. The leaven she will hide is the truth that I now teach, which people find hard at this time to understand. But the woman will bring to remembrance all that I have said and done, and all who believe will do the works that I do and more."

I and my fellow apostles, when we heard these words, looked from one to another and took great comfort once again from explanation given by our Master. We knew now that his truth would never die.

We continued on through Peraea, the land beyond, with Jesus teaching in cities and villages wherever people gathered. We journeyed slowly toward Jerusalem located afar across the Jordan River.

Someone once asked Jesus, "Are only *a few* people to be saved?"

Jesus answered, "Only those will be saved who enter through the strait, narrow, and difficult entrance, for once the master of the house shuts the door and one seeks to be admitted, they will be unable to enter in. When they knock to have the door opened, the Lord will say, 'I know not from where you come.'

"They will explain that they've eaten and had drink in the Lord's house and taught His way in the streets. But He may say, 'I don't know where that was. Depart from me; you have worked unrighteousness.' Then they will weep and be wordless when they see others in the kingdom of God while they themselves are kept out.

"Many *will* come from east and west, north and south, and will be welcomed into the kingdom of God. Some who come last shall be allowed in first, and there will be some who were first, who shall enter last.

"Salvation may come early to those who live by the truth of God. Those for whom it comes late are they who in time will repent and keep the commandments and learn righteousness through the laws of God. All who make this effort to know the grace of God will find salvation."

Later that day, certain amicable Pharisees came to warn Jesus. "Leave here. Depart quickly. Herod wants to arrest and kill you."

"Thank you!" Jesus replied. "But go and tell that fox, 'Today I heal and cast out devils, and tomorrow do it again. On the third day I shall be finished, my work completed. Yet I must walk today, tomorrow, and the day following also, for it cannot be that a prophet hid and wasted away out of Jerusalem.'"

Then he lamented, "O Jerusalem! Jerusalem! You kill prophets and stone those sent to you. How often I would have gathered all your people together, as a hen gathers her brood under her wings. But you would not allow me. Behold, your temple is to be left in ruins, and truly I say to you, you will not see me until the time comes when even you shall say, 'Blessed is he that comes in the name of the Lord.'"

From then on, Jesus spent his time teaching more than doing anything else.

On one occasion, he went into the house of a chief Pharisee to break bread on a Sabbath day. Of course, all eyes were on Jesus. But also present was a man who had a condition of dropsy. Knowing that the lawyers and Pharisees present were testing him, he asked them, "Is it not morally correct to heal even on the Sabbath day?"

All present ignored the question. No one answered him. So Jesus walked up to the man, spoke a few words very quietly to him, and with that the man turned and left the Pharisees' house, the swelling gone from his body, his feet moving in a normal gait. He was healed.

Then Jesus answered his own question, "Which of you, if you have an animal, an ox or an ass, which falls into a pit, will leave him there in the pit because it is the Sabbath? I venture each of you would straightway recover your animal." No one gave back words disputing his answer.

"Then let me ask you this," Jesus said. "When invited to a wedding, one doesn't take the chief seat at the marriage feast. Why? Because a person of greater honor may have been invited, and you would be uncomfortable when asked to take a lesser seat or even ashamed because you had to go down to the lower room to be seated. But if you go first to the lesser seat, your host might bid you go higher. Then all present will respect you and wonder who you are to be so honored. Whoever exalts himself shall be abased. In humbling yourself, you will be elevated."

Then Jesus turned to his host, "When you make a special dinner, don't just call your close friends and rich neighbors or kinsmen or brothers. Do you hope to be invited back to dine at their place?

"Instead, call the poor to your feast, those who are maimed, lame, and blind. You will surely be blessed, but not by those you've called for they cannot repay you. But as a loving and just person, at the resurrection you will certainly be recompensed."

At these words, the tongue of one of the diners was loosed, and he said, "Blessed is this man—he shall eat bread in God's kingdom."

Jesus said to him, "A man once prepared a great supper and bade many come to his feast. At suppertime his servant called them, 'Come, supper is ready.' But, as if it was agreed among them, all began to make an excuse to not attend. Each one had a different reason.

"The master of the house became very angry and told his servant to go into the city and quickly bring poor people, those maimed, those who limp, even those who are blind. The servant did so, and when there was still room, he was sent to bring people in from the highways and places out of the way. 'Just urge them to come that my house may be filled with people receptive and ready, for I say to you, none of those invited shall taste the feast that I have prepared.'"

Even as he was speaking these words, many people arrived at the Pharisee's house, having heard that Jesus was dining there.

Seeing this, Jesus went out to speak to the multitude, saying, "If any man comes loving me more than his father, mother, wife, children, brothers and sisters, yes, loving me even more than his own life, he becomes my follower.

"Whosoever does not carry bravely the troubles and afflictions resulting from their devotion to my spirit and ideals cannot truly be my student. Who among you, intending to build a tower, *does not* first estimate the figures, so he knows he can afford to build and will be able to complete it? One who finishes only his foundation is ridiculed by men who say, 'This fellow began to build and now can't finish.'

"What king making war against another doesn't first sit down with counselors to determine if he has ten thousand men able to go against another king who has twenty thousand troops? Knowing the other king is still far off from the battlefield, he then sends a delegation to him to discuss conditions of peace.

"Just so, if any of you, who, having counted the cost, has not the willingness to forsake all else to follow me, you cannot become my disciple. Salt is good. But if salt loses its taste, what can make it savory again? It is not good for anything. It is simply discarded. You who have ears, hear this."

Now even publicans and sinners came to learn from Jesus. When the scribes and Pharisees took note of this, they complained that Jesus was welcoming sinners and eating with them. But Jesus paid no attention to their grumbling. Instead he gave an illustration of his purpose and intent.

"Which of you men, if you have a hundred sheep and one is lost, won't leave the ninety-nine, even if you are in a wilderness place, and look until you find the lost one?

"When you find it, you tenderly carry it on your shoulders, being very happy that you recovered the one which was lost. Coming home, you call out to your friends and neighbors, 'Share my joy! Come celebrate with me. I found my lost sheep.'"

"Just so," said Jesus to his audience, "when one sinner repents, there is more joy in heaven over that one, than over the ninety-nine good persons who never had reason to repent.

"Or," he continued, "if a woman have ten pieces of silver but loses one piece, won't she light a candle and sweep the whole house if need be, looking everywhere for it until she finds it. Then she calls her friends and neighbors together, asking them to rejoice with her, saying, 'I have found the coin which I had lost!'"

"Likewise," Jesus said, "there is joy in the presence of the angels of God over each sinner who repents."

He continued teaching: "A man had two sons. The younger asked his father for his portion of the inheritance he would someday receive. So the father divided unto *both* sons his living. The younger son went off and wasted his inheritance, living riotously. When his money was spent, he was in sore need, for a famine grew in that land and he had nothing to sustain him.

"So he went to a landowner who sent him into his fields to be a swineherd. He was hungry enough to think even the pigs' corn would taste good because no one in that place gave him good food. He thought of his home, his father, and all the household servants who had plenty to eat, while he was almost starving to death.

"*I will leave here and go to my father*, he thought. *I will confess, I have sinned against heaven and against you, my father. I'm not worthy to be called your son. Just make me a servant.*

"He returned home. His father saw him from a far distance and rejoiced greatly. He ran to meet him and embraced his son, welcoming him with kisses. The son confessed his sin against heaven and his father. But his father called to the household servants, 'Bring a new robe and a ring for his finger. Bring shoes for his feet.' Then he instructed them to kill the fattest calf in his herd and roast it. They would celebrate his son's safe return with all his friends. 'My son was dead and is alive again. He was lost and found his way home to me,' he explained to the servants.

"The older son was working in the field. As he came home, he heard music and dancing. Calling one of the servants, he asked what was going on. 'Your brother has returned. Your father is celebrating because he has received him safe and sound.'

"The older son became angry and would not join the celebration, so his father went out to bring him in to the feast. But the older son refused, saying, 'For many years I've worked for and obeyed you, never refusing to do your asking. Yet you never gave me even a young goat for a feast with *my* friends. But when my brother returns—he who asked for his share of your wealth and then wasted it with harlots—you kill the fatted calf to celebrate his homecoming.'

"Filled with compassion, the father comforted him. 'My son, truly you have never opposed me. All that is now mine is also yours. It is right that we rejoice with merriment and gladness for your brother was dead to us. Now he is alive and back in our hearts, worthy of forgiveness and love. He was lost and is found. Come and welcome him home.' Soon after, brother met brother with genuine joy."

Jesus then turned away from the scribes and Pharisees to us.

"Hear this, my students: A rich man discovered that his steward was dissipating the profit from sales of wheat and oil. He called the steward and said, 'What am I hearing about you? Give an account of your dealings or you'll be dismissed.'

"The steward wondered, *What will I do? If the stewardship is taken from me, I'll become a beggar. I am so ashamed. I know, I'll work this out some way so that when I am put out of this man's house, others will still hire me.*

"The steward then called all those who owed his lord. 'What do you owe?' he asked one who owed for a hundred measures of oil. The steward said, 'Sit down quickly and take your bill and write fifty measures and pay your bill.'

"To another he asked, 'How much wheat is owed for?'

"'One hundred measures,' he answered. The steward said, 'Take the bill and write fourscore measures. Then pay at once!'

"And so the rich man commended the unjust steward because he covered his mismanagement cleverly, protecting himself. This commendation was proof that the children of this world are more astute than the children of light.

"Now," Jesus said directly to us, "*you* must learn to be wise in this way but *for the truth*, instead of in the ways of this world. A man who is faithful will be always faithful, in this world and for truth. A man who is just will always be just; an unjust man will always be found unjust. But if you are found unfaithful in the unrighteous riches, who will trust you with the true riches? If unfaithful with another's goods, who will give you what is due you?

"You cannot serve two masters. If you hate one, you will love the other. When holding to one, it is right to despise the other. You can't serve God Almighty and make also a god of worldly riches."

The Pharisees were listening to this discourse. They were covetous and made fun of Jesus's teachings.

Jesus responded, saying, "You justify yourselves before men, but God knows your hearts. What you esteem so highly is detested by God. Until John Baptist, the law of Moses and the lives of the prophets were morally in force in man's life.

"Since the time of John the Baptist, the kingdom of God is preached, and men are urged to enter into it. It is easier for heaven and earth to disappear than for one point or small line in the letters of the law of Moses to fail to be rightly written, and each law must be obeyed.

"Whoever puts away his wife then marries another commits adultery, as does the man who marries the woman put away by her husband. This is the law. You must learn that Moses's law supports my new Gospel also. For instance, the law of kindness.

"A certain rich man lived and dined lavishly. A beggar named Lazarus lay at his gate, his body full of boils. He hoped to be fed a morsel from the rich man's table. Instead dogs came and licked his sores and he died in agony; then angels carried him into the comfort of Abraham's bosom.

"The rich man also died and was buried. But since there is no death, he also found he still lived beyond his flesh which died, but he was not comforted. He was in torment, in the mental hell he earned through selfishness in this life.

"He could see far off to where Lazarus was comforted in Abraham's care. He cried out to Abraham, 'Father Abraham, have mercy on me. Send Lazarus to dip his finger in water to cool my tongue, for I am tormented in the heat of my discomfort.'

"Abraham answered, kindly calling the rich man *son*. 'Son, you received good things in your life, and Lazarus had only evil things. Now he is comforted, and you are in torment. Besides this, there is great distance fixed from us to where you are, and any who would cannot pass from here to you, and no one can pass from there to here.'

"'I pray then,' the rich man said, 'send Lazarus to my father's house. Let him tell my brothers of my situation now, so they live in a way to avoid such torment.' But Abraham answered, 'They have Moses and the prophets. They can listen to them and obey their words.'

"The rich man said, 'No, Father Abraham. They would perceive no more than I did. But if one went from the afterlife they will repent.' But Abraham answered, 'If they won't hear Moses and the prophets, one risen from the dead will not persuade them either.'

"Does not Moses also command this:

> If there be among you a poor man of one of your brethren within any of your gates in your land which the Lord your God gives you, you shall not harden your heart nor close your hand from your poor brother. But you shall open your hand wide unto him and shall surely lend him enough for his need in that which he wants.'"

Many who heard these words of Jesus took them to heart and resolved to be more compassionate. Others also heard but cared little about changing themselves to be kind to those less fortunate.

It was a nice spring day, and we were still in the land beyond the Jordan. Jesus was pacing his slow return to Judea. He told us to find a quiet place off the traveled road, a place where we could listen while he taught a few important lessons.

He began, "Offenses will come. Nothing can change that, but woe to him through whom they come. I have told you that it is better that a millstone be hung around the neck and that person be cast into the sea, than for one to assail or wound a little child. There is no offense more worthy of punishment than this. But take care concerning your own thoughts and acts, that they give no offense to anyone of any age.

"If any of your brethren commit an offense against you, rebuke him; reprove to heal the breach between the two of you. If he repents and regrets his action, then you must forgive him. Even if he trespasses against you seven times in one day, and seven times in that day says to you, 'I am sorry,' then you shall forgive him."

One of us—I think it was Thaddeus—said, "Lord, increase our faith."

Jesus responded, saying, "Do what is right to do. If you have trust as small as the tiny mustard seed, you could say to a sycamine [fig] tree, 'Be uprooted, and be planted in the sea.' With faith in your request, that tree, responding to your command, will obey you.

"You murmur at my words," Jesus said, for we had all gasped!

"Nevertheless, I tell you, as I have told you before: When praying, believe when you pray. You have learned that all things are possible to God. That one can walk on the sea, heal all who are sick, forgive and redeem weary sinners, and raise to life those who have died. Why should not a fig tree transplant itself at your command?

"It all depends on your *knowing* that you are capable of performing wonders. But always your purpose must be righteous. Of course, there is no real reason to transplant a tree into the sea." At that, we laughed with him.

"If you have a servant working for you, which of you will say when the work is accomplished, 'Go sit down to eat'? Instead you say, 'Change out of the clothes worn working in the fields with the cattle, then fix my supper and serve me. When I have eaten and quenched my thirst, then you can eat and drink.'

"Does one thank the servant because he does what is asked of him? I think not. If you thank him, it is because you are kind. So when you have served— doing all required of you—you will not expect thanks for your obedience. Instead you will say, 'We have done that which it is our duty to do.' This is true service to God: That you learn to perform God's wonders among men. It is a duty for all who understand God."

Having taught us in this way about faith, forgiveness, and service, Jesus rose to his feet, and we followed him, talking little among ourselves but rejoicing in just being with him.

In Peraea, a messenger came from Bethany seeking Jesus. Hearing that Jesus was teaching north of where the Baptist had baptized just a few years previously, the messenger hastened to find us.

When he arrived, he went straight to our Master and said privately, "I bring you word from Bethany. The sisters of your dear friend Lazarus have told me to say, 'Lord, behold, he whom you love is sick.'"

Jesus thanked the messenger and quietly said to him, "Tell the sisters, 'This sickness will not mean death but will be to the glory of God, that the Son of God might be glorified.'"

Jesus did not return at once to Judea but continued to teach the news of the kingdom of God to people in Peraea for two more days. On the third morning, he said to us, "Now we will go back to Judea."

We apostles were concerned with the hostility of the Jews there for they had sought to stone Jesus on several occasions. "Why do you want to go there again?" we asked.

Jesus gave a strange answer. "There are twelve hours in this day. A man walks in the daylight hours and doesn't stumble because he sees the light of this world. But if one walks in the night, he stumbles, having no light." Then he said, "Our friend Lazarus sleeps, but I am going to wake him out of sleep."

We answered, "If he's sleeping, he will be fine." But Jesus spoke of his death, not of a restful sleep, so he said plainly to us, "Lazarus is dead. I am glad for your sakes that I was not there, because you will believe and not be shocked when you see him alive. At any rate, I go unto him."

Thomas Didymus said, "Let us go with our Master. If he dies, we will die with him."

A day later we arrived in Judea and were about to enter Bethany when we learned that Lazarus had been placed in his grave four days before.

When Martha heard that Jesus had come, she walked to meet him, but Mary stayed at home. When Martha met us, Jesus embraced her; and she wept as she said, "Lord, if you had come at once, my brother would not have died."

Jesus assured her, "Your brother shall rise in life again."

Martha answered, "I know . . . I know he shall rise again in the resurrection at the last day."

Jesus said, "I am the resurrection and the life; he who believes in me, though his body is dead, lives."

When these words came from the mouth of our teacher, Martha's eyes opened wide as she listened closely. "Whoever lives and believes in me shall never die. Do you believe this, Martha?" Jesus asked.

She said, "Yes, Lord. I believe! No . . . I *understand* that you are the Christ, the Son of God, prophesied to come into the world."

So saying, Martha hurried home and, finding Mary, quietly told her, "The Master is here and calls for you."

At once Mary went to Jesus, in the place where Martha had met him, for he still hadn't come into Bethany.

Because Bethany is quite near to Jerusalem, many Jews had walked out to comfort Martha and Mary. When the friends who came from the city to comfort the sisters saw that Mary left in a hurry, they followed her, thinking that she was going to Lazarus's grave in her mourning.

Meeting Jesus, Mary fell at his feet, saying sadly, as had Martha, "If you had been here, my brother wouldn't have died."

When Jesus saw her tears and those with her also weeping in tender sympathy, his spirit uttered a deep mournful sound of sorrow, for he was disturbed at the copious weeping and felt keenly their sense of loss.

"Where have you placed the body?" he asked.

"Lord, come and see," she said. All noticed that Jesus himself was weeping.

The Jews marveled, saying, "See how he loved him."

Some wondered aloud, "Could not this man who opened the eyes of the blind have caused this man to live?"

Hearing this, Jesus again groaned in sorrow, as he came to the grave which was a stone-lined chamber in the hillside, with a large stone covering the entrance.

"Please," Jesus said, "take away the stone."

But Martha cautioned him, saying, "Lord, by this time his body is corrupting and stinks. It has been four days since he died."

Jesus said, "Oh, Martha, didn't I say to you, that if you would believe, you would see the glorious power of God?" For a moment, he held her small hand in both of his.

When three men succeeded in rolling the stone from the entrance to the place where the body of Lazarus was laid, Jesus stepped closer, looked upward, and said, "Father, I thank you that you have heard me. I know that you hear me always, but because so many people stand near, I said it that they may believe that you have sent me to do this thing."

With a loud voice Jesus cried, "Lazarus! Come out!"

A few heartbeats later, we sensed movement in the shadows of the cave. Then Lazarus appeared in the entrance even though his feet and hands were bound with funeral bindings, and his face was covered, in fact, bound about with a napkin.

How he was able to rise and walk will forever be a puzzle to me. It appeared that his feet shuffled as he came into view. When his form filled the entrance to the place where minutes before he lay lifeless, we murmured in amazement.

Very quietly Jesus said to his sisters, "Loose him and let him move freely." Stunned, they looked to the Master with a sense of awe mixed with fear. Again Jesus said, "Loose him, and let him go."

Martha, ever the helper, stepped forward with trembling hands to untie the napkin knotted to cover the face of Lazarus. When the napkin was removed, Lazarus's eyes were closed, and a yawn was coming to his lips.

Martha untucked the binding under her brother's chin, loosening the burial strip as it fell away from his form, unwinding until his arms and hands were free. Mary helped pull away the bands. She let them fall downward until they lay in a heap at his feet.

Each sister then took a hand on either side of their beloved brother and Martha bade him, "Open your eyes." He did so, looking for a moment slightly puzzled. Then a small smile cupped tears falling from his eyes.

Friends who were there began to marvel, first with gentle murmuring sounds of wonder, and then with cheers, softly voiced so as not to startle the man. Only the pungent odor of fragrant spices which had anointed the body wafted sweetly through the air.

Lazarus flexed one arm, then the other, as his sisters stood close to him, enraptured by their brother's return to life. He took a step or two and then reached out both arms to gather close his loved ones. His eyes opened wide in wonder and gratefully sought the face of Jesus.

Everyone present was trembling with joy, and many tears fell to the ground as Jesus walked into the embrace of the Bethany family.

A quiet voice from somewhere in the throng said, "Praise God! Oh, praise God!" At that, we also began to make inwardly a silent hymn with those words in our hearts.

Then two strong men crossed their arms to make a seat for Lazarus, and he was gently lifted and quietly carried to his home by friends who loved him.

Nothing can express the wonder of those moments when Lazarus came back from his four-day sleep in the clutch of death.

I, Andrew Bar-jona, looked upon the assembled witnesses, and thought of them as having God's own joy upon their face. Words cannot convey the inspiration of those few moments which proved again our Master's dominion over death.

Some of those present at the resurrection of Lazarus, stubborn with previous doubts about the miracles they had heard of Jesus, now believed.

Others left, hastening back to Jerusalem to tell the Pharisees what Jesus had done in Bethany, raising Lazarus from his grave four days after death. They hoped the Pharisees could accept this supreme proof that Jesus had come to earth from God.

The Pharisees and chief priests quickly gathered a council and posed the question, "What shall we do? This man does many things beyond the power of the usual laws affecting body and life. If we do nothing, all men will come in time to believe in him. Then the Romans will deny our influence and presence as a nation."

Caiaphas was high priest that year. Later we were told that he spoke up, "You all say nothing worth my consideration. It is expedient for us that this one man, guilty or not, die for the people, in order that our entire nation does not perish.

"The people begin to call this man a king because of his spiritual dominion, and soon we shall never be able to rise against Rome. I speak not my own attitude toward this Jesus, but as high priest. Jesus should die for the nation, but not for that reason only; this death will also gather all of God's children who are scattered abroad from Israel."

From that day, plans were made to secure the death of Jesus.

And so it was that Jesus resolved to no longer work among the Jews in Jerusalem.

We left the area and walked, not westward through the valley to Samaria, but directly north. The land here is hilly and barren, sere, almost wasteland.

Our destination was the village of Ephraim, near the border of Galilee. There we spent a little time in quiet seclusion.

Soon it would be the week to celebrate the Passover. Many pilgrims go early to Jerusalem to purify themselves in the temple before the celebration begins. Therefore, the authorities were on the lookout, hoping to see Jesus among those in the courts of the temple. Not finding him, they wondered among themselves, "What do you think? Maybe he will not come to the feast?"

Now, the chief priests joined the Pharisees and gave a command that if anyone knew where Jesus was, he should report this so they might seize him. But no one knew where Jesus was.

We left Ephriam, crossing upper Judea to the Jordan River, then passed again into Peraea. As usual, scribes were amongst us to keep their eyes on our Master. Jesus didn't seem to be bothered. He just went about his work, healing and teaching. When they demanded when the kingdom of God should come, he answered directly and pointedly. Sometimes he turned away from lengthy debate with them, and taking us aside, he privately instructed us. We kept growing in spiritual wisdom and understanding.

"Do you remember when we traveled through Ephriam, in a certain nearby village we saw ten men standing far off, watching us?" Jesus asked.

"We were told that they were lepers. When they called, saying, 'Jesus, Master, have mercy and pity us,' I answered them, 'Go show yourselves unto the priests. They will certify your cleanness.'

"I knew they would be cleansed and they *were* healed as they went," Jesus continued. "Remember though, only one of the men, when he saw his flesh restored to soundness, came running back and with loud voice praised God. When he reached our group, he fell down on his face at my feet, giving thanks again and again.

"I asked him, 'Were not ten men cleansed of their leprosy? Where are the nine?' Only one returned to give glory to God. That one was a Samaritan. With gladness, I sent him on his way for it was his own faith that healed him."

Later someone again questioned Jesus as to *when* the kingdom would come. He answered, "The kingdom of God doesn't come with observation. Nor should any say, 'lo, here! or lo, there is the kingdom!' Remember this: the kingdom of God can only be found within."

Jesus warned us, "The time is coming when you will want a day like this of teaching and healing, but you will not be able to see it.

"You will be told to look here or look there. Don't go after those who claim to teach as I teach. Do not follow them.

"Lightning flashes from one place in the sky and shines across the whole spread of heaven. So shall it be for the truth spoken by the Son of man. But first, I must endure many things and be rejected by those among whom I have lived and taught.

"As in the days of Noah, so it shall be in my time. Then people ate, drank, married, and were given in marriage. But the day came when Noah alone obeyed the voice of God. He entered into safety and deliverance with his kin when the flood came that destroyed all else.

"As in the day of Noah, so shall it be in my time: few will heed or obey the message of God given through me.

"In the days of Lot, men also ate and drank, bought and sold, planted and built. But on the very day that Lot, obeying the angels, fled from Sodom, fire and brimstone rained from the sky. All in Sodom and in Gomorrah, cities of the plain, were destroyed. Even every plant growing out of the ground.

"When the truth of the Son of man fills thought on the great day of understanding, and you are on the rooftop of your house, don't come down to take any possessions. If one is in the field, don't return to the house. Remember Lot's wife. Don't look back.

"Whoever seeks to save anything from life in the flesh will lose it. Whoever loses his life in the flesh shall find his life is preserved spiritually. Your body is yours, but not you. You are an outlined consciousness in the thought of God.

"Things in the Mind of God alone will endure. Of two people, one will endure the change when good prevails over all evil. One will be taken, another will choose to remain behind."

We asked, "Where, Lord, shall the one left be found?"

He answered, "Wherever the body is, the vultures shall gather and then nothing shall remain to be found."

The next morning Jesus decided to go again into Jerusalem.

When we arrived, the city was quiet. We went directly to the temple.

As he was teaching, the chief priests and elders confronted him. They asked, "By what authority do you do these things? *Who* gives you authority?"

Jesus replied, "Let me ask you something. If you answer me, then I'll tell you the authority behind my words and works. The baptism of John . . . was it from heaven, or from men?"

His adversaries reasoned quietly among themselves. "If we say 'from heaven,' he will say, 'Well then, why didn't you believe John?' If we say John got this notion from men, the people will rise up against us; to them John was a prophet sent from heaven."

So the priests answered, "We cannot tell if it was from heaven or of men."

"Just so," Jesus replied, "neither do I tell you the authority by which I heal and teach."

He returned to his discourse.

"A man had two sons. He came to the oldest and said, 'Go work in my vineyard today.'

"'No,' said the son, 'I don't want to.' But afterward, he changed his mind and went and worked hard.

"The father likewise asked the other son to go to the vineyard. 'All right, sir, I will!' But he did not go."

Jesus asked the chief priests and elders, "Which of the two did the will of his father?" they said, "The first son."

"Truly," Jesus said, approving their answer, "but now is the telling. The publicans and harlots will enter God's kingdom before such as you.

"John the Baptist came to you teaching a way of righteousness, but you did not believe him. Publicans and harlots afterward did believe him. When you hear now of John's righteousness you still do not regret that you didn't believe him then.

"In fact, hear this parable: A certain landowner planted a fine vineyard, hedged it all around, prepared a winepress, and built a tower. Then he rented it to a farmer and took a trip away from home. When the vintage time came, the man sent his servants to receive payment from the farmer. The farmer took the servants, beat one, stoned one, and killed the other.

"The landowner then sent several more men to collect the money due him. The farmer also beat, stoned, and killed the second servants. As a last attempt the owner of the vineyard sent his son, expecting the son would be esteemed and respected.

"But no! The farmer saw the son, caught him, threw him out, and finally killed him, thinking he could then claim the son's inheritance. The landowner came home." Jesus asked the elders, "What do you think he will do to the wicked farmer?"

The answer came swiftly. "He will make him miserable and destroy him. Then he will rent out the vineyard to those who will make the payments which other renters failed to give."

Then Jesus said, "The scriptures say,

> The stone which the builders rejected, the same is become the head of the corner. This is the Lord's doing, and it is marvelous in our eyes!

"Therefore," Jesus continued, "the kingdom of God shall be taken from you in Israel and given to a nation who will bring forth the fruits of God's kingdom. Whosoever shall fall on this rejected stone shall be torn asunder. But he on whom *it shall fall* will be pulverized to powder."

As the chief priests and Pharisees heard these parables of Jesus, they realized that he was talking about them. They wanted to arrest him but feared the multitude of people who considered Jesus a prophet.

Jesus had more to say to them. "The kingdom of heaven is like a king who made a marriage for his son and sent servants to invite certain people to attend the wedding, but they did not come.

"So the king sent out other servants with the invitation telling all invited that the wedding dinner was prepared and things were now ready, even the fatlings and the oxen are killed and roasted, so come quickly to the marriage and the feast.

"Again no one accepted. The event wasn't important to them. One man went to his farm and another to his place of merchandize. Others took the king's servants, whom they mistrusted, and killed them.

"The king was furious at this, and calling his armies sent them to slay the murderers and burn their cities. Then he said to his servants, 'The wedding is ready, but the invited guests were not deserving. Go out on the highways, and whoever you find, bid them to the marriage.' Everyone, both good and bad, then came. Thus many guests were furnished for the wedding.

"But one guest had not bothered to dress in the wedding garment furnished to guests from afar. When questioned about this, he could not explain why this was his case. The king had his servants bind this guest's hand and foot and then take him away into gross darkness . . . where regret for lost opportunity calls forth ceaseless weeping and gnashing of teeth in the anger and pain of self-condemnation. His sin was—minor though it may have been—that he had no reason to give for not being at his best in the clothing provided."

The Pharisees took counsel even more frequently to determine how they might trap Jesus when he was teaching.

They sent their lackeys out in company with men from Herod's court who said, "Master, we know you are true and teach truth about the ways of God, but you don't care for any man because you don't pay attention to persons or men of position. Tell us therefore, is it lawful to pay tribute to Caesar or not?"

Jesus knew they were trying to trap him. He said, "Why do you tempt me, you pretenders? Show me your tribute money."

They gave him a penny.

He asked, "To whom does this superscription and image belong?"

They answered, "Caesar."

He said, "Then render to Caesar the things that are his. Render to God the things which are God's."

His adversaries all marveled at these words and left to go about their usual business.

Later in the day several Sadducees—who believe that the soul dies with the body and do not believe in resurrection of the dead—asked Jesus, "Master, Moses said if a man dies having no children, his brother should marry the widow and raise up children, as his brother would have done had he lived.

"There was once among us seven brothers. The first died and left his wife to his brother, for he had no children. Likewise, the same happened to each of these men in turn. At last the woman died too. In the resurrection of these seven, whose wife shall she be?"

Jesus said, "You mistake, not knowing the scriptures or the power of God. In the resurrection, no one marries or is given in marriage, but in heaven one is as an angel of God.

"As far as resurrection of the dead, God has spoken unto you, saying, 'I AM the God of Abraham, the God of Isaac, and the God of Jacob.'

"God is not a god of the dead but of the living. How then can you not believe in resurrection of the dead?"

Everyone who heard this doctrine of Jesus was astonished.

In time, the Pharisees heard how in this way Jesus silenced the Sadducees. They gathered together again to plan how to trap Jesus.

One of them, a lawyer, tried to tempt our Master. He asked, "Which is the great commandment in the law?"

Jesus in answer said to him, "'You shall love the Lord thy God with all your heart and with all your soul and with all your mind.' This is the first and great commandment. And the second is like it: 'You shall love your neighbor as yourself.' On these two commandments hang all the law and the prophets."

While the Pharisees were still gathered together, Jesus asked them, "What do you think of Christ? Whose son is he?"

They answered, "The son of David."

Jesus said to them, "Note then how David in his spirit calls Christ 'Lord,' saying,

The Lord said unto my Lord, sit thou on my right hand till I make
your enemies your footstool.

"If David calls Christ LORD, how is Christ David's son?"

No man was able to give an answer to Jesus, and from that day forth no one
questioned Jesus any further to entrap him.

But a young man came to Jesus and asked, "Good Master, what *good thing*
shall I do that I may have eternal life?"

Jesus studied the fellow silently for a moment, then said, "Why do you call
me good? There is but one who is perfect, that is God. But to enter into eternal
life, you must keep the commandments. Do not kill, commit adultery, or steal, or
bear false witness. Honor your parents, and love your neighbor as yourself."

"I've done these things all of my life, from childhood. What do I lack?"
the man asked.

Jesus said, "To be perfect, sell all that you own and give to the poor. Have
treasure in heaven. Then become one of my followers."

The lad turned and walked sadly away from us, for he was very wealthy
and had many possessions.

Jesus turned back to us. "Truly, I must say to you, a rich man hardly enters
into the kingdom. It is easier for a camel to go through the small hinged doors
set in the large city gates than for a rich man to enter the kingdom of God."

We were amazed at the words. No, we were dumbfounded. "Who then can
be saved?" we asked.

Jesus looked silently toward each of us. Then he answered reassuringly,
"With men it is just impossible, for to become rich is the goal of many. But with
God such things are possible."

My brother Peter, ever cautious, said to Jesus, "We twelve have abandoned
all else to follow you. What will we gain by so doing?"

Jesus, before answering, looked again with compassion into the eyes of each
one of us. Then he said, "Truly, I say, you who have followed me in the new
birth are separated from God no longer. You are in a different and better state
of understanding, which you must prove anew each day. In this state of newness
as children of God, when I, the Son of man, shall sit upon my throne of honor
in the presence of God among men, you too shall each sit upon a throne. You
shall be the standards by which one shall judge the children of Israel.

"All who have left houses, kinfolk, parents, wives, children, or lands for
my sake shall obtain ten times more than was forsaken and shall inherit eternal
life. But many that are first shall be last, and those last shall be first.

"The kingdom of heaven is like the man who went out early to hire workers
to work in his vineyards. He hired them for a penny a day and sent them to
gather fruit from the grapevines.

"Three hours later he saw other men standing idle who wanted to work. He hired them. He did this again about the sixth hour, and at the ninth hour hired even more workers, for the grapes were just perfect for harvest. Even at the eleventh hour, he hired some men found standing idle because no one had need for them.

"He sent these workers into his vineyard, saying each time that he would pay them what was right. That evening the steward called all the workers in from the vineyard, and starting with those hired last he gave every worker a penny.

"Those who had worked in the vineyard the full twelve hours were paid, but they thought they should receive more than all others. When they didn't, they grumbled discontentedly against the landowner, saying, 'The last worked only one hour and received as much pay as we who worked hard and long in the heat of the day.'

"The householder said to them, 'My friends, I don't wrong you. Didn't you agree to work for me for a penny? Take your pay and go home in peace. It is my business if I give unto the latest worker the same as I promised to you. My vineyard has been harvested when the fruit is at the point of perfection because I was able to hire as many as needed to complete the work today. Isn't it lawful for me to use my own money as I choose to? Must you see this as evil because I am good?'"

Jesus looked up. "As I said, Peter, those who are called first may be paid last, and the last may be paid first, for many are called. Few are chosen, for few choose to work. All who work to enter heaven will have the same reward, eternal life."

Chapter 14

Things were changing every day. We were back in Jerusalem when Jesus unexpectedly led us away from the multitude to the Mount of Olives.

"You must be made aware now of things to come," he said. "People will continue to join us everywhere we go. We will go daily into the city but not abide there. There will be tumult and danger, but have no fear.

"If any of you would find comfort, send for your kin to come as usual for the celebration of Passover. When they arrive, I will sit down with them and explain what will soon come to pass.

"But first, I have to tell you. A few days from now, I, the Son of man, will be betrayed to Pontius Pilate and ultimately handed to the chief priests and scribes and Pharisees, who will condemn me to death. They will deliver me then to Gentiles who will mock and scourge me, for they don't know who I am or why I have come to the Jews. I shall be crucified . . ."

We all gasped in protest to our Master's announcement and spoke in a babble of sorrowing words.

Crucified! The horror that word evoked was among us like the fear one feels when earth rumbles and quakes, causing houses to fly apart, trees to uproot, and one's legs to collapse beneath one's body.

We had seen crucifixions along the byways and highways where Imperial Rome flies banners over people who die upon wooden crosses because of some offense to the empire or emperor. It is a frightening scene.

It was unbearable to think that Jesus, this good man of God who taught us for so many, many months, should be considered criminal because his doctrine is not yet comprehended. His message of perfect humanhood must have seemed farfetched to one lacking faith in God. It is unthinkable to us that our Master will be sentenced to hang upon a cross because religious authorities find offense in his teachings.

If he led a revolution against Rome, people would be willing to perish from the earth if given the opportunity to challenge the yoke Rome has placed upon

Israel. But to introduce a new concept of God brought the threat of death by crucifixion instead.

Jesus broke through our dismay and sorrow. "On the third day, the Son of man shall rise again to life," he said quietly.

This is the third time our Master told us of the fate which would befall him. Yet here he was standing before us, unbowed, unafraid, certain of his immortality. He expected us to see him as able to withstand the terrible ordeal which he would endure.

We tried to rest that night, but no one could sleep.

Early the next morning James and John sent a messenger to Capernaum urging their parents to come at once to Jerusalem. Messages also went to Joanna and Chuza, Cleopas and Mary, Alphaeus and his wife.

Another messenger was sent to Cana to Jesus's mother telling her, "My time has come. Please be near. Bring my sisters and brothers with you. Travel with the family from Magdala and my dear sweet Mary."

The messages went forth as our Lord desired. It seemed from that moment on that our entourage swelled with men and women who had been blessed by the healer from Capernaum.

The widow woman from Nain and others who never dreamed what was soon to take place, laid aside their tasks and came early—they knew not why—to celebrate the Passover.

Our father Jona arrived with Zebedee and others from Capernaum. Some families stayed in Jerusalem. Some came to the house of Lazarus.

Jesus walked among them, greeting kin and friends and neighbors. He carried on his teaching and healing. His peace was profound, communicating itself to all, even to the Pharisees who were present everywhere he went.

One evening after our kinfolk arrived, Jesus's aunt, Salome, wife of Zebedee, came to where we apostles were eating our supper around the fire in the grove in Bethany.

She came alone, quietly emerging from the gathering shadows. She approached Jesus and fell at his feet, looking up into his face. The Master sat there smiling lovingly, as he did to all who came close worshiping him.

"O, son of my dear sister, may I ask something in the nature of a special request?"

"What would you ask of me, dear Salome?" he said.

"Please grant that these two sons of mine may sit beside you, one on your right hand, the other on the left, when you come into the kingdom of your Heavenly Father." Her face held both hope and doubt.

Jesus answered, speaking to James and John, "Your mother asks this for you, but you don't know what she requests. Are you able to drink of the cup of sorrow and suffering that I shall drink from? Can you endure the baptism of fire with which I shall be baptized as I finish the work given me by my Father in heaven?"

He was looking at his cousins, waiting for their answer.

"We are able," they replied. But shame was in their eyes.

"Yes," Jesus kindly answered Salome, "your sons shall surely drink of my cup and be baptized by this fiery trial which awaits us all as I go forth. But to sit at my right hand and at my left is not mine to give. It shall be given to those for whom it is prepared by my Father. We all await God's grace and favor."

Salome slipped away into the darkness, but sobs of her sadness remained on the night air.

Well!

The ten of us sitting around that fire exploded indignantly against James and John, each of us setting forth our own worthiness to be accorded a place of special closeness to our teacher. Had not we *all* been faithful in following Jesus? done his bidding? loved even the pesky scribes and overbearing Pharisees when we could have been baited into cursing them? The night air was filled with many words of selfish justification for each one's worthiness.

"Quiet!" commanded Jesus. "This is no time to seek to succeed me or gain our Heavenly Father's favor among the sons of earth. You know that nobles among the Gentiles exercise supreme governance over the Gentiles. Those who are greater exert control over even the nobles. But that is not the way it is among God's offspring.

"Whoever among you wishes to be great, he must minister to the needs of others. And whoever wishes to be most eminent among you, let him be your servant. The Son of man came into this world not to be ministered unto but to give to all the one thing most needed—an example of what it means to be the image and likeness of God. To give one's life is redemption. It is deliverance from bondage to the flesh and alienation from the spirit of God."

Our hearts burned within us. I felt so ashamed.

James and John rose and followed their mother back through the vineyard to the house. The sisters of Lazarus and the other women who supported our Master spent hours trying to comfort the misguided wife of Zebedee.

But not one word was spoken amongst us the rest of the evening or throughout the night.

The next day Jesus took Thaddeus, Simon Zelotes, Judas Iscariot, Nathanael, Philip, and Thomas, and walked east from Bethany to Jericho.

We who had brothers, Matthew and James the Less, John and James, and Simon and I, remained in the vineyard to tell the women and other close friends what Jesus had told us about his betrayal and crucifixion.

We explained that Jesus knew before he began his work in the name of his Heavenly Father that the most important lesson he could impart to the children of man would be that there is no death. Proof that if one dies, he would not be dead, for God is the eternal life of all men.

For the women it was a day of sorrow from the start, but before the sun went down, there was also hope. We explained to them how Jesus had already proven dominion over death. First for a dear little maiden. Then for a young man, the son of a widow bereft of other children or husband. And finally, the restoration to life of his dearest friend, Lazarus, who had lain in the grave four days yet came forth without even the odor of corruption upon him.

Mary of Magdala was also able to reassure them. She told how Jesus had spent many hours teaching her the truth about the God-given dominion of man in heaven and on earth. "I know our dear elder brother, Jesus, is the Son of God, the All-loving and Eternal," she said. "I know also that he will soon prove to all that the love one has for God and others is one's very life. Through love we can become the image of God who is divine Life and Truth and Love."

Peter and I were amazed to learn that Jesus not only taught this to his disciples but had also imparted to Mary truths of great depth and promise, some seeming to surpass even the truths he had taught us.

The apostles who accompanied Jesus to Jericho that morning told us later how, as they neared the city, a blind man was sitting along the road, begging. He heard and sensed many people walking by and asked what it all meant.

"Jesus and his followers are passing," he was told. At that he cried out, "Jesus! Son of David, heal me!" The people who walked ahead of Jesus told the man, "Be quiet and hold your peace!" The blind man instead called more loudly, "Jesus, thou Son of David, have mercy on me."

Jesus stopped and asked that the man be brought to him. He said, "What do you want me to do for you?"

The blind man said hopefully, "Lord, I so much want to be able to see."

Jesus said, "Then accept your God-given ability to see. Your faith can save you from blindness."

Immediately the man was able to see. Straightway he joined the pilgrims and followed Jesus. As he walked along with the multitude, he glorified God, thanking Him for his healing. Others seeing this also gave praise to God.

Jesus continued walking through the streets of the old city of Jericho.

A very rich man named Zacchaeus—who was eminent among the tax collectors in Judea—heard that Jesus would be passing that way. He wanted to see Jesus but couldn't because he was small of stature. So Zacchaeus ran ahead and climbed up into a sycamore tree to be able to see the Master.

When Jesus came to the place, he looked up; and, seeing him, he said, "Come down, Zacchaeus. Hurry! Today I'd like to stop at your house." In no time at all, Zacchaeus came down and, gladly welcoming Jesus, took him to his home.

Townspeople like the Pharisees were critical. "He's gone to be a guest in the house of a wrongdoer," they said. "The Master has just invited himself into the home of one we know to be a sinner."

Suddenly the little man, who had become very rich in his activity as a tax collector, realized he could no longer justify wealth gained by extortion. Zacchaeus knew Jesus would never countenance such wrongdoing.

While they were eating, Zacchaeus stood up and announced, "Behold, Lord, I shall give half of my wealth to the poor. In addition, wherever I have taken anything from any man by false estimation of the tax owed, I will now restore to him four times what I took."

Jesus looked deep into the man's heart and saw sincerity. He said, "Today salvation has come to this house, for Zacchaeus has proved to be a son of Abraham. As the Son of man, I am come to seek and to save that which may have been lost."

Late that day returning to Bethany, from the crest of a certain hill the six disciples and Jesus watched the setting sun gild the heights of the temple in Jerusalem, as shadows began to bring in the darkness of night.

We ran to greet Jesus and the apostles when they neared the house of Lazarus. We entered through a gate into the loggia of the house of the Bethany family then exited through their back courtyard and went on down the hill, but Jesus remained to tell Lazarus and the others what happened that day.

We settled around our fire and contentedly ate the fruit and bread we pulled from the purses each of us carried. Those who accompanied the Master to Jericho said that the mood of the pilgrim followers was tense.

Again and again it had been asked of Jesus, "Lord, will you restore soon the kingdom to Israel?" Sometimes the people said, "We hope the kingdom of God is near and will come as soon as you bid it to appear." How little they really understood.

Later that evening, Jesus came into our circle of firelight and sat down. "Hear this," he said. "A certain nobleman traveled to a distant country to receive a kingdom bestowed upon him. He had ten servants and gave each of them a pound to invest while he was away, saying, 'Look after my investments until I return.'

"Now the citizens of that place did not wish to have this man rule over them, but each servant knew he had to do his Master's bidding. When the nobleman returned, he asked the servants to give an account of how they had managed his estate, wanting to know how much each man had gained by trading with the money entrusted to him.

"The first man showed a gain of ten pounds. To this servant he said, 'You have been profitable for me. I give you authority, when I leave, to rule in my stead over ten cities.'

"The second increased his one pound to five and was given authority over five cities. Both men had proven themselves good and faithful in investment of the money.

"But then the third servant, when asked of the increase he had made, handed forth the nobleman's money. He had kept it hidden, tucked away in a linen napkin. He explained, 'I know you are a conservative man. You claim what you have not procured by yourself. You reap where you have not sown.'

"The nobleman was angry with this steward. 'Yes! You knew this of me, so why did you not take my money to the bank? Then when I returned I might have received interest paid for the use of my money.'

"He told a servant standing there, 'Take this pound from him and give it to the servant that has ten pounds.'

"Everyone present protested, 'He already has ten pounds—a great increase!' The nobleman answered, 'I say, everyone who has shall be given more. From him who *has not*, even what he has shall be taken away from him. Now any of you who wish that I had not been given authority over these men, all of you who oppose me as an enemy, come and be destroyed.'"

Having taught this hard lesson, Jesus said, "The day after tomorrow we go into Jerusalem. So shall it be done to me."

There was no hopeful end to this day. We did nothing that night but pray for strength to endure the events which lay ahead in the Holy City.

The next day we joined the guests and family of Lazarus for a modest repast, served in an atmosphere of faith and love and budding sorrow. That evening we went to the house of Simon, who had been healed of leprosy. While there, Mary of Bethany came with a casket of spikenard and poured it on Jesus's head as we sat at meat.

When we saw this, we became indignant and asked among ourselves, "To what purpose is this waste? This ointment might have been sold and the money given to the poor."

Jesus sensed our dismay and said, "Why condemn Mary this way? She has done me a kindness. You will always have the poor with you, but I will not always be with you. She poured this ointment on my body because my burial will soon take place.

"Wherever the good news of my triumph shall be told, this shall be added to the telling. What this woman has done shall be a memorial to her, of her love for my work in this world."

We knew then that shame was mixed with our sorrow.

The next evening we were invited to eat with Lazarus and his sisters. Jesus's mother and Mary of Magdala were houseguests of the family, and we sat down together to break bread. Lazarus, fully recovered, was at the table, his usual gentle self, conversing and eating, with just a hint of homesickness in his eyes.

I often wonder, what did Lazarus experience when he left his earthly body for four days in the hereafter? Simon Peter and I were both more than curious.

At the finish of the supper, as we sat talking, Mary, her sister Martha, and young Mary of Magdala disappeared from the room. Jesus sat quietly with his mother close by, and both of them listening to and observing us. We disciples chattered away, fearful of silence that might lead our thoughts ahead to the coming days.

Then the three women returned. Martha carried several linen cloths over her arm, and her sister Mary carried a vessel holding a pound of spikenard, the costly ointment grown in the highest mountains in the world, far to the east of our land.

Mary of Magdala knelt at Jesus's feet beyond the table, at the edge of the cushioned platform on which we diners were reclining on either side of a low table.

While Mary of Bethany held the spikenard, the second Mary then gently anointed Jesus's feet with the fragrant balm and then wiped them with her tresses. It was an act of veneration eclipsing affection, and we were moved beyond words.

Mary never raised her eyes as she undertook the reverent task. I thought of another woman, the penitent, who had bathed Jesus's feet with tears as she sought forgiveness for her sins.

But Mary of Magdala shed neither tears nor smiles. Her adoration was selfless; and as I watched her silent benediction, deep gratitude was invoked in my own thought. I realized that she was honoring the Anointed One of God for all of us, rendering thanks to God in the presence of those who best knew and loved this Savior of the world.

Completing her task, she modestly rose to her feet and turning her sweet face away from all of us, left the room. The other women present silently followed her; and we men were left in the clutch of a loneliness of mind, a deep sense of individual unworthiness in the sight of God and man, but penitent and submissive to the divine will. The room was silent, filled with the lingering odor of the ointment.

It was Judas, son of Simon of Kerioth, who broke the spell.

"Why was not this ointment sold for three hundred pence and given to the poor?"

Jesus answered, "Against the day of my burying has this dear one kept this. You will always have the poor with you. But me you have not always."

He said no more, for people were thronging the dooryard, wanting to come in, knowing that Jesus was here, but also wanting to see Lazarus whom Jesus had raised from death. But they were all sent home.

The next morning Jesus said, "My time is at hand. We will now go into Jerusalem."

We left Bethany walking the middle road which crosses the Olivet range known as the Mount of Olives. We walked up the east side, almost to the summit of the mount. The road is rugged and steep. Before we reached the crest, we stopped for rest and drink. Jesus sent two of us, Thaddeus and Simon Zelotes, into Bethphage.

"You will find there a she-ass tied up and her colt with her," our Master instructed. "Loose them both. If the man says anything to you, tell him, 'The Lord has need of them,' and at once he will let you bring the beasts."

From the top of the mount as Jesus led us over the hill, all Jerusalem lay at our feet, spread out and shining. I was walking beside our Lord. He spoke suddenly with tears in his eyes and in his voice. "Jerusalem! O Jerusalem. If you had known even the least of the things which belong to your peace! Now they are forever hidden, and you cannot discern them.

"The days shall come when your enemies will dig a trench around you and imprison you on every side. They shall level you, and the inhabitants dwelling within your walls shall be thrown to the ground. One stone of the temple will not be left upon another. You cannot know how long it will be before you will be visited again for redemption to the glory of God."

The men returned with the she-ass and her foal. We put our cloaks on the back of the donkey, making it comfortable for Jesus to sit upon. Multitudes began to gather around us. Some spread garments in our path. Others cut fine branches from trees and leaves of palm and strewed them in the road before us as we descended the mount.

Others went before and a few followed Jesus. All raised their voices, saying, "Hosanna! Praise to the Son of David. Blessed is he who comes in the name of the Lord. Hosanna! Praise to the Highest. Blessed be the king who comes in the name of the Lord! Peace in heaven, and glory to God, the highest."

When we reached Jerusalem, all the city roused at the sight asking, "Who is this?" The throng accompanying us said, "This is Jesus, the prophet of Nazareth in Galilee." Then all people began to rejoice, praising God with loud voices, for many had seen or heard of the wonderful things done by Jesus in the name of God.

One of the Pharisees said, "Master, rebuke your disciples."

Jesus answered, "I tell you, if these people were to hold their peace, the stones would at once cry out!"

We entered the city and soon arrived at the temple. Jesus walked around, looking things over. Midafternoon, we twelve returned alone with him to Bethany.

The next morning we left Bethany very early before daybreak, and when we got as far as Bethphage we were hungry. Especially our Master. When we saw a fig tree with leaves fully grown, he walked over to it, expecting to find ripe fruit. It really wasn't time for this fruit, but since leaves develop after the tree has formed its tiny figlike blossoms, Jesus expected to find fruit ready to be consumed. In his disappointment he said, "No fruit will grow on you, from henceforth forever."

As simply as he might say to a lame man, "Take up your bed and walk," he said of the tree, "Never again will fruit be found on you." We disciples heard his words. He had taught us to see false appearance and all hypocrisy as evil and worthless because pretentious and unfruitful. Then he remarked dryly, "*Bethphage* means 'house of unripe figs.'"

Even in our sorrow, we smiled at his witticism.

We went on into Jerusalem and entered the temple. As he had at the beginning of his work, so also now, as the days grew few in which he could work, Jesus drove out all who bought and sold in the temple. He overthrew the tables of the money changers and prevented anyone from carrying vessels through the temple.

He cried out, saying, "It is written, 'My house shall be called by every nation the house of prayer. But it has been made a den of thieves.'"

The chief priests and scribes saw how many people were impressed with his doctrine. From then on they thought only to destroy him, simply because the people came to listen to his words and left believing his messages.

When next we walked the crest road to Jerusalem we saw the fig tree, its leaves were withered and the tree was dried up from the roots. Jesus told us, "If you have faith, with no doubts at all, you shall not only do as I have done to the fig tree, but if you say to this mountain, be removed, be cast into the sea, it will happen.

"All things whatever you ask in prayer, believing in the power of God, you will receive for your asking. You must never doubt. Then you will have whatever you have said. But you must never think or seek or speak things evil or harmful.

"I say to you, all things you desire when you pray, believe that you receive them, and you will have them. When you pray, forgive if you have anything against anyone, then your Father in heaven will also forgive you your trespasses. If you don't forgive, you will not be forgiven.

"The scribes and Pharisees sit in Moses's seat," he began to say to those who now gathered around him. "Whatever they ask you to comply with, do. But do not do anything their way, for they say and do not. They interpret the law and lay upon men heavy burdens and make no effort to ease them.

"Instead, they do all their works to be seen by others. They make their own phylacteries broad, wearing wide scriptural texts to seem more devout than others. They enlarge the borders of their robes, seek high seats at feasts, and prominent positions in the synagogues.

"They love to be called 'teacher, teacher.' Don't call yourselves teachers. You have one teacher, even Christ, the Truth. All of you are brothers, none greater than another. The greatest among you will be a servant to all. Whoever exalts himself shall be abased, and whoever humbles himself shall be exalted and honored with praise from others."

Temple authorities, scribes, and Pharisees were standing close in the shadows. Jesus began to rebuke them.

"Misery and calamity will come to you scribes and Pharisees, hypocrites!" Jesus said. "You waste and consume widows' houses while pretending to make long prayers to help them. You shall be condemned for this.

"You go over land and sea to make one convert, then you make him the child of hell twice more than yourselves. You guide others blindly, saying that one who swears by the temple does nothing, but swearing by the gold of the temple makes one a debtor to use the temple for righteousness.

"This is foolish blindness. Which is greater, gold or the temple which sanctifies the gold? The same goes for swearing by the altar which is nothing; but if one swears by the sacrifice placed upon the altar, he is responsible for its right use. Whoever, as I, seeks divine revelation in prayer at the altar, swears by it and the gift given upon it.

"Affirm by the temple of God and you affirm the presence of God therein. Affirm heaven, and you solemnly affirm the presence of God's power and the glory of God who sits upon the throne in the heaven of God's everywhereness.

"You pay tithes of mint, anise, and cummin and omit the weighty matters of the law which are judgment, mercy, and faith. Both the tithes and observance of the law should have been done by you!

"You strain at gnats, yet swallow camels. You make your consciousness seem clean, but inside you fill it with extortion and excessive tributes imposed on others. You who are authorities on righteousness, cleanse first that which is the content of your own thought, then the outer appearance will likewise be free of all that is impure and injurious to others.

"You know, you are like whitewashed burial places—beautiful outside, but within full of dead men's bones and corrupted bodies. In like manner, you outwardly seem religious and righteous, but within you are filled with hypocrisy and inequities.

"You are hypocrites when you build tombs for prophets killed by your fathers, then try to redeem the fathers by decorating the sepulchres of their victims who are the truly righteous ones.

"You say, 'If we had lived in that time, we would not have taken their blood.' By such saying, you witness truly that you are children of men who killed the prophets. So be it; you fill the measure of your fathers.

"You are subtle as serpents are subtle, yet venomous. You are vipers. How can you, being mischievous and malignant, escape the sentence and condemnation of hell?

"Observe this: I send unto you persons inspired with godly teaching, wise men, and scribes, skilled in the law of God. Some you will crucify to kill; some you will scourge in the synagogue. You will persecute my students from city to city.

"But back upon you will come the righteous blood shed on the earth. From the blood of Abel, unto the slaying of Zacharias—son of Berachias also known as Jehoiada, who was martyred between the temple and the altar—will come judgment.

"Truly," Jesus continued, "these things shall come in punishment upon your generation. Oh Jerusalem, Jerusalem, you who kill the prophets and stone those sent to you! How often I wanted to gather your children together even as a hen gathers her chickens under her wings, but you will not let me!

"Behold, your house is left unto you, empty. For I say, you shall not see me from now on until you can say, 'Blessed is he that comes in the name of the Lord.'"

With those words, Jesus prepared to depart from the temple. We gathered around him and took him through the buildings, showing him one last time where he had taught and healed and condemned the vain traffic among the money changers.

Sadly he turned to us and said, "See all these things? Truly I tell you, there shall not be left here one stone built upon another that will not be thrown down." We wept as we walked away.

When we reached the Mount of Olives, Jesus sat down to rest. We gathered at his feet, for we were alone with no others crowding to hear his voice.

"Tell us," one of us said, "when shall these things be? What shall tell us you are returning? What will be the sign that the end of the world is near?"

Jesus answered, "Be alert! Let no man deceive you. Others shall come in my name, saying, 'I am Christ.' Many shall be deceived. You will hear of wars and rumors of wars. Don't be troubled. These things must come to pass, but the end is not yet.

"Nation shall rise against nation, kingdom against kingdom. There will be famines, pestilences, and earthquakes in various places. All these are but the *beginning* of great sorrow.

"As I have told you before, you will be delivered up and subject to great affliction, and many shall try to kill you or make all nations hate you because you walked with me. Others will give offense and betray and hate each other. False prophets will rise up and deceive many. Iniquity will abound and cause many to be less loving. But anyone who endures to the end of all this, he shall be saved.

"When the good news of the dominion of God is preached throughout the world for a testimony to all nations, then the end of this world shall come.

"Therefore, when you see the abomination of desolation—spoken of by Daniel—stand in the holy place, in the place of God's glory, then let all in Judea flee into the mountains.

"Remember, I told you these days will come. Write them on your hearts. Then you will know that the time of the end is near."

Jesus said, "The Passover is also near . . . two days hence. It is then that I shall be betrayed."

Even as we were being told this, the chief priests, scribes, and elders of the people were meeting. They had been called to the palace of Caiaphas, the high priest. There they consulted together how they might take Jesus unaware and kill him. But all agreed, "This must not be done on the feast day; otherwise, there might be an uproar among the people."

What we didn't know then was that Judas Iscariot also went to the chief priests and asked, "What will you give me if I deliver Jesus into your hands?" The chief priests answered, "We will give you money. After the fact."

Judas rejoined us later that day—but none of us dreamed that he was seeking to deliver Jesus to them at a time of absence from a multitude of followers who, being close by, might protest the arrest.

Then Jesus asked us a strange question. "When I sent you out on your first healing mission, I sent you without purse, scrip, or shoes. Did you lack anything?"

The answer was a chorus of nos.

"Now," Jesus said, "you who have a purse, take it, and also your scrip. If you have no sword, sell a garment and buy one.

"I tell you, that much written of me in the scriptures has yet to be accomplished. As once did Peter, those who think to protest I consider transgressors, for things concerning me will have an end; but first all must be accomplished."

But we, not listening, were thinking about his request that we acquire swords; and one of us spoke up, saying, "Lord! Observe this, we already have two swords among us."

Jesus said in answer, "It is enough. Your happiness lies in doing what I have asked you to do." We were now only waiting. Waiting and fearing.

The fourth day after the Sabbath came. We were all at loose ends, not knowing what to do.

Our Master was quiet in the house of Lazarus, where Jesus's mother, his kin, and Mary of Magdala were also guests.

We apostles decided to go into Jerusalem. Simon and I would go to our uncle's home. Our father Jona would have arrived there by now.

James and John walked with us; in fact, all of the apostles came along, knowing that their kinfolk would also be arriving in the city.

After a short visit and a trip to the Temple Mount with our father, Peter, I, and the others left the city and went back to the garden on the Mount of Olives. I had an overwhelming desire to spend the rest of the day in consecrated prayer. Simon and I separated from the others and, setting an example, we entered into bodily comfort and quietness and began to silently affirm our love for and from our Heavenly Father and our beloved teacher. In supplication, we invited angels to fill our hearts with selfless devotion of thought to our Master's forthcoming proof of eternal life. We prayed that nothing would interfere with his ability to raise himself from death, that no resistance to his teaching could nullify his God-given power and purpose to prove that with God all things are possible.

The day seemed long, the night even longer. Yet I arose the next morning with a clear head and confident strength. We all did. To a man, we knew that our Master had also spent his night in prayer. We were all wrapped in his gift—a covering of surety and quietness. I, for one, had devoted every prayer, asking divine Love to be my Lord's ever-present Comforter.

It was a very busy day for Jesus. He taught us as usual on the Mount of Olives, and seemed loathe to see the day end. He spoke to us again of the kingdom of heaven. This time he likened it to ten virgins, readying themselves to go out to meet the bridegroom.

"Five of the virgins were wise; they took oil in their vessels along with full lamps. Five were foolish and did not prepare. While the bridegroom tarried, they all slumbered. At midnight the cry was made, 'The bridegroom is coming, go out to meet him.'

"They arose, trimmed and lit their lamps, but the foolish found their lamps would not stay lit for they had no oil in them. They begged the wise, 'Give us some of your oil.' 'No,' replied the wise. 'There isn't enough for us and you. Go find someone who sells oil and buy for your own lamps.' They did so. But while they went out, the bridegroom came, and those who were ready went in with him to the wedding. The door was shut. Later the other five virgins came, saying, 'Lord, Lord, let us in.' But he answered, 'Truly I don't know you.'

"If they had really been friends, they would have been prepared," Jesus explained. "Just so, I say to all, WATCH, for you never know what day or hour the Son of man will come.

"When the Son of man comes in his glory and all the holy angels with him, then shall he be seated upon the throne of the Christ. And before him all nations shall gather, and he shall separate peoples one from another, just as the shepherd divides his sheep from the goats. He will place the innocent and inoffensive at his right hand, the brash, denying, and hateful ones on the left. Then he will say to those on his right hand, 'Come, you who are blessed of my Father, inherit the kingdom prepared for you from the foundation of the world.'

"'I was hungry, you gave me meat. I was thirsty, you gave me drink. I was a stranger, you took me in. Naked, and you clothed me. I was sick and you visited me. In prison, and you came unto me.'

"The righteous then will inquire, 'When did we see you hungry and fed you, or thirsty and gave you refreshment? When as a stranger did we take you in, or you were naked and we gave you needed clothing? When were you sick or in prison and we came to you?'

"The Lord will say, 'Truly, because you have done it unto one of the least of these, my brethren, you have done it to me.' But then the Son of man will say to those on the left hand, 'Depart from me into everlasting fire prepared for the pretender of evil and his messengers.'

"'When did we see you in need and *not* help you?' they will ask. The Lord shall say, 'When you did *not* do it unto one of the least of these needy ones.' Now you have the everlasting pain of loss; but the righteous have life eternal."

Then Jesus said, "It is two days until my Passion, when the Son of man will be delivered to be crucified. Remain at peace, for my Father gives me strength to do His will."

We walked back to Bethany in the twilight, and in silence. No words could divert the grief I felt.

I could not rest. I could not even pray. In time, I yielded to this intuition: "Just listen. Divine thoughts will fill you."

I thought of all the things I had learned from Jesus, things which enabled me to heal and even show others how they could be their own physician. My mind no longer looked upon the things of the world as enduring, but rather on the things of God. God's things are thoughts, I had learned. So it is and ever shall be in the world of perfect mind, God's world. All things therein are created by Spirit, not of flesh or of perishable substance. The world of Spirit is a world of light and love. All that is manifested comes from the perfect mind of God. Our Master said that everything is tangibly real, even as it seems to the sight of mankind. But all is eternal with nothing of temporal nature or condition. I cannot imagine this yet.

How much I have learned! How little I know! And yet the one thing I do know is this: I am set upon a course to infinity and for eternity. May I never abandon the quest, the journey, or the necessity to prove what I have been taught by Jesus the Christ.

This day has been so fraught with fear and so blessed with activity! One fear is that I may not see my teacher after a few more days. Upon our shoulders will fall the burden of bearing his works and words of Truth to an indifferent, uncomprehending world.

For many hours our Master has drilled into us the reality of perfection as the truth of God's creation. How often he has proven the fact of spirituality by taking flesh from a state of illness and failure to freedom and perfection of function.

Jesus destroyed our belief in dust as the ingredient from which God created man as this image, His likeness.

"Live Truth," he has thundered to us in urgent tones. "It must be lived," he said. "In thought. In act. In word. In deed.

"I, Jesus," he once said, "am sent to waken the world from Adam's dream. Now you, my students, must sound the trumpet to rouse all mankind and then sing my song to teach them. You must heal the sick and raise the ever-dreaming dead to life in God."

Chapter 15

The day of Passover arrived. The day of dread. The day when our Master would be taken from us.

We went to see Jesus. We met him in the loggia of Lazarus's home. It was very early, the sun barely risen above the distant hills toward Moab and the nearer eastern ridges. "Where shall we prepare to eat the Passover?" we asked.

"You two go into the city," he told Peter and John. "You know where the mother of young John Mark lives in the upper heights of the city, on Mount Zion. Next to her home is the house where her brother Barnabas Joses, of Cyprus, lives when he comes for Passover.

"Go there and say to him, 'The Master says, my time is at hand. I and my disciples will keep the feast today at your house.' He has a large room furnished and ready." They went to Barnabas and found everything arranged.

Lazarus and his guests were to observe the feast at the home of John Mark's mother. She was a widow of some wealth and was welcoming also the families who were to come from Galilee.

Jesus's mother, his kin, and the family from Magdala arrived early that afternoon at the home of John Mark's mother. Lazarus and his sisters came shortly after. Jesus went into seclusion with us in the house of Barnabas. We tried to keep busy in any way we could. Prayer seemed the best way.

Next door, the women fixed an early paschal meal for both houses. Two lambs were ritually slain and set whole to roast on a spit. Later when the meal was ready, the lamb, unleavened bread, and the bitter herbs were placed before us on the table, as was wine mixed with water, crushed fruits moistened with sweet vinegar until they had the quality of soft mortar, reminding us of the strawless bricks our forefathers were forced to make in Egypt. All this was consumed as the age-old Passover tale was read aloud.

The first cup of wine was blessed and served. We cleansed our hands and said a prayer. We ate the bitter herbs. When the lamb was presented, John, being the youngest, asked for us the meaning of Passover. Our Master responded,

And it shall come to pass, when your children shall say unto you, what mean ye by this service? That ye shall say, it is the sacrifice of the Lord's passover, who passed over the houses of the children of Israel in Egypt, when he smote the Egyptians and delivered our houses. And the people bowed the head and worshipped.

Then the second cup of wine was blessed and consumed as we sang the Hallel:

Praise ye the Lord. Praise, O ye servants of the Lord, praise the name of the Lord. Blessed be the name of the Lord from this time forth and for evermore. From the rising of the sun unto the going down of the same the Lord's name is to be praised. The Lord is high above all nations, and his glory above the heavens. Who is like unto the Lord our God, who dwelleth on high, Who humbleth himself to behold the things that are in heaven, and in the earth! He raiseth up the poor out of the dust, and lifteth the needy out of the dunghill; That he may set him with princes, even with the princes of his people. He maketh the barren woman to keep house, and to be a joyful mother of children. Praise ye the Lord.

When Israel went out of Egypt, the house of Jacob from a people of strange language, Judah was his sanctuary, and Israel his dominion. The sea saw it and fled; Jordan was driven back. The mountains skipped like rams, and the little hills like lambs. What ailed thee, O thou sea, that thou fleddest? Thou Jordan, that thou wast driven back? Ye mountains, that ye skipped like rams; and ye little hills, like lambs? Tremble, thou earth, at the presence of the Lord, at the presence of the God of Jacob which turned the rock into a standing water, the flint into a fountain of waters.

We partook of the unleavened bread and the lamb after the thank offerings, the bitter herbs, and the fruits. The third cup of wine—the cup of blessing—was blessed, given, and consumed.

After the fourth cup of wine, we sang the second half of the Hallel, the Passover hymn, all verses from three psalms. My gloom and sorrow lifted a bit. But there was no joy. We were celebrating an old tradition and at the same time holding our breath on the cusp of a new one, as we celebrated this last supper with our beloved Master.

Jesus reached forth his hands to us, looking up and down the table into each man's face with such gentleness and love we had to wipe our eyes when his glance moved on to the next apostle.

Then Jesus shook his head in profound sadness. I had seen that look on his face before. He was plainly upset now.

"One of you shall reveal me, making known, just who I am, to those who will take me into custody for trial," he said.

John was lying beside Jesus on the highest couch at the table, his head at the level of Jesus's bosom. I noticed Peter beckoning to John, urging him to make inquiry as to of whom Jesus spake.

Jesus continued, "Sadly, but truly I must tell you . . . one of *you* will deliver me to the authorities." With that our sorrow was complete, and to a man we were undone. "Is it I?" one asked. Then another, "Lord, is it I?" We all voiced our fears that we might be requested to betray him, making him known to his enemies that he might be taken to his death.

"He who dips his hand with mine in the dish, the same shall bring them forth and give me over to my captors." Judas Iscariot quietly asked, "Master, must it be I?" Jesus answered almost silently, "You have said you would."

Jesus then took bread, gave thanks for it, then broke it, and gave the several pieces to be shared around the table. "Take, eat of it. This symbolizes my body."

He took his cup of wine, gave thanks for it, as he had for the bread, and passed it. Each man drank from the cup. "This symbolizes my blood, in the new agreement, for I shed my blood pardoning the sins of the world. But now I shall not, from this time forward, drink the fruit of the vine until that day when I can drink it new with you in my Father's kingdom."

Jesus broke a crust of bread and dipped it into the bowl of olive oil just as Judas Iscariot did the same. Jesus said to him, "That you are to do, do quickly."

Judas received the bread, then taking his scrip which held the money used for our collective needs, he rose from the couch and slipped out of the room as we drank the wine.

Jesus then said, "The Son of man indeed must go, as it is written of him,

> He was wounded for our transgressions, he was bruised for our iniquities . . . he shall see the travail of his soul and shall be satisfied; by his knowledge shall my righteous servant justify many, for he shall bear their iniquities.

Jesus repeated, "The Son of man indeed goes to his death, but infamy will rest upon that man by whom he is delivered up! Good were it for that man if he had never been born. All of you shall be offended because of me this night, for it is written, 'I will smite the shepherd, and the sheep shall be scattered.' But after I am risen, I will go before you into Galilee."

Peter, poor Peter, he *had* to say something. The rest of us simply groaned inwardly, but Peter had to be brave. "Although all shall be offended, yet *I* won't be," he said.

"Peter, truly, sadly, I tell you . . . even in this night before the cock crows, you will deny me three times!" said Jesus.

But Peter spoke even more vehemently, "If I should die with you, I will in no way deny you." And we all agreed and said, "Nor will I. Nor will I. Nor will I!" Then, foolishly, we began to strive among ourselves, who would be accounted greatest among us.

Jesus put an end to that fuss. "He who would be greatest among you let him be as the younger, and he that is chief as one who serves all others."

We recline on couches as you know, around the festive board. So when the lamb had been eaten, we were gathered still around the table. Jesus rose from the dining couch. He stripped off his robe—that soft seamless garment he always wore.

He laid it aside and girded himself with a towel. He poured water into the basin previously provided for us to cleanse our hands as we ate. Then our Master began at the couch furthest from his seat, kneeling at the feet of Simon Zelotes, who started to protest. Jesus motioned him to silence and proceeded to wash his disciple's feet. After wiping them with the towel, he moved to Philip and repeated the act. And so it was that each of us in turn were taught abject humility and service to one another.

Simon Peter was the last one before whom Jesus knelt to perform his astounding act of subservience. Our Master before us as a slave!

We were all speechless, all that is except my brother.

"Master, do you wash *my* feet?"

Jesus replied, "What I do, you can't realize now. But hereafter you will know."

Peter responded with loud indignation, "You will never wash my feet!"

Once again my heart lurched. *Peter! Oh, Peter, don't be proud. Don't be profane. Learn humble acceptance! This man is willing to die for the world,* I protested silently against him within myself.

Jesus looked into my brother's eyes and said, "If you will not let me wash your feet, you have no part in my sacrifice."

To his credit Peter answered at once, stretching forth his hands, "Lord not my feet only. Wash my hands and my head also."

Jesus replied, "Whoever is washed needs only to wash his feet for he is otherwise every bit clean; I would have you all clean."

Judas is not here, I thought, *so we are not all clean.* Jesus affirmed this.

"But not all of you are clean," he said. And then he knelt at the feet of my brother and finished his task.

Our Lord rose, reclothed himself, and sat down again. "Do you know what I have done to you? Do you realize what it means? You call me Master. You call me Lord. Rightly so, for this I am. If I have washed your feet, you must also wash one another's feet.

"I have given you an example. Do as I have done to you. No one is better than another. You each are chosen to serve my Father's cause from among all the people of the earth. Truly, no one of you is more or less than God's servant. No servant is greater than His Lord. Nor am I, the one sent of the Father, greater than the Father who sent me.

"If you understand and do these things that I have done, you are indeed happy. Now, henceforth, strive to refresh each other, just as you stand. Know this: I speak not of you all. I know those whom I have chosen. One of you will fulfill these words of scripture: 'One that eats bread with me has lifted up his heel against me.'

"Now, before this is proven, I tell you, so when it comes about, you will know that I am the one chosen of God to do this work among the inhabitants of the earth. Truly, I would have you know that he who receives whomsoever I send forth, by accepting my gift, accepts God who sends me."

"Do not grieve. Let not your heart be troubled," Jesus said. "You believe in God; believe also in me. In my Father's house are many dwellings. I go to prepare your place. I will return and receive you to myself that you may be where I am. Where I go, and the way, you know."

Thomas spoke up, "Lord, we don't know where you go, or the way."

Jesus said, "I AM the Way, the Truth, the Life. No man comes to the Father but by me. If you know me, you know my Father also. You shall know Him even better from now on. You will know what to look for and how to recognize God's presence."

Then Philip said, "Show us the Father—that would be enough to reassure us."

Jesus said sadly, "Have I been so long time with you, Philip, and yet you don't know me? Seeing me, you see the Father. Why then do you ask me to show Him to you?

"Believe this: I am in this Mind that is God, and this Mind that is God is in me, as my very mind and life. At least believe me on the basis of the wondrous works that God shows you through me.

"Know this: Whoever accepts me as true, the works that I do will he also do, and greater works even, because I go to my Father. Whatever you request in my name, I, the Christ, will enable you to have it.

"If you love me, do as I have commanded. I will entreat the Father, and He shall give you another Comforter, one who consoles in a way that abides with you forever . . . even the meaning and essence of the Truth. The world cannot receive it because it has not understood this Spirit of Truth nor accepted it, seeing me not as the promised deliverer. But you know the Truth, for Truth dwells with you and shall be in your heart and mind.

"I will not leave you alone and without comfort. I will come to you even to your thought, recalling all I've given you to understand and all you have proven to be God's Truth.

"In a short time, the world will see my presence no more. But you will see me, because my Truth shall live eternally, as henceforth will I. You will also, when you have completed your work for my cause on earth.

"You have my commandments. Keep them because you love me. All who love me shall be loved of my Father, and I will also love him and manifest my risen self as Christ to him."

Judas Thaddeus asked, "Lord, why do you manifest yourself as the Christ to us but not to the world?"

The Master explained: "Not everyone loves me. If anyone does not love me, he ignores my sayings. But these sayings are not mine but are the Father's, for He sent me.

"If one loves me, he will retain my words, and my Heavenly Father will love him, and we will come into His heart and remain in His thoughts.

"The Comforter I have promised to send to you is the Holy Ghost, sent by the Father in my name. This Comforter, the Christ, shall bring to remembrance and teach again all things of which I have spoken. I have many things to say to you, but you can't grasp them yet. When the Spirit of Truth comes, he will guide you into understanding all truth. He will reveal things to come.

"He will glorify me, for he will explain to you all that is mine. So for a while you will not see me. Then a while later you shall see me—understand me—and you will rejoice to know me spiritually.

"Your joy then can never be taken from you. At that day, you will not ask of me but of God—in my name, and it will be given you. Ask, and you will receive.

"I've spoken to you in proverbs. But then I will show you the Father plainly. The Father loves you because you have loved me, and you have believed that I have come from Him. Now I am to leave the world and go to the Father.

"You shall be scattered in the coming hours . . . leaving me alone. But I will not be alone. The Father is always with me. Peace. I leave peace with you. My own peace I give you. Not as the world gives do I give you peace. Don't be troubled nor have fear in your heart.

"I've told you that I am to go away. I go, yet will come again to you. If you loved me, you would rejoice that I go to the Father. My Father is greater than I. I tell you this before it all happens, so when all this comes to pass, you might know and understand.

"After this I won't talk much. The things which govern this world will try to distract me but will find in me nothing which responds or yearns.

"The world will soon know that I love and trust the Father, and as God gave me commandment, so I do what is required.

"Let us go forth."

Only later did I realize the ordeal that lay before our Master; and then I knew it only because my brother, Simon Peter, was witness—a furtive witness hiding in shadows, pretending to be one of the rabble.

It began after our Passover supper, when we went forth from the quiet room in the upper city. The streets of Jerusalem were empty. A few beggars and homeless people were about, but we made our way quickly to the quiet olive groves in the place called Gethsemane.

"Sit here," Jesus suggested to us, "I will be at prayer yonder." We settled ourselves and soon were asleep, sated as we were with the dinner the women had served us.

Jesus took with him his cousins James and John and, of course, Peter, eager Peter—always ready to do the Master's bidding.

But did they do what he asked of them?

This is what Peter told me occurred.

They were only a stone's throw away from where we rested, but we could not see them. Jesus explained to the three companions, "My soul is heavy with sorrow, even to the point of death. I must pray. Watch with me. I will go a bit further but remain in your sight."

Peter said they watched Jesus fall upon his knees, bending his face nearly to the ground. They heard him say, "O my Father, if it be possible, let this cup of sorrow pass from me. If not, let it be as you will."

That is all Peter heard, for his eyes closed in sleep. "We did not keep our watch; at least I did not," he told me. He wakened to hear Jesus who was standing above his students who had fallen into sleep. "What?" he said with disappointment etching his words. "Couldn't you watch with me for one hour?" Peter and the other two stood up and stretched, shaking sleep from their limbs as they moved about.

Jesus said, "Watch! Pray that you don't give in to the temptation to let down your guard. Your spirit is willing, but your flesh is weak."

With that he went back, and prayed again. This time he said, "O Father, if this cup of sorrows may not be taken from me, except I drink it, I bow to your will."

Peter confessed to me later that his eyes were too heavy – he struggled to stay awake, but simply could not. They all slept. Jesus came again to them, and then left, to pray for the third time the same words. Apparently one of them did not sleep, for the story later was told in detail of Jesus's passion.

"The next thing we knew he was rousing all of us: 'You may as well sleep on, and take your rest now. The hour is come, when I am delivered into the hands of sinners. But if you are with me, rise and join me as I go forth, for the one who delivers me is coming.'" Tiny beads of blood were as sweat on his brow.

Even while he was speaking, and we were rousing from sleep a multitude advanced, carrying swords and curved staffs, some in the hands of the elders of our people and chief priests from the temple. Leading those who were upon us was one of our own: Judas Iscariot!

He signaled to halt the mob, and he advanced to Jesus, saying, "Greetings Rabbi," then he kissed him for Jesus had said, "Deliver me with a kiss."

Jesus held forth his hands, saying, "My Friend, for what reason have you come?" The multitude closed in around him, and took Jesus into custody.

It was more than Peter could bear. He drew the sword Jesus had bid us obtain, and struck out with it defensively, and of all things, it came down on the right ear of the man who was servant to Caiaphas, the High Priest. The ear lay severed, held only by a thread of flesh upon the cheek of Malchus. We all knew his name for he was pompous, vain and arrogant, and given to displays of self-importance.

Blood spurted from the side of his head.

Jesus said, "This is enough suffering," and he touched the ear, pushing it into its natural place – and then healed the man who was nearly faint with fear and loss of blood.

By now the elders, the captains of the temple guard, and the chief priests surrounded Jesus. They were awestruck, seeing for the first time Jesus's power to heal.

"Why have you come for me with swords and clubs?" Jesus asked. "I was in the temple with you every day; you never touched me then. But this is your hour, and you have come in the power of darkness."

With that, they led our Lord from the Garden of the Oil Press and took him at midnight to the residence of Annas, father-in-law of Caiaphas, the high priest this year. We apostles fled into the safety of darkness.

Only Peter followed the mob, mingling with those in the rear darkness as they returned triumphantly to the city.

A fire was built in the great hall of Annas's house; and since it was cold, the room soon filled, and Peter sat down among those getting close to the fire for warmth.

My brother could not tell me this later without sobbing. It seems one of the maidservants recognizing him, scrutinized him for a while, then proclaimed, "This fellow walked with the prisoner. I followed them once."

Poor Peter. He must live forever with his response. "Woman, I know him not," he said.

But a little while later another person saw and recognized him, saying, "You are one of those who follow him." Peter denied, saying, "Man, I am not." A second man confidently approached and declared, "Of a truth this fellow *was* with him; I tell you he is a Galilean."

Peter became totally undone when he revealed all this to me, for, said he, "I told this second man, 'I don't know what you are saying.' Just then Jesus—oh, dear God—Jesus turned and looked deep into my eyes, and I recalled his warning, 'Before the cock crows you shall deny me three times,' for when I answered, 'Man, I know not what you are saying,' I heard a rooster crow before the false dawn when the third hour of this new day began."

"What did you do?" I asked him.

"I fled . . . I ran from the hall, into the streets, back to the garden where they arrested him. Only there could I vent my regret in bitter tears and loud vehemence as I cursed my weakness. In whimpered whisperings I begged God to forgive my weakness and I begged Him to repair my loathed selfhood, should that be the will of the Almighty whose gift to this world of His only begotten Son was at that moment being cruelly rejected and would soon be returned to Him. Then I went shamefully back to be witness to our Master's trial." Meantime, Annas had Jesus bound and taken to appear before Caiaphas, the high priest.

While Peter warmed himself again at a fire in the judgment hall of Caiaphas's palace, Caiaphas was asking Jesus about us, his disciples, and his teaching. No mention was made of the miracles and healings. Jesus was here before the Sanhedrin, the governing body, the senate of the nation of the Jews. Seventy elders were present, joined by one more person, the high priest who presided over the council. They held the power of life and death but had no authority to execute the sentence of death. That task was delegated to the Roman authorities.

The Sanhedrin is a priestly clique. The judgment hall, where Jesus stood trial in the middle of the night, was filled with elders and scribes, none mandated by law to sit as judges. They had conspired against our Master and could not try him in a daylight court, for they had nothing with which to charge and find him guilty and subject to death. They sought witnesses against him. Many false witnesses came, but none dared to accuse him.

At last, two men stood forth, willing to testify they'd heard Jesus speak of destroying the temple and rebuilding it in three days. Even then they testified falsely, one saying that Jesus said "I can destroy this temple." The other claiming he said "I will destroy this temple." What Jesus had, in fact, said was, "Destroy this temple, and in three days I will raise it up." We now understand that he was speaking of the temple which is his body. So there was no proof on which to base an accusation.

Caiaphas asked, "Don't you answer this witness made against you?" Jesus made no defense. At this the high priest shouted, "Tell us if you are the Christ, the Son of God."

"If I tell you, you won't believe. If I ask you, you won't answer me," he replied.

To a man, the members of the Sanhedrin rose up and asked, "Are you then the Son of God?"

They had their answer in Jesus's words courageously spoken, "You have said."

Caiaphas instantly tore the blasphemy seam of his judicial robe and declared, "He blasphemes. We need no further witness." The voices of the council were raised in chorus with the onlookers, "He is guilty of death!"

Jesus had never dishonored the name of his Heavenly Father. He never failed to give credit and honor to God. But now, contrary to procedure of law in the Jewish council, Jesus was taken into the courtyard of Caiaphas's palace; and there, the waiting mob, shouting insults, mocked him."

Simon Peter witnessed this from the shadows. How thankful I am that Peter ventured forth that night and saw this.

When I left Barnabas's house to search for my brother, the streets were half empty. I had put on a hooded tunic to better shield myself from baleful stares and malignant eyes. I first heard a rumble of sound coming from the Gabbatha—the place called The Pavement—in front of the governor's palace where Pilate, a Roman procurator in Judea, was continuing the trial. I hurried there and found a spot on the fringe of the growing crowd.

I saw the priests and elders and guards from the temple milling around beneath the high veranda where the judgment seat, used by the governor when making pronouncement of his decision, is placed.

At that moment Jesus, unseen by us, was standing before Pilate who asked if he was indeed King of the Jews. "You say" were the only words given in answer.

From without came loud cries as the temple contingent railed loudly against Jesus, hoping to influence Pilate.

Amazingly, Jesus simply stood silent before the verbiage, for in truth he was receiving angel messages from His Father in heaven and was comforted with a quiet fearlessness.

Pilate was amazed, impressed. "Don't you hear the many things being witnessed against you?" he asked.

Jesus gave no reply. Pilate marveled exceedingly.

When there was a lull in the strident voices, Pilate went out and said to the chief priests and the people, "I find no fault in this man."

He was then informed, "He stirs up the people, teaching Jews everywhere, from Galilee to Jerusalem." Then Pilate asked, "Is he a Galilean?" When that fact was confirmed, Pilate knew Jesus belonged in the jurisdiction of Herod Antipas, who happened to be in Jerusalem at that time. So Jesus was sent to Herod's palace for trial because Herod Antipas was tetrarch over the region of Galilee.

Herod had heard of Jesus but had never seen him. He wanted to see a miracle done by him. He interrogated Jesus at length. But Jesus answered him not a word.

Again the retinue from the temple made accusation. But Herod and his soldiers simply set the case aside, except for dressing Jesus in a gorgeous kingly robe, after which they mocked him and had him escorted back to Pilate's palace. That night Pilate and Herod became friends, whereas previously they were sore enemies.

At the Feast of the Passover, it was a custom that the people could choose a prisoner and ask for the release of anyone they wished to set free. Pilate asked of the crowd, "Whom shall I release to you? Barabbas or Jesus called Christ?" He knew there was the vengeance of jealousy in the air.

He sat down in the judgment seat, ready to respond to the call of the crowd. But then, a message sent by his wife was given to Pilate: "Have nothing to do with that just man. I have been in anguish, suffering, because I had a dream of him."

The chief priests were inciting the multitude. "Choose Barabbas. Destroy this Jesus." Barabbas was a known thief and murderer committed to prison.

When Pilate spoke, he asked again, "Which of these two shall I release to you?"

The crowd roared "Barabbas. Barabbas."

"Then," said Pilate, "what shall I do with Jesus, called the Anointed?"

"CRUCIFY HIM! CRUCIFY HIM!"

Pilate held high his hand, until silence reigned.

"Why? What *evil* has he done?" There was no answer to that question.

Now the crowd's response was even louder.

"LET HIM BE CRUCIFIED."

Pilate knew there was nothing more he could do or say. It was all tumult and bedlam, uproar and confusion.

He called for a basin of water and a linen towel; and there, in plain sight and in silence given at his command, he washed his hands before the multitude, proclaiming, "I am innocent of the blood of this just person. See ye to it."

He ordered Barabbas to be released from prison. Taking the sash of the robe he was wearing, Pilate symbolically whipped Jesus and so delivered him to be crucified.

The governor's guards then took Jesus into the common hall and gathered the whole band of the governor's company. They stripped Jesus of the royal robe placed on him at Herod's command and put on him a scarlet robe. They platted a crown of ugly thorns and placed it on his head and a reed in his right hand. They made fun of him, hailing him as "King of the Jews." They spit on him, then broke a reed and beat on his head with it. Then they took the robe off, put his own clothing on him again and led him away to be crucified.

The new day dawned bright and cloudless. But upon the sweep and heights of Galilee and Judea, a sad darkness was creeping. The cock that always sang before the morning star arose did not greet the sun. Nor was the dawn chorus of the birds heard that day.

The grebe birds—rook and raven—did not croak or caw. The bulbul, crested lark, chiffchaffs, and great tits called no one to rise up from sleep at the song of a bird. Cranes and swallows did not chatter; the wryneck did not cry *kew, kew, kew*; and the doves mourned in silence.

I could not swear that my breath would continue to come without great effort. Nor could I make one foot rise from the ground and know that the other one would follow in step.

"I AM the Way. The Truth. The Life," our Master had said.

Yet I could think of no way to go. No truth to know. No will to live. "Where are you, God?" I found myself asking.

"Everywhere, in everyone," my Master's voice penetrated my grief as I remembered his teaching.

I'd dared not go close, but from a safe vantage I'd heard the rabble of men raise their voices time and again. I knew Pilate to be a hard administrator of justice, being a man who put his own interests above our nation's.

Later we learned in fuller detail that our Master had been alone before Pilate in the judgment hall. The scribes and Pharisees and elders could not enter, for to so do would mean defilement.

Pilate had come out to them and asked what accusation they brought against Jesus.

"He is a criminal, or we would not have brought him to you," they answered.

Pilate replied, "Then you take and judge him according to your law."

Their response was, "It is not lawful for us to put any man to death." (That is what Jesus knew, and why he told us he would be crucified by the Romans.)

Pilate went inside to ask Jesus, "Are you the King of the Jews?"

We learned later that Jesus had answered, "Do you ask the question of your own knowledge, or did others tell it to you about me?"

Pilate bristled. "Am I a Jew? I was told this about you. *Are you* the King of the Jews?"

Jesus said, "My dominion is not of this world. If it were, I would fight—I and my students—that I not be delivered to the Jews. My kingdom is not of earth."

Pilate asked, "But are you a king?"

"*You* say I am a king," Jesus answered. "For one purpose I was born, for one reason only I came into the world. It is this: That I might bear witness to the truth. Everyone who seeks truth will hear the words I speak."

Pilate asked scornfully, "What is truth?"

Jesus gave no reply, I was told.

Then Pilate went out to report to the Pharisees, saying, "I find no fault whatsoever in him. But your custom is that I release one criminal to you at Passover. Is it your wish that I release to you the King of the Jews?"

A mighty protest rose from the crowd. "No! Not this man. Free Barabbas! He is only a thief."

Pilate went in and took Jesus and lashed him with cords. And the Roman soldiers made a new crown of thorns and put it on his head. They stripped him of his tunic and clothed him with a robe of royal purple. They slapped Jesus with their hands and did mocking obeisance to him.

Pilate went out to the people gathered there and said, "I'll bring him to you, so you know that I find him to be without fault"; and he saying "Behold the man!" brought forth Jesus, wearing the crown of thorns and a robe of royal color,

Immediately the chief priests, elders, and officers cried out, "Crucify him! Crucify him!" But Pilate answered, "No, you take and crucify him. I find that he has done no misdeed."

But the Jews protested, "We have a law; and by our law, he ought to die because he made himself the Son of God."

Pilate went back into the judgment hall, taking Jesus with him. "From where have you come?" he asked.

Jesus gave no answer.

Pilate said, "You don't answer me? Don't you know I have power to crucify or release you?"

Jesus answered, "You could have no power at all concerning me, if it was not given you from above. Those who delivered me to you have by far the greater sin."

Pilate was now determined to release Jesus.

But the Jews called loudly to Pilate, "If you let this man go, you are no friend of Caesar. Anyone who makes himself a king, as does this Galilean, speaks against your Emperor."

Hearing this, Pilate again brought Jesus out of the judgment hall. Then he sat down in the judgment seat on the terrace above the pavement.

I, Andrew, could see none of this and dared not show myself, but I heard it. It was nearing midday when Jesus was brought again for all to see. "Behold your king," said Pilate.

A yell went up. "Away with him. Crucify him!"

Pilate asked, "Shall I crucify your king?"

To this, seven chief priests answered, "We have no king but Caesar!"

A ripple of shock went through the mass of Jewish citizens.

I recalled Jesus once identifying for the elders the coin with Caesar's image on it, telling them to render to Caesar that which is Caesar's and to God what is God's. The Jews, who considered themselves God's people, now declared "We have no king but Caesar!"

"Take him, and do with him as you will," said Pilate.

Later I learned that Pilate wrote on a plaque, "Jesus of Nazareth, King of the Jews" in Hebrew, Greek, and Latin so many could read the inscription.

The chief priest, Caiaphas, then asked Pilate to write, "Jesus Christ of Nazareth. He said, I am the King of the Jews," instead of "King of the Jews";

but Pilate refused, saying, "What I have written stays written." And the plaque was affixed to the center of the cross piece upon which Jesus would soon die.

When the procession left Gabbatha to go beyond the city walls to the place called Golgotha, where death and burial take place, I was standing deep in the shadow of a doorway.

I saw a soldier grab a reed and place it as a scepter in Jesus's hand; he first smote our Lord atop his head then spit in his face mocking him. The thorn crown pierced Jesus's brow, and blood dropped on the front of the white robe which he was once again wearing.

A procession formed, with elders and scribes mingling in the contingent of guards and escort officers. A man was summoned from the throng to come forward. He was ordered to heft the timber which would be the cross arm on the gibbet from which Jesus would hang until his death. This man was Simon of Cyrene in Libya.

I feared I might be identified as one of the disciples and be subject to arrest and certain death. This kept me from rushing forth to help carry the heavy crosspiece. But eventually, I did leave the shadowy doorway and was swept along as the noisy crowd surged forward out of the city.

Hundreds struggled up the grade toward the high point where two of the three gallows were planted in the ground; these two already holding crucified felons. Rock had long ago broken away at the crest of the hill, falling to settle below, and it is there that the stone outcropping suggestive of a human skull gives this place its name—*Golgotha*, "the place of a skull."

I looked into the throng but saw no one I knew. I was on the outer edge of the rise, so stricken with grief I could hardly climb. I saw a tall bushy castor bean plant which could allow me to remain present but out of sight.

I reached the spreading foliage and hid there. Yes, I was in that much fear. I heard my name called. It was my brother, Simon, struggling through the mob to reach me. He grasped my arms, and we fell to the ground.

His face was white and his breathing labored. He was pitiful to look at. His eyes were bloodshot, and his voice hoarse. He was bedraggled, unkempt, soiled. He clung to me like a drowning man.

We were safe because we were hidden where we could see, though not hear, what was being done at the top of the hill.

We saw the women gathered there. Mary, Jesus' mother, in the arms of Zebedee's wife, Salome. And Mary of Magdala. Close by was Mary the wife of Cleopas. Oh yes, and not to our surprise, Mary and Martha of Bethany were there with young John, son of Zebedee, who sheltered from time to time each of the women in his sturdy arms.

I arose, intending to go to them, but Simon commanded me, "No!" His voice was like a horn: "We CANNOT show ourselves. It would distract our Master! John is his cousin. Kin are allowed to be near. Our appearance would distract our teacher and cause him concern. The crowd might call for more blood!"

I knew Simon was right, and I fell again to my knees weeping. Then I turned my back and prayed to God as I had never before prayed to Him, wanting, needing to feel the presence of the One who alone owns both heaven and earth.

As my anguish subsided the thought came, I am the first to know Jesus. It seems right that I should now be nearby praying for him.

Simon was very agitated. I reminded him, "With God all things are possible. Regardless of what takes place before our eyes, the spiritual victory of which Jesus has assured us lies within him."

I no longer marveled that Jesus had moved so resolutely into this hour through the cruel persecution of these past weeks. I felt strangely at peace, yet I knew great danger would confront all of us in the days to come.

The babble and hissing of the multitude increased. We could barely see what was occurring on top of the hill, for we hunkered down trying to remain unseen. But then, suddenly, we heard a cheer as the crosspiece borne by Jesus was being drawn up by ropes, to be secured by a soldier who was to mount a ladder at the rear of the central post to bind the crosspiece with ropes. It was with an awful thud that the foot of the cross fell into the pit dug to anchor the gallows stem. A soldier placed Jesus's feet on the wedge provided to permit the crucified one to bend his knees instead of having his legs hanging free and swinging to search for footrest comfort.

Jesus's head was bowed—that we could plainly see.

His arms were stretched wide with cruel spikes driven through his wrists into the crosspiece, holding him immobile. At the sixth hour, the deed was done. Jesus was on the cross. Death was in the air.

John later told us the four executioners who had completed their cruel task stayed at the foot of the cross. It had been previously determined that they would take his clothing. Possession of his coat was to be decided by the casting of lots to determine which soldier would own it. That precious, luminous garment, woven from top to bottom without a seam, Jesus's mother's gift to her holy Son, was gambled for!

Thus the scripture again was fulfilled which prophesied, "They parted my raiment among them, and for my vesture they cast lots."

The turmoil around us lessened as droves of people began to leave, for darkness was falling in daytime and fear set in like a dry grass fire sweeping across the land. Simon Peter and I were anxiously praying as people departed. We wanted to leave our castor bush refuge and creep closer to the top of the rise. The women were clustered at the foot of the cross. Jesus could see them as they looked up to his face. John was there too, now comforting Jesus's mother.

After some time we heard that our Master spoke to his mother, saying, "Woman, see him as your son."

Then to John, "See to her welfare as if she were your mother."

Mary wept, and John gathered her close to his side. How like our Lord and Savior to knit together the mother he tenderly cherished and the young cousin and disciple whom he especially loved for his pure strength, goodness, and faithfulness.

Having made certain that his mother would be cared for, Jesus seemed to know that he could now depart from his earthly temple.

"I thirst," he said. At hand was a vessel full of vinegar, and one of the soldiers filled a sponge with the fluid and held it up with a stem of bunched hyssop and offered it to him to relieve his thirst.

He had been on the cross for three hours. We were exhausted with grief, knowing that our Master must be tormented with pain. He suddenly cried out in a loud voice, "Eli, Eli, lama sabachthani?" My God, my God, why have you forsaken me?

Our hearts were pierced with his words. We knew them to be from a psalm of David which prophesied the suffering of God's anointed.

Again the soldiers offered him the sponge, but he refused the soporific. We heard him say, "Father, into Thy hands I commend my spirit." Then he cried again with a loud voice, saying, "It is finished."

With that, he ceased to draw further breath.

The temple authorities who remained had asked Pilate to have the soldiers break the legs of the three men on the crosses to hasten death, for day was now declining and a dark storm was closing in. They fractured the legs of the man crucified on Jesus's right, and then of the other felon on his left. Coming then to Jesus, they saw that he had breathed his last. There was no need to hasten his death.

But one of the soldiers put his spear to the side of Jesus's torso and thrusting it upward pierced his body. Blood and water flowed out, proving that Jesus had indeed died.

Peter and I turned away heartsick, filled with fear. Darkness came sweeping in like a sandstorm. There was a sudden wind and a sharp earthquake. The rocking of the earth sent boulders flying and men falling. On the hill, three crosses swayed in the tempest, then rain fell in streams, and streamlets formed and ran down in cascades of mud mingled with blood.

Afterward, we learned that at the moment Jesus expired, the veil which hid the Holy of Holies in the temple was rent from top to bottom. Men nearby dropped to their knees, fearing that the end of days had come and all flesh was doomed to die.

We slogged down the hill through mud until our feet were once again steady under us. Just as authorities began the descent of our Master's body from the cross, we sadly left the scene and made our way to the house of Barnabas in the upper city.

It was here that we all had agreed to meet at the close of this day. When we arrived, several apostles were already there. Each one was heartbroken, cowering in disbelief, asking, "What could we have done? What should we have done?"

Simon Peter—exhausted, muddied, and disheveled—broke through the cloudy self-condemnation with these words, "From this moment forth, we must not fail him. He left his message in our hearts and minds. Now we must prove our worthiness of all he taught us. We have no choice but to love each other as he loved us."

Later, under the cloak of evening, James and Matthew left the house and went back to the place where Jesus had died. Nothing moved atop the hill. But a bit beyond, outside of the city wall at the foot of a nearby rise, there is a burial garden. They saw lights flickering there. The apostles went to the place where there was a new sepulchre, hewn into rock, with a great round wheel of stone ready to be rolled across the entrance to seal it.

Within the walls of the tomb, two men were wrapping the bathed body of Jesus in linen as it lay on a narrow hewn ledge.

One of the men was known to the disciples, for Jesus had told us of him. He was Joseph of Arimathaea, a kin of his mother. He was prominent in Jerusalem. Secretly, for fear of the Jews, he was also a disciple of Jesus. He had gone to Pilate to ask that the body of Jesus might be taken away for burial and Pilate gave him leave.

Nicodemus, who came to Jesus by night at the beginning of Jesus's mission, was there. He had purchased seventy-five pounds of spices, which they were now using as they swathed the body for entombment.

James and Matthew remained without, for the tomb was small. Mary Magdalene and Salome the mother of Zebedee's sons were also waiting there to be witness to the gentle care being given to the body of Jesus.

When the task was done and the stone was rolled to prevent entrance to the sepulchre, the men left; but the women wrapped in their woolen shawls remained through the night. Conscious of the love of God, they felt endless gratitude for the life they'd shared with God's son. Only angels could have made their watch-guard holier.

The next morning, Pharisees went to Pilate, saying, "That impostor, Jesus of Nazareth, said while he yet lived, 'after three days I will rise again.' Command, we beg you, that the sepulchre be guarded until the third day. His disciples could come by night and steal his body to fool the people into believing that he has risen from the dead."

Pilate answered, "You have guardsmen. Do as you wish. Make it as secure as you can." So they came to the burial ground.

They opened the tomb just enough to see that the body was still there. Then they rolled the stone back across the entrance and sealed it with a large peg driven deep into the earth, which prevented anyone who might try to gain entrance. They set three watchmen to hold guard so no man could try to enter the tomb. It was still the Sabbath, the day for rest.

Chapter 16

I can't tell you if the next day was bright or gloomy. We were all stunned. Frightened. We didn't talk to one another. We didn't eat. No one left the house of Barnabas. We didn't open the door, even when the women, who were mourning next door in the house of John Mark's mother, came to comfort us. They just entered at will, bringing food and assuring words of comfort. We, in our deep grief, only ignored them.

I tried to pray. It helped when I turned my back and sat in a corner of the main room near a window covered with a towel so there was only a little light.

We were praying as best we could, but the day passed very slowly. When it began to get dark, several of us ventured out one by one into the streets nearby, but nothing important was learned.

That night *everyone* slept, for we were numb with wearied grief. Then the pain of an empty stomach began to rouse us to the need to eat, and we awakened long before daybreak.

The women had brought food the night before—fruit and loaves. I ate two bites and could take no more. Others ate to the full. As we began to stir and converse, our stomachs rebelled; and the food we'd just eaten spewed out of our mouths, showing how upset we inwardly still were. We fussed and cleaned up the mess.

It was the first day of the week, and in the predawn darkness we tried to quiet our thoughts with prayer. But all I could think was, "He is gone, and we are left." And I, for one, had little heart for prayer.

Then, barely noticeable, there was a sound outside the entry to Barnabas's house. "A rat," someone said. But then it was heard again, a muffled sound of someone knocking at the door.

We were still very frightened. Instant silence reigned. Again came the sound. But no one moved to open the door. We were cowering in fear.

Again, the knocking; this time it was louder. There was no pounding, no assertion of authority, simply the gentle insistence of someone wanting to enter through the door we'd locked late the night before.

Thaddeus put his finger on his lips to warn us to be very quiet. Then he crept to the door and put his ear to better detect if the person seeking to enter was a friend or foe.

He heard a voice, a woman's voice. "Mary, young Mary," he whispered hoarsely. "Open!" commanded James, Jesus's brother who had joined us late the evening before.

Thaddeus sprung the latch block and opened the door. There was Mary of Magdala, trembling with fear.

"They've taken our Lord out of the sepulchre, and we know nothing as to where he now lies."

Peter grabbed a torch and with John bolted out of the house and ran through the still sleeping city, to the cemetery where Jesus was entombed.

John, being the younger, outran Peter and was first to reach the sepulchre.

The stone indeed was rolled away. Stooping down, John looked in and saw the linen burial clothes lying there. The guards were nowhere in sight.

But he did not go into the tomb.

Simon Peter reached the place, breathing hard, but directly he entered in and investigated. He saw the linen clothes and the napkin which had covered our Master's head in death. The napkin was not lying with the wrapping bands but had been folded neatly and was lying nearby.

Then John entered the tomb, saw what Peter was seeing—that Jesus's body had indeed been taken from the place.

The fact is that Jesus several times spoke of his rising from death after three days, but he never quoted to us from scriptures the prophecy that he would rise again from the dead.

And so Peter and John returned to us furtively and, with much sadness, told us what they had seen. Jesus's body had been stolen.

Mary, stricken with sorrow, had followed them to the burial place; but now she remained outside of the tomb, weeping, when the two disciples hastily departed from that place.

As she wept, she stooped down and looked into the place where the body of Jesus had lain.

She was stunned to see in the tomb two angels clothed in white, sitting there on the ledge, one at the head, the other at the foot where Jesus's body had been laid.

"Why do you weep?" each angel asked in turn.

"Because they have taken away my Lord, and I don't know where he now lies."

Mary turned away from the angels, for she saw someone standing near her in the darkness. She supposed it to be the gardener who asked, "Woman, why do you weep? Whom are you seeking?"

Mary answered through her tears, "Sir, if you have carried him from this place, tell me where you have laid him, and I will go to him."

She heard her name spoken: "Mary."

She turned and saw that it was Jesus who was standing there, clad in a white tunic.

"Master!" Her voice rang with joy, and her arms reached forth to embrace her Lord. Her heart was racing, her mind exultant.

He had explained to us how he had given to friends and foes alike word that the sign he was giving was the sign of Jonah who had been three days in the belly of the whale. Like Jonah, he would come forth in three days to live again.

Now Jesus said tenderly, "Do not touch me, Mary, for I am not yet fully risen from the earth in ascension to my Father in heaven. Go, dear one, to my brethren. Say to them 'I am ascending to my God and your God.'"

"Oh yes!" Mary told us she replied. She then came straightway to Barnabas's house and brought us this joyous news.

"Then we will see him again! Surely he will, in some way, show himself to us and the world!" This came from my brother. Peter needed to see him. "Let us consume our morning meal and make ourselves and this place ready to see him."

This time our bread stayed down and our stomachs grew peaceful. We ate in thoughtful silence.

Thereafter we made neat the house, bundling up our soiled clothing, ordering our pallets and few possessions. Taking our laundry, we went out wearing garments not fresh but serviceable to cloak us somewhat from being identified. We were still fearful of the temple authorities.

Two by two we made our way into the lower city, some of us to public fountains, some going farther to the spring in Ein Karem, taking muddy garments worn the day of the crucifixion. Others of us went to Gethsemane or to public bath cisterns to bathe and dress in fresh garments.

To say our hearts were lifted is to beg your understanding of how we had despaired for three days and now felt reborn, renewed, and filled with holy hope. It seemed natural that we go about our tasks in quietness.

I, for one, stood in awe of the glad turn of events. Words could not convey the depths of sadness my heart had endured. Now, words could not express the height of gladness my heart had risen to. We all were sobered with quiet joy. Tenderly we worked together. Compassionately we answered each other. Courteously we forgave one another when one blundered, misspoke, or gave mild offense.

In some gentle way eleven men became more like their teacher—kinder, more patient and tolerant, less judgmental, less prone to self-assertion.

We separated to refresh our bodies and came together again at midday, and without a word, our reunion took each of us into the sanctuary of prayer. To a man, we found that lessons from our Master surfaced in our minds; and we, without planning, spent the rest of the day rehearsing inwardly what we had learned from this man who had proven death to be no part of one's life.

Expectantly we waited within the walls of Barnabas's house and courtyard for our Master. The women brought more food from next door, their faces radiant with joy and hope and acceptance of the fact that Jesus had indeed raised himself from death, as he had raised others from the grave, the underworld, and hell.

I prayed, thanking God, yet asking more beneficence in words from the Psalms: "Open Thou my eyes that I may behold wonderful things out of your law."

Jesus had taught us, "God's allness is God's law."

And so our hearts found peace.

Mary Magdalene, filled with rejoicing, was grateful when Joanna, and Mary, wife of Alphaeus and mother of Matthew and James the Little, along with Salome the wife of Zebedee, asked her to go with them to the tomb. Though we did not hear until later that young Mary went along, we learned that when they reached the place, the great stone was rolled back from the door. This time the angel of the Lord sat upon it. His face was radiant with moving light, and his clothing was whiter than any whiteners known to earth. At his feet the two watchmen posted to guard the tomb lay as dead men for they had been shaken when the angel appeared and the earth quaked again.

"What has happened?" the women asked the angel. The angel's answer: "I know you seek Jesus who was crucified. He is not here. Come see the place where your Lord lay. Then go quickly. Tell his disciples that he is risen from the dead and will go into Galilee before them and there shall they see him. Tell them I have told you this good news."

The women were leaving the garden sepulchre, having great joy and strange fear. But on the way Jesus met them! He greeted them, saying, "All Hail!" The women fell before him. Gently touching his feet, they worshiped him, saying, "Thank God! Thank God! Thank God!"

Jesus said, "Have no fear. Go tell my brethren to return into Galilee, for there shall they see me."

As the women left the garden, the watchmen, who had been startled to stillness at the appearance of the Angel of God, hurried past them on their way to tell the chief priests what had just happened.

The elders heard their story, took council, and came forth with a large sum of money for the soldiers, telling them to say that Jesus's disciples came by night and stole the body while they were asleep on their watch.

The men were assured that if the governor heard this untruth, the elders would give an explanation to him, protecting the watchers. So they took the money and did as they were told, and many believe to this day that this lie is the truth.

Later we heard from Mary Magdalene how she and Mary the mother of Levi and James the Little, and Salome the wife of Zebedee brought sweet spices to the tomb to anoint the body again the day after the Sabbath. The two older women insisted on going, taking the spices with them. Young Mary had already visited the tomb, but she went again.

The women reached the sepulchre hoping to find someone to roll back the stone which sealed the entrance.

When they arrived, they saw the stone was removed. Entering the sepulchre, they saw an angel clothed in white sitting on the right side of the chamber. They were startled and frightened.

"Don't be afraid," the angel said to them. "You have come seeking Jesus of Nazareth who was crucified. He is risen. This is where they laid his body but he is not here."

The women departed, leaving the unused spices behind. They were shaken and trembling. They were amazed but did not cry out with joy to those they met. Yes, they too were cautious and fearful, but young Mary was not. She was radiant with joy.

This is now the third time that Mary came to assure the apostles. At first we had not believed her, but now we knew it was a fact. Jesus had risen from death.

Joy began slowly to creep into each heart and mind. All who heard these witnesses were comforted and rejoiced. Words which at first had seemed to be tales had been proven true.

That very evening, before we laid down to rest, the apostles, except for Thomas who was out on a family errand, were assembled to plan the return to Galilee.

Unexpectedly Jesus came into our midst, saying, "Peace be unto each of you."

He parted his belted garment and showed us the healed wound in his side. He spread forth his hands and showed where the spikes had been driven through his wrists to hold him to the crosspiece.

To say we were excited is to make less of our true emotions. We were overjoyed. We pressed close around Jesus, being careful to not touch him, yet wishing mightily to be able to embrace him and hold him to our hearts.

Again he said, "Peace be ceaseless in your hearts and minds.

"My Father sent me hither, and now I send you into the world." So saying, Jesus closed his eyes and breathed deeply. Then he said, "Receive the Holy Spirit to inhabit your hearts to the exclusion of all else.

"Go forth. Challenge the sins of the world; remit punishment to those who believe in my name, for thus are their sins remitted. Whoever holds to sins through carnal desire, in them sin is retained. Their belief of life in sensual flesh binds them to earth and renders them unready for eternal existence."

Raising his hands in benediction, Jesus disappeared from our sight, even as he had appeared unexpectedly in our presence. No door had opened to admit him. None was needed for his departure. We ten witnesses to his spiritual ability stood in hushed and reverent awe of our Master.

Thomas returned a short time later. We told him what we had experienced. But Thomas wanted only to see for himself, saying, "I will truly believe when I see in his hands the print of the nails and touch with my fingers the wound in his side. Then I will truly be witness to his resurrection."

Two of Jesus's close followers decided that afternoon to walk to Emmaus, a village three score furlongs from Jerusalem. Joses and Clopas his son ventured forth.

Several furlongs out of Jerusalem, a man drew near and joined them.

The man said, "What sort of conversation are you having one to another as you walk in such sadness?"

Clopas answered, "Are you a stranger in Jerusalem that you don't know what happened here a few days ago?"

The stranger asked, "What happened?"

"Jesus of Nazareth, a holy man who walked among us healing and preaching for nearly three years was condemned to death. He was crucified at the instigation of the chief priests and rulers. It is the third day now since he was laid in a tomb.

"Early this morning certain women who often walked with him and his disciples went at daybreak to the sepulchre. His body was not there. The tomb was open. Angels close by told them that he was alive."

Clopas and Joses were startled when the stranger replied, "You are fools and slow of heart to believe all that has been prophesied and has now come true. If this was God's intent that Christ should suffer death and return to his glorious spiritual estate, should he not have entered into the proving?"

Then the man said, "Hear what Moses and all the prophets said of this man and wrote of him in the scriptures." And he recited all that was prophesied.

They reached the village of Emmaus. The stranger acted as though he would journey on, but Clopas said, "Abide thee with us. It is near the close of day." The man agreed to tarry with them.

Later they sat at meat and watched him take bread into his hands. As he thanked God for the blessing of food, he broke the bread, and handed portions to Clopas and Joses to eat.

At once the two men saw clearly that this man blessed and broke bread as Jesus had done. No longer blinded by the fear and belief that Jesus was dead, they saw clearly that their teacher was right there, alive, alert, and loving.

At once Jesus vanished from their sight, and they hurried back to tell us of his conversation with them as they walked to Emmaus.

Early the next day we set out to return to Galilee. Taking the shortest route northward, we reached Jacob's well near Sychar before sunset and stopped there to rest through the dark hours.

A small fire shed warmth as the night air grew cooler, and fire light reflected in our faces as we sat talking about Jesus's resurrection.

Later, as we grew sleepy, Peter, James and John seated themselves across from the rest of us. The fire between us was now merely glowing coals.

Peter began to speak. "Do you recall when we were in Caesarea Philippi and then went up the foothills of Mount Hermon?" he asked. "Jesus voiced his intent to climb the high mountain and asked James and John and me to accompany him. Remember?" We nodded yes.

"It was quite a climb. We reached the top, and the view was wide and far reaching. I wondered why our Master requested only the three of us to scale the mountain with him. I had enjoyed the climb for it distracted me from the pronouncement Jesus made earlier that day about his coming passion when he revealed that he would soon suffer death but rise in resurrection the third day thereafter."

Now Jesus *had* come forth from the grave and I, Andrew, wondered why the trek up Mount Hermon was being brought to mind again.

James took over from Peter and described the scene which one beholds from such heights. "We saw the Jordan River threading through Galilee and Judea toward the inland brine sea. We saw the Great Sea spread beyond the shore of Syrophoenicia. To the north we could see the dark shape of Lebanon's cedared mountains. To the east stretched the ridged uplands of Gaulinitis southward along the sea of Galilee. We could see almost all the land through which we had journeyed with Jesus."

John continued, "But on the mountain, something occurred which Jesus asked us to not tell until he was risen from the dead."

For a few moments we were silent, having no idea of what was coming next. I found myself recalling the holy calm which enveloped the Master as he looked into the stunned faces of each one of us after predicting his crucifixion. I felt now as I had then, scarcely able to breathe.

John continued, "I didn't know why Jesus had taken the three of us that day, but I understand now what he was doing. He was teaching us to see far beyond the present scene and times, beyond the sameness of the world we know so well path by path, rock by rock and face by face.

"What happened next is hard to describe—almost too sacred to try to explain—but this is what he asked us to tell to no one until he was risen from the dead. We three have not even talked among ourselves about the happening, but tell you we must and do our best to help you understand.

"We stood there on the mountaintop, appreciating the wide and wondrous view," John said, "and heard Jesus behind us talking to someone. We turned at once to see who was there.

"Jesus stood only a short space away from us, earnestly conversing with two individuals. His visage and his countenance were altered from head to sandals.

His face shone with a radiance brighter than the sun. His garments were as luminous as his face. His form was changed. Enhanced, he seemed to exude strength and gentleness at the same time. He seemed no longer embodied by flesh and bones but clothed in light.

"At first I was stunned by the changed appearance of our Master. Then I saw the others also had glorious bodies, glistening, and radiant."

Peter continued, "It will help if I tell you we saw three individuals, each of them embodied by light, of light, as light. How can I say it so you can see what we beheld? Their bodies were not flesh. The wonder of beholding three individuals wrapped in light is . . ."

James broke in before Peter could say more. "Let me tell it Peter. We knew at once who was talking with Jesus—it was Moses and Elias! Yes, dear brethren, we were in the presence of Moses and Elias, both having glorified forms, as did our Master."

"How could you recognize who they were?" asked Thomas. "Moses has been dead for eighteen hundred years and Elias lived eight hundred years ago, how could you be seeing them when they've been so long dead!"

"Not dead," the three disciples declared in unison.

"Apparently not as we think of death. Do you recall Jesus telling us of Moses disappearing when a bright cloud came down upon him on Mount Abarim and he was never found?" said Peter. "And scripture records Elias ascending in a chariot of flaming fire with thousands of angels.

"Our thoughts were inspired with the view on the mountain," said Peter. "But consciousness was lifted even higher when we saw our Master transfigured."

James spoke up. "These men were clad in the garments of immortality. Here we were, three mortals awestruck in the presence of immortal beings."

Peter nodded in affirmation. "Such light is too bright for men to live with yet."

I spoke up. "We disciples are utterly amazed. Did they see you?" I asked.

James answered, "They gave no heed to us as they quietly talked with Jesus. We heard one say to Jesus, 'You know whence you were before you came to earth.'

"We heard the other say, 'Heaven is within you, Jesus, as heaven is within all. Go forth now and reveal eternal life to those who sleep in Adam's dream.'

"Both Moses and Elias then embraced Jesus."

Peter, James, and John were silent, letting their words sink into our minds.

"I should not have spoken," confessed my impetuous brother, Simon Peter, "but rashly, I now realize, I said, 'Lord, it is good that we are here and have seen all this. If it pleases you we will now build three habitations—one for you, one for Moses, one for Elias—to dwell in here.'

"Before I had finished speaking a cloud bright with living light descended upon us; and from the cloud a voice rebuked me, saying, 'This is my beloved Son, in whom I am wholly pleased. Listen to him.'

"It was the voice of God! We were hearing words from the voice of the Almighty!"

"I fell on my face to the ground," said James.

"We all did," added John. "We were taken down in awe. But Jesus rescued us from our trembling prostration. He touched each one of us, saying, 'Rise up. There is nothing in God to fear.'

"We opened our eyes. Moses and Elias were no longer with us. Only Jesus.

"'Come now,' he said, 'we must go down from the mountain while it is still day.'"

"As we descended we talked of what we had experienced," said Peter. "Did we really see Moses and Elias?" I asked Jesus.

"'Yes,' he replied. 'Nothing that lives ever loses life. And nothing that dies ever has real life. All things made by God live, abiding forever in the infinite realm of Spirit. All that God creates expresses infinitude and eternal existence.'

"'You have seen two men who did God's will on earth,' said Jesus, 'and as on earth, they continue to serve God in the eternal realm.'"

I thought, *What can we say to all of this?* Nothing.

We sat wide awake, talking through the night. Peter kept the fire blazing. We were absorbed in a wonder too great to understand, but too promising to forget. We were lost in a new resolve to follow our Master, wherever we would be led.

As the morning star rose in the darkness before dawn, we still sat deep in thought, hopeful in heart, and gratified in spirit. Three of the twelve of us had seen the reality of glorified existence. They heard the voice of God instructing them to listen to His beloved Son, our Lord and Master, Jesus the Christ.

"Lord, open my ears that I too may hear thy voice" was my prayer for days afterward.

Back in Capernaum we gathered daily at the house in Chuza's grove. Sharing our own family homes at night with apostles from Cana and elsewhere, we met each day in the grove to discuss how we would go forth into the world to preach the Gospel of the kingdom of God.

We also shared sentiments after hearing about the suicide of Judas Iscariot, whose body had been found midweek after the crucifixion, hanging from a samuda tree in a small obscure canyon on an upper slope of the Mount of Olives.

It is easy to judge and condemn those who fail a trust. Our Master had urged us to avoid opinions. "Have spiritual convictions," he often said, "but avoid opinions for they are based on what an eye sees or an ear hears rather than on what God knows."

Simon Zelotes, who sometimes paired with Judas, sadly told us how Judas feared that our Master's cause would be endangered if the Jewish elders arranged his death. Judas told Jesus of his fears, and Jesus told him that it was necessary for someone to deliver him into the hands of those who would put him to death.

As we talked about these things, Jesus came suddenly into our presence, simply appearing in the midst. "Peace . . . ," he said. "Peace be to each of you.

"Thomas, you have not seen . . . reach forth your finger now," he said, "and touch the nail print. Put your hand into my side and believe that it is I myself. No longer be without faith or unbelieving."

After Thomas did as he was bidden, he humbly said, "My Lord and my God."

Jesus said, "Thomas, because you see me, you believe. Blessed are all who have not seen yet believe." Then the Master was no longer present, he simply disappeared before our eyes.

The days went by. We eleven apostles tried to keep the faith. We went into outlying regions and healed all who sought healing.

One day I sat alone seaside, thinking deeply about our Master. A few minutes later he walked up and sat down beside me. "How is it you are still here, Lord?" I asked. "How is it you have not gone to your glory in God?"

"I am still teaching, Andrew. In time I shall depart, but for now I am here to prove that life endures after death."

"Master, you often told us that you are the Way, the Truth, and the Life. You said also, 'If a man keep my saying he shall never see death.' I do not understand this as I should. Please enlighten me."

Jesus looked deep into my eyes, seeming to read my need. Then he told me truths too deep for me to repeat quite yet. Perhaps later I will sometime find words to tell you.

No, I will share with you *now* the most incredible things Jesus revealed to me. As I've said, I don't know what he has shared with any of the other apostles. But I recall in detail what he told me that day.

First, the importance of loving. "Love as God loves His offspring," he told me. "The more you love, the more you will see the results of love; the fruitage of healing through God. God's love meets all human need," he said.

"Your love reflected from divine Love will heal. Man is found to be the image of our Heavenly Father wherever love blooms."

Then he explained to me the water being made wine. And the multitude being fed when only a few loaves and fish were at hand to meet the hunger of the multitude.

As a rabbi engages the thought of a child, Jesus said to me, "Andrew, in time to come, the earth and all therein will no longer seem what we think it now to be. The fleshly mind will yield to the divine, and man will be conscious only of good. Things will be seen as thought. They will have outline, form, and substance, but not in matter as they are now perceived."

"That is what I have. Intelligence and goodness are reality as the substance of the thoughts of God," he continued, "and they are seen in men as spirit, as action, as practical.

"In fullness of time, mankind will learn that the carnal mind—its thoughts, its beliefs, opinions, and convictions—are false.

"Ages may come and go before God's creation appears in its perfection, harmony, abundance, and glory; yet it all exists right now in Spirit.

"In time, men will seek to understand that what one's eyes behold as fleshly and carnal is unreal. Men will discern how enduring substance, form, function, cause, and effect can be known. Body will be the expression of conscious existence, individuality and identity.

"Men will understand that all physical things are actually only temporal. They will learn that true substance is not what is seen with bodily eyes and touched with fleshly hands. They will learn that there is no elemental substance other than thought from the Mind of God.

"Someday they will discern that infinitesimals, though not seen, exist in omnipresence and proceed from intelligent concept to manifestation as ideas, mentally brought forth for divine purpose of goodness and God's glory.

"This then is the beginning of true knowledge. Men will want to understand the omniscience and omnipresence which is God. They will understand the power given to those who image the likeness of the one infinite divinity.

"One may thus access every needed thing as thought and bring forth the manifestation thereof."

And then Jesus said solemnly, "Only the pure in heart can reflect this God-given power. When this day of understanding comes, mankind will perceive how I produced such abundance of loaves and fish without process of planting, harvesting, or baking the bread. Or trolling to gather fish."

My mind was reeling. We were staggered with such abundance! Apparently aware of my curiosity as to how he was able to do this, the Master gave explanation.

I recall Jesus referring first to a psalm which he recited in part that day.

> Praise the Lord. He heals the heartbroken. He binds up their wounds.
> He numbers the stars and has names for them all. Our God is great,
> and His power is great. His intelligent Mind is boundless. He covers
> the heaven with clouds, preparing rain for the earth, making grass
> to grow upon the mountains, giving creatures food—both beasts and

fowl. He grows snow like wool. He scatters frost like ashes. He casts ice like small bites of food. Then he sends his word and melts them. He causes his wind to blow and the waters, before straightened in ice, begin to move and flow again. He shows his word to Jacob and his wisdom to Israel.

"This world," he explained, "is but a limited sense of the spiritual reality from whence I come. This life is limited. When mankind learns that the spiritual creation is the expression of God's perfect intelligence, men will gradually abandon all except the divine consciousness as reality."

Jesus continued, "I discipline my thought to bear witness to only what confirms God's goodness. "You now have no idea, Andrew, of the reality of God's power and goodness. But you know that the kingdom and power of God is within you. It is within every man's and every woman's heart and hope. All who learn of me can shape their earthly lives according to the pattern I have shown. Every act of my life of teaching and healing will eventually awaken the race out of Adam's dream and Eve's bewilderment."

I was breathless. To have laid before me the solution to the sadness of human life was almost more than I could take.

"As to how the loaves and fish were multiplied, Andrew," said Jesus, "when there is no limitation or fear in thought, all good and only good is available. Someday man will study mind and find it to be God. Then, they will easily attain the kingdom of God on earth.

Jesus continued, "Andrew, you now understand why I gave the parable of the talents, saying, 'everyone that hath shall be given and he shall have abundance, but whoever has not gained the wisdom that is profitable, even the little understanding that one has, shall be taken from him!'

"There is a perfect awareness and understanding of the power of God. When God is known as the loving and productive source of all that exists, creation will be seen in all of God's glory. Everything divine intelligence brings into being, man will embrace and use. In man the glory of God will be forever displayed."

When Jesus finished teaching this wonder of being, I felt baptized in love and wisdom and could say nothing. I simply took my Master's right hand and held it first to my cheek, then to my heart. My flood of gratitude fell to the depths of my soul.

Jesus said, "There will be a new heaven and a new earth, but it will be nothing more, nothing less, than the reality of heaven and earth as it has always existed and exists right now spiritually."

We walked together a short distance along the sea, deep in thought. The Master lightly touched my shoulder and then vanished from my presence.

But . . . I do not forget. I do *not* forget!

Chapter 17

Again we were in Chuza's grove, awaiting our Master. The day passed, but he did not come.

Weary, disappointed, even heartsick, Peter broke our anguish, saying, "I'm going back to the sea to work." He arose and walked off. Before he was out of sight, I called, "Wait brother! I'm coming too."

Then Zebedee's sons and Nathanael and Thomas Didymus and Matthew and James the Less decided to go with us. Three disciples stayed to watch should Jesus come.

Among the eight who returned to the sea, four of us were fishermen. So we teamed up, experienced fishers working with those who were not. We sailed out in two of Zebedee's larger boats as soon as darkness set in.

Soon we were trolling waters three hundred feet offshore. It was good to be on the sea. Good to feel the cool night breeze. Good to hear the gentle lap of the waves against the hull of the ship.

We talked very little but worked very hard, pulling in the dragnets then throwing them back. They were always empty when drawn, but at least we were doing something.

All night long we worked, only to haul in the fishless ever-collapsing nets. "How is it," I asked, "that nothing seems to be working now?" No one had an answer.

Near daybreak we pulled in the nets and headed to shore. A voice came through the light morning fog. "Children, have you any meat?"

Someone yelled back, "No. Not one fish."

We heard the voice again, "Cast your nets on the right side of the ship, for there are fish and you'll draw many."

We felt strangely compelled to obey, and as we cast the nets, the water roiled with a huge school of fish, as though we were chumming for a catch.

"Light of heaven," Peter whooped, "it's the Master!" He grabbed his fishing tunic and, fastening it about his waist, plunged into the sea and swam to land.

We others manned the rudder and oars and turned the skiffs shoreward. When we were only a few yards from the stony beach, our nets were bulging with fish. We thought to drag them toward land rather than take the time to dump the catch into our vessels.

We anchored in water deep enough for the fish to swim while in the nets. After securing the nets, we leaped out and splashed ashore, abandoning the boats. We ran to greet our Master, then Nathanael left to fetch the other three disciples watching and waiting in Chuza's grove.

There was joy and much babble when they returned.

We gathered around our Teacher but did not embrace him. Was it really him? He seemed lighter in weight, somewhat delicate, somehow less physical. And radiant with an inner light. Stalwart, yet with his usual gentle repose. How we revered him!

A little way from where he stood, there was a small fire burning around a center pile of flat stones. Jesus said, "Bring some of the fresh fish you've just caught, and I'll add them to our morning meal."

The seven of us went with Simon, and drew one of the dragnets to shore. It was full of fine large fish, a hundred and fifty-three of them. We chose a few then drew the nets out of the shallows and let them down in deeper water to open, setting free the fish.

Off they swam, with our gratitude that they had obeyed our Master's command to fill the nets. We looked and saw that not one web of the netting was broken, despite the abundant harvest. Another miracle! Would this man never cease to amaze and inspire us?

We took the few fish, freshly gutted, and gave them to Jesus who laid them on the broiling stones. He had removed the loaves warming there and, placing a small already cooked fish in each rolled flatbread, he gave to us to eat. We ate in contented silence as the strengthening morning sun burned away the shoreline mist. All eleven were together again, joyous to be with our risen Master.

I cannot say what the others felt, but it seemed that my heart was being emptied of sorrow and despair, even of the terrible grief and burdening images of having watched so helplessly while Jesus hung upon the cross. The morning meal diminished the sadness of the Passover supper.

Here he was, and joy and gladness seemed to rise both in our songs and in our tears. One of us was actually weeping bitterly. It was my brother.

No gladness welled up in his heart, so excruciatingly sad was he. His tears fell ceaselessly, shamelessly down his cheeks, onto his dark, curly beard, to his chest, then to his feet, and the sand beneath his feet. His attempt to smile was shadowed with shame and deep regret.

Jesus noticed this.

"Simon, son of Jona," he asked, "Do you *love me* more than these friends?"

"Oh yes, Lord," he answered (somewhat blithely to my thought). "You know I love you."

"Then feed the lambs of my flock," Jesus said.

Simon's mood brightened, but the question came again: "Simon, son of Jona, *do* you love me?"

The same answer came forth, "Yes, Lord, you know I *love you*." He spoke slowly, solemnly this time.

Jesus answered, "Then feed my sheep."

Peter's face flushed, for now both he and we knew that our beloved Master was restoring Peter, forgiving the denials he had uttered in the doorway of the house of the high priest on the night before the crucifixion.

Again Jesus asked, "Simon, son of Jona, *lovest* thou *me?*"

We could see that Peter was undone with sadness and regret that Jesus asked the third time, "do you love me?"; and his face crumpled and a river of tears poured again from his eyes despite his efforts to choke them back.

I saw my brother weeping—Cephas the Rock, named by Jesus, weeping in huge contrition. I wept in sympathy for him and with him. I felt his grief. I wanted to cry out to our Master, "Does he *love* you? Master, he is dying of sorrow and shame that he denied you"; but I uttered not a word in defense of my brother's tears.

I knew that Jesus loved him. In the questions, he was showing all of us how to bring sin to repentance and sorrow for wrongdoing. He was teaching us to have compassion even while calling for correction. Then there is forgiveness following the tears of repentance which abjectly fall.

Peter, with his head bowed and his body trembling, walked forward a few paces to stand close to his Lord and Savior.

He answered the third query in a voice so low we almost missed hearing his words.

"Lord you know everything; you know I love you."

Jesus placed both hands on Peter's shoulders for just a moment and said, "Feed my sheep."

Peter looked directly into Jesus's eyes. He saw nothing but holiest love.

Jesus then spoke words we all heard. "Truly, I remind you, Peter, when you were a child you dressed yourself and walked any place you wanted to go or to see. But when you become old, you will stretch your arms out, and someone else will put clothes upon your body and carry you where you yourself would never want to be taken."

My heart sank. What could this mean? Will Simon, like Jesus, also be crucified? Perish such thoughts. But again they came to me in cold fear.

Jesus said two words to Peter, and then spread his arms wide to include all of us symbolically, as he repeated them, engraving these words upon each of our hearts.

He said simply, "Follow me."

"Follow me."

We breathed more easily. Peter humbly stood aside. Jesus turned away from us, the remnant of his followers, and began walking back toward Chuza's grove for a farewell visit to the nobleman's family.

John fell in step to walk with Jesus. Peter fell back. Moments later he called out to Jesus, "Lord, what shall this man be asked to do?"

Peter! Peter! Peter! My heart cried out in a silent but inwardly shrieking protest. *Jesus said to you, "Follow me."*

I was almost raging against my brother in the secret chambers of my heart. *Be silent brother! Close your mouth! Utter no words! God will direct the Cause of Christ. You cannot take charge of the whole world when our Master departs from earth.*

I was so busy trying to quiet my thoughts that I almost missed Jesus's answer to Peter's question: "If I decide that John wait on earth till I return, what is that to you? I've bidden you to follow, not succeed me."

Peter fell to the very back of our troop and walked alone. I left him there, for I was deep in thought wondering what John must be thinking about Jesus's answer to Peter's question.

Late that afternoon we eleven apostles sat together on the lower slopes of the Horns of Hattin where Jesus had given the sermon on the ethics of his cause months before.

We'd had but few tidbits of dried fruit and a few kernels of nuts for the wonderful seaside breakfast was still in our bellies. But now we rested.

Jesus sat apart, gazing eastward across the sunlit sea. He might have known my thought for I was remembering every experience I'd had with him.

He turned and looked back straight into my eyes and gestured with a backward nod of his head that I should come to him.

He arose as I joined him, and we walked over a small rise in the land and sat down together just out of sight of the other ten.

"I shall now spend less time with each of you," he explained, "but you are the first one who sought and followed me, Andrew."

I smiled. Perhaps I should have been silent but I was full of questions. "I have something to ask," I said. "It wraps up all other queries I might have."

"Say on," Jesus replied with a smile.

"I go back to the first miracle when you changed water into wine. You explained in words then hard to grasp, it was all so new to me.

"Since then, however, I have had infinite reason to marvel how it is that you so unerringly heal. You restore life. Make rigid muscles work. Foul flesh is made pure and touchable. You lengthened a man's arm. You taught us to see God's perfection in every man. We have been enabled to do works similar to yours. But I would learn more that I might even walk on the water and multiply loaves."

Jesus smiled with that penetrating love that seemed to want to confirm and match my motives to his heart's pure offering. He sat silently a few minutes and then began to speak.

"The substance of God's perfect thought is goodness. This substance, mental in nature, is not like changeable physical corporeality. Substance is perceptible as thought. The mental substance which endures comes from verities always at hand.

"Things of flesh and blood, all growing things, all moving creatures, in the process of birth, growth, and fullness of being, then decline into death. In this world the pattern sometimes becomes disrupted. Young things die before they have developed. Or if developed, the carnal thing may languish, become violently disturbed, or perish in some affliction or danger. None of this is so in the kingdom of God.

"You have seen all sorts of bodily afflictions healed. You have seen multitudes fed; the wind and sea controlled. You have seen abundance and quietness bestowed. It is God's consciousness that is the source and origin of life and being. There is no enduring substance in things of this world. They exist for a time but ultimately perish. Such substance may be either good or evil.

"In God, substance is intelligence and goodness is all. Man has access to God's goodness and power. Do you understand this, Andrew?"

I did, and I didn't. I told Jesus this; and he said, "Use what you can. The key is to think of God the ever-present, all-powerful, and all-knowing Mind as true substance. Then know yourself to image God, not in corporeal form, but through spiritual consciousness."

These words were hard for me to understand. I know I shall grow weary trying to fathom all they promise. But at least I have recorded them.

Forty days had passed, one by one, since the resurrection of our Lord Christ Jesus. We continued our healing efforts. We sometimes slept in the olive grove in Gethsemane, other times in the hills and valleys of Galilee. Or among rocks in desert places. We saw Jesus less often but heard from others of appearances he made to other followers—once to five hundred at one time.

Then one morning our Master appeared in the olive garden. Saying little, he simply embraced each one of us for a moment. Then he led us out to Bethany, into the walled courtyard garden where Martha grows potted wild mountain roses and Mary culls the spent blossoms.

There in the shade of the terebinth tree where Lazarus takes his midday rest and recites Psalms-sourced prayers, our Master stood peaceful and calm before us.

He seemed a bit remote.

No one said a word. We gathered there not knowing why he had brought us to the Bethany family home. Jesus's mother was there. The Marys also, and others who cherished Jesus and had provided so much for him and for us. Here we all were, and there our Master stood smiling benignly upon each of us.

He stepped then from shade into pure sunlight which seemed to waft warm fragrance on the gentle breezes stirring the grass and palms leaves.

He looked at us as if seeing but one man. We felt his love as tangibly as we felt the gentle breeze and sun-sent warmth.

He bowed low to his mother with his hands crossed over his heart.

Then he lifted them in benediction upon all of us and breathed a blessing in these words. "You are children of God, blessed of the Lord most High. Leaving you and my body, I now go from earth to the fullness of harmony, to the God, from whence I came."

And then . . . then . . .

He no longer stood upon the earth but seemed to stand in the air; and he slowly rose until he looked down upon us, his love pummeling our hearts, our minds, and quickening even our flesh. An enveloping cloud of light enfolded him and his form seemed to slowly dissolve until we could no longer see him. Within the glory cloud we saw a host of angels of purest light, with forms not unlike our own, but more radiant, with cloudbow colors outlining each face and figure.

Jesus was soon gone from our vision into his heaven—into the ascendant harmony of the reality from whence he came to earth to show *us* the way to heaven.

We stood transfixed, privileged beyond reason to have witnessed the most profound happening the world can ever know—the ultimate defeat of birth and death and evil.

He, who taught mankind that God is the perfect Intelligence in whom we all, in truth, live and move and have our being, ascended into the eternal reality, his spiritual life in God.

No one wept. No one spoke. We just continued looking to the radiant heights, hearing angel songs until the heavenly chorus also dissolved into this Genesis light.

The day resumed but a brightness remained, and the air above us seemed charged with a living and a powerful presence.

One by one, we each left the scene, not speaking, just thinking, rejoicing, remembering. We departed in quietness. What more could be said?

Before long we were again all undone. The inspiration of the day when our Lord forsook the world, the flesh, and all evil to rise into heavenly existence, faded.

Uncertainty crowded out the glory of that hour, and we eleven close followers of Jesus squabbled among ourselves. What were we to do? Where will we be safe? How shall we be directed and protected? Who amongst us is wise, steadfast, impartial, and generous enough to follow Jesus's example and lead the way wherein eleven others might faithfully follow?

"I AM the Way," Jesus had promised. But he was gone. He had disappeared, and we were left in uncertainty. Indeed, we were paralyzed with fear of the unknown. Our thoughts grew into angry words. I was sickened by all this. We agreed then to separate for seven days to regain our peace and inspiration. When it was suggested that we each return to our own homes in Galilee, assent quickly followed. We vowed to come together again in seven days, meeting at the shore beneath the Horns of Hattin.

Simon and I walked home in silence having agreed that our greatest need was for prayer.

I tried to review every moment—from the first time I saw Jesus until the last time when he spoke to me alone. I realized that I possessed a great treasure of truths. The truth that God was not *a*, but *the one* perfect Mind, accessible to everyone everywhere. The truth that God is not just loving, but Love itself. That God's Love is ever present, everywhere. I learned that God is not just source, origin, beginning, and substance of all being, but Life itself, expressed in things forever existent and known only for good. That God is the intelligence, conceiving and connecting all things with intelligence, making ideas manifest, uniting all to God's infinite, eternal being.

As we journeyed homeward, my thoughts grew more profound, more conditioned to expect that each apostle was experiencing a similar thought process in order to refocus on the lessons our Teacher had taught us.

By the time we reached Capernaum, peace had returned to Simon's and my own heart and mind through our silent prayer. We reached our father's place and went to the back where we usually found him sitting beneath the tiel tree. He was not there. We entered the house, calling our names so as to not startle him.

He was lying abed, half asleep. Simon gently roused him. He made no effort to rise. He looked weary. His voice was so soft we could barely hear his words. "Are you all right?" we asked.

"I have heard the news. Your Master has gone," he replied.

"Oh, Father!" said Simon. "We saw him ascend to his glory beyond the flesh."

"He's gone from earth the right way," said Jona, "and I suppose you are to carry on; but I am too old, and I desire to forsake this flesh. Tell me when you last saw your Master."

We sat beside the bed where our father lay nestled in comfort and resignation. He listened, eyes closed, as we told him all we'd been through that week. We told him of the glory cloud which took Jesus from our sight and of the angels that sang him to his home in God where all things live never to die and where man will realize he is home and alive forevermore.

For a moment Jona's eyes opened wide, and there was on his face no fear, no pain, just bliss. Then his eyes closed, and we knew our Abba was in the presence of angels, lifting him into continuity of conscious life in God.

We saw no death.

Simon and I looked into each other's eyes. We both knew Jona had set us free to do the will of God according to the gift of having shared in the life of Christ Jesus, and so we buried our loved father late that very day, grateful that he stayed until we could be present when he left us.

A week later we apostles met again peacefully at the shore beneath the mountain where Jesus had last called us to meet him for individual guidance.

No one knew what others had been told that day, for it was agreed that each of us should hold sacred our last individual teaching from the Master. Thus no one could claim dominance or special commission to lead.

To our surprise, Mary of Magdala came to this meeting. She arrived with Jesus's brother, James, just as we began to determine the course we should take to continue the work begun by Jesus. We greeted them; and following our Master's example, we allowed Mary to remain in our presence.

A debate began. What would he expect his chosen apostles to do now? What did he tell us to do?

"Go into all the world," suggested Matthew.

"Continue to heal," said another.

"Do the work he showed us how to do."

"Cleanse lepers."

"Cleanse lepers? . . ." one wondered aloud.

"Yes, even cleanse lepers."

"Cast out demons."

"Preach the Gospel."

"Raise the dead." There was no murmur of assent or dissent to do this. It was expected that we could and would raise the dead and dying to continued life.

Mary was sitting to one side listening quietly, adding nothing to the discussion.

We made plans to travel through the Galilee into Peraea then across the Jordan in returning to Judea. This journey was designed to prove unbroken the presence of the Christ in teaching Jesus had entrusted to his students. The next day we went forth.

Again multitudes turned out to listen and follow us as witnesses to the continuity of Christly words and works.

As before, scribes and Pharisees came to listen and sometimes to debate, accuse, or even belittle our sincere efforts which brought healing and redemption to many.

For several months we met time and again on the slope of Hattin. And time and again we went forth two by two or four by four. Many were added to the Cause of the Christ in each place where we preached and healed. Our surety increased as we realized the fact of Jesus's promise that the Christ would be with us wherever we were.

One day my brother, Simon called Peter, declared that we were told to go into all the world, and perhaps it was now time to go beyond Palestine, into Egypt, Syria, and even farther abroad.

Seven days later we gathered on the shore of the Sea of Gennesaret.

Again James, Jesus's brother, was there and with him was Mary of Magdala. "We are here because our Master asked us to meet with you to help determine how to continue the work he has given you to do," said James.

At this I felt my brother grow tense, even as I did. *Be patient. Let them speak,* my better self whispered to me.

The atmosphere changed. A cloud settled over the sun above us. The gentle breeze stiffened, and wind-whipped white foam broke atop waves as they washed up on the shoreline. No one spoke.

The silence grew rigid.

Then Mary stepped forward, saying with outstretched hands, "Brethren . . ."

I am ashamed to say I turned my back to her.

"Listen," she begged. "The Master has asked me to knit you together, should disaffection ever take you off the course he set for you."

As she spoke, my days of peaceful prayer vanished!

Imagine! A *woman* venturing to return us to a spiritual basis of thought!

"Do not despair; don't be dismayed, dear ones," she said. "Our beloved Way-Shower set the example for the coming days and years of your lives and of mine."

James, brother of our Lord, confirmed her right to speak. "Jesus knew the time would come when women would walk equally with the sons of man. Now, hear her. As you were each given special counsel in the last of Jesus's days amongst us, so too was Mary."

We gasped, individually and collectively. I watched as disbelief communicated itself eye to eye amongst us.

Then, in my mind, it was as though I heard our Savior's voice: "Love for each and all is key to the kingdom of God within you."

I had heard these words before, and hearing them now when he was not present was startling; then I remembered his pledge to be always with us.

I lowered myself to the ground. Simon Peter did the same.

Mary, beloved of our Lord, and dear to each one of us, stood there deep in thought. Finally she spoke, "Jesus taught us that though our bodies return to nothingness, that which remains alive forever of each of us is our consciousness, for we are made in the image of God. Thus we are in truth spiritually mental beings. God is our Soul, our Life, our Mind. As such, we must all grow to know, and man must be known as the perfect likeness of God.

"Salvation is real, the fact of all things being perfect and spiritual. It is the thought's ascent to God."

I could not argue with Mary's words.

"There is no place called hell," she said. "Hell, like heaven—Jesus taught me—is a state of thought. Hell is brought about by wrongdoing. Heaven is holiness of thought experienced through love and righteousness."

We nodded as she spoke these words; we had heard the same from the mouth of our Lord.

Mary continued, "You have also been taught that all things evil in this world will disappear. All that is good exists in the Mind of God, and we individually experience this good as we claim it through spiritually understanding God. Good thought appears as good things."

We had heard Peter argue with Jesus on the subject of sin. Jesus taught us, "Sin is action based on ignorance of the truth of God's Love which redeems the victims of ignorance. Then men learn God's truth and repent of wrong thought."

Mary continued, "One's Mind must be spiritual, for God is the only creator. We have witnessed the triumph of Jesus's deathless life as proof that as a man understands, loves, and serves God, he is able to love as God loves, and live eternally. All sense of being material dissolves in the light of one's spirituality."

We listened, questioningly, then began to fidget.

"Why," I wondered, "do we sit here at the feet of a woman?"

Peter, irascible Peter, stood up. "Tell us something new, Mary, something we've not heard from our Lord, if you know any such."

Mary stood there, not speaking. Hateful thoughts filled each prejudiced mind.

"Where the divine consciousness is, there is one's treasure," said Mary. "This world is not the reality of the heaven and earth of God's revealing," she continued. "The spiritual, the eternal—that which is of God—is real."

I thought then of our Master's words: "Be of good cheer, I have overcome the world."

Now my ears were open. I looked toward Peter. He sat down and no longer fidgeted.

"Sister," he said, "tell us everything the Lord told you, whether we can agree with you or not."

That was too much for me. I leaped to my feet again. "You have said things familiar, but other things are strange because new to us."

Peter rose to support me. "How could you have had private talks with Jesus and we not know about it. I can't imagine his asking *you* to give us further teaching."

There was a general murmur of agreement among the other apostles. James, the brother of Jesus, stood aside, letting us foment our disbelief and discomfort at being instructed by a woman.

Peter continued, "Do you suggest that Jesus had a special affection for you, Mary? Perhaps you are the only woman outside of his family that he has held in his arms. We were witnesses when he healed you, remember?

"Permit me to dishonor your talking. I do not believe you." Thus Peter challenged her veracity, and I could only agree with him. He sat down.

Mary wept. We had greeted her with tender affection, but now animosity was elevenfold in the air.

But one of us thought differently.

Matthew rose and went to Mary, offering her his shoulder and wiping away her tears with the hem of her sheer shawl.

"Peter," he said sternly to my brother, "you are heated as usual, vexed and fretted on the side of adverse thinking instead of standing on the side of peace.

"If Jesus loved Mary more than us, it was because he found her faithful. Again we are losing our unity of thought. Togetherness must be preserved. We are going forth to preach his Gospel, so we must be united in truth and love."

Matthew kissed Mary of Magdala on her brow and said to her, "I am grateful for all you have told us of our Master's words to you."

And to us he said, "I am now leaving this assemblage of his students, as he said we should, to take the good news so every individual on earth may learn about God's kingdom and power through righteousness and understanding developed in one's own consciousness."

Matthew departed from the assembly.

Then other disciples began to leave, wordlessly, one by one. I looked at my brother. Simon was abject, his misery unbearable to see. Soon we were the only apostles remaining except for Mary who stayed, and with her James, the brother of our Lord. I took Peter's arm and guided him to Mary's side. She stood there moist-eyed. Lovingly, she reached forth to embrace us.

"I apologize, dear Sister," I said.

"It's all right, Andrew, I know in time you will repent and welcome spiritual wisdom in women."

I left her then in Peter's presence and walked out of earshot while they conversed. Peter never told me what they said to each other, but I know it was good, for James and Mary walked back to Capernaum with us.

As we walked along, we vowed to never again tolerate dissension among the twelve of us.

Peter and I apologized again and again to Mary, humbly pledging to prayerfully accept and protect her discipleship in every way. Hopefully we will never repeat opposition such as was made that day. Without Christly love, our lives and work would become unfruitful,

There is a stirring in Israel. A fellow named Paul has ceased persecuting those of us now known as The Way. He had a vision of the Master and heard the voice of Jesus instructing him to be an apostle to the Gentiles.

James, our Lord's brother, will now head the work in Jerusalem.

Of many who followed Jesus almost from the day of his baptism at the hands of John, we chose two of the most faithful, Joseph also called Barsabas Justus and another named Matthias. We voted by lots for one to take the place of Judas Iscariot. Matthias was chosen. He will work with James here in Jerusalem.

We met again two weeks ago on the shore of Gennesaret to give each other blessings before we go separately into the world to preach and teach the good news that the kingdom of God has come! Mary Magdalene and the Bethany sisters came to bid us Godspeed. This is our plan:

Thomas has already gone toward Parthia en route to India.

John goes first to Rome, Peter to Corinth.

Philip heads into Asia Minor.

Matthew and Thaddeus to different cities in Syria.

James the Less sails to Spain.

Nathanael Bartholomew plans to walk to Armenia.

James of Zebedee will remain for a time in Judea.

Zelotes plans to work in Egypt.

I will travel to Greece, along the shores of the Great Sea. It is my hope to someday reach the isles beyond the sea. I am outfitted to sail tomorrow.

It is in my heart and prayers that every man, woman, and child on earth may come to understand and love God as I have through the teachings of our Lord Jesus Christ.

Farewell . . .

Acknowledgments

Dorothy Pendleton, for twenty-eight years, has shadowed my path, waiting for me to write this book. Without her, this would not exist. She took miles of handwritten foolscap and letterheads, deciphered every page of each version and revision, typed and retyped the book into her computer. Every writer should have a friend like De De. Thank you! Thank you!

Marlene Fabian took an early interest two years ago when I began to write. Days became weeks and months as she gave support and practical attention to grammar and punctuation. You have my endless thanks, Marlene.

A longtime sister to my heart, Marjorie Scott Eichelberger, and her husband, Dr. Robert Eichelberger, listened to, read, and reviewed the book during the writing process and offered valuable corrections along the way. Writers to writer, they were a special blessing. I'm very grateful to you, dear friends.

Lastly, Dr. Christopher Wye read the manuscript critically. His appreciation of my effort to tell the story of Christ Jesus the Healer encouraged me to elucidate the spiritual meaning I've always found in the Gospels. So thanks to you, Chris, for your respect, support, and guidance.

And of course, to those at Xlibris who have shepherded in design, copyediting, publicity, promotion, and elsewhere and in other ways the publishing of this book, I am mindful and deeply grateful. You have made it a wonderful adventure for me. Thanks again and again to all of you.